DOWN RANGE

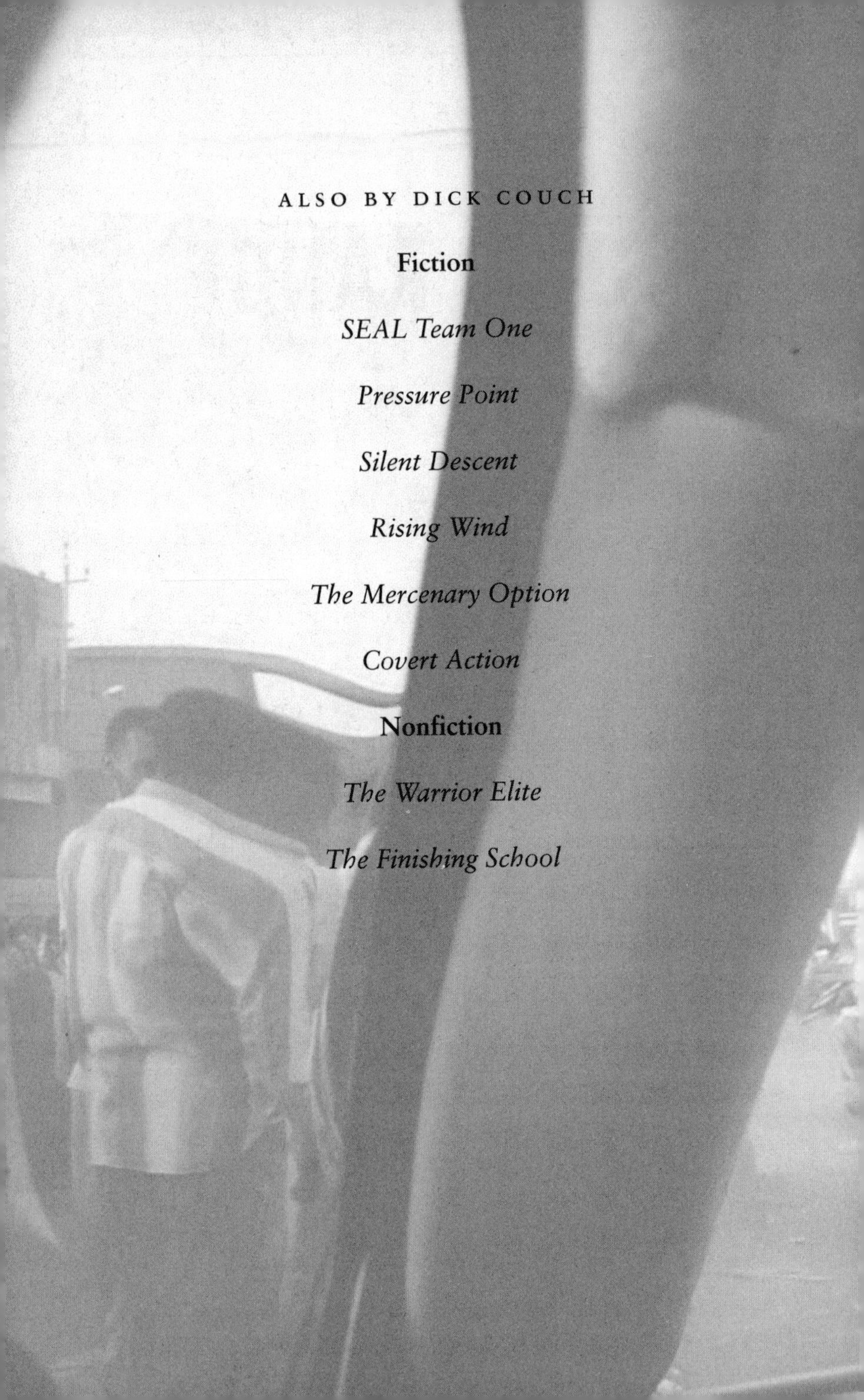

ALSO BY DICK COUCH

Fiction

SEAL Team One

Pressure Point

Silent Descent

Rising Wind

The Mercenary Option

Covert Action

Nonfiction

The Warrior Elite

The Finishing School

DOWN RANGE

Navy SEALs in the War on Terrorism

DICK COUCH

Foreword by Richard Danzig

THREE RIVERS PRESS

NEW YORK

The United States Navy and Naval Special Warfare Command
do not endorse this book.

Published in the United States by Three Rivers Press, an imprint of the
Crown Publishing Group, a division of Random House, Inc., New York.
www.crownpublishing.com

Three Rivers Press and the Tugboat design are registered trademarks of
Random House, Inc.

Originally published in hardcover in the United States by Crown Publishers,
an imprint of the Crown Publishing Group, a division of Random House, Inc.,
New York, in 2005.

Library of Congress Cataloging-in-Publication Data
Couch, Dick, 1943–
Down range: Navy SEALs in the War on Terrorism / Dick Couch;
foreword by Richard Danzig.—1st ed.
1. Afghan War, 2001– 2. Iraq War, 2003. 3. United States. Navy. SEALs. I. Title.
DS371.412.C67 2005
956.7044'345—dc22   2005006048

ISBN-13: 978-1-4000-8101-1
ISBN-10: 1-4000-8101-7

Printed in the United States of America

Design by Leonard W. Henderson

10 9 8 7 6 5 4

First Paperback Edition

For the Families

Navy SEALs are now going back down range on their third and fourth combat deployments. When they return "home" they are often away at a remote training site as they prepare for the next deployment. And there is no end in sight. When these men take their guns back to the fight, there are families who stand by these fathers, brothers, and sons—loved ones who anxiously wait for their return. They all live in fear of that phone call or knock on the door, the sedan with government plates that pulls into the driveway. We must not forget that the families of SEAL warriors, in their way, are downrange as well. Those of us who enjoy America's blessings owe them a debt of gratitude for their patriotism and support. Thank you for your sacrifice.

In Memoriam

Since the hardcover edition of this book was released in early June of 2005, eleven Navy SEALs have been killed in action in the global war on terrorism:

Lieutenant Commander Erik S. Kristensen
Lieutenant Michael M. McGreevy
Lieutenant Michael P. Murphy
Senior Chief Petty Officer Daniel R. Healy
Chief Petty Officer Jacques J. Fontan
Petty Officer First Class Jeffrey A. Lucas
Petty Officer First Class Jeffrey S. Taylor
Petty Officer Second Class Danny P. Dietz
Petty Officer Second Class Matthew G. Axelson
Petty Officer Second Class James E. Suh
Petty Officer Second Class Shane E. Patton

May God Bless these warriors and those they leave behind.

ACKNOWLEDGMENTS

A great deal of effort and attention went into telling the operational story of the Navy SEALs while respecting security protocols, as well as the privacy of individual SEAL operators. Fortunately, I had a lot of help from men returning from the fight and from various levels of command within the Naval Special Warfare community. My thanks to those whose stories appear within these pages. I hope I got it right, or as right as possible under my "rules of engagement." For those of you who told me some great stories, but for security or editorial reasons could not be part of this work, thank you as well. And for those of you who courteously listened while I swapped a war story from another era, thanks for your kindness and patience. Finally, for all the SEAL operators who continue to take your guns back down range, I and the rest of America cannot thank you enough.

CONTENTS

FOREWORD

You can read this book in any of four ways. Most narrowly, it is, of course, a portrait of that singular and typically secretive band of warriors, the Navy SEALs. In these pages, you will hear the voices of the silent and see the faces of the invisible. Dick Couch, who retired in 1997 from the Naval Reserve, was one of these warriors. The SEALs have given him access that no one else enjoys. In two previous books, he has compellingly described their rigorous selection, grueling training, and intensive mission preparation. Here, after a brief recapitulation of their physical, mental, moral, and skills training, he chronicles their most recent exploits. We see how the SEALs meet very diverse challenges underwater in the Persian Gulf, in the mountains and valleys of Afghanistan, and in the cities of Iraq. And we observe how these challenges transform the SEALs, so that their twenty-first-century command structure, mission planning, and deployment patterns are notably different from those envisioned at the end of the twentieth century.

A second approach to this book is to read it for its insight into our military as a whole. Because the SEALs don't work alone, these pages are populated by soldiers, marines, sailors, and airmen. (Nor are all of them American. The British and the Poles appear here to play important roles.) Because war is a come-as-you-are activity, unpredicted combinations and permutations of forces are called into play. This study of the SEALs in action accordingly, inevitably, and properly becomes a study of how our forces are—and are not—marshaled, deployed, and coordinated to meet diverse ends.

More broadly, these pages provide a close-up view of some of the most important fronts in the war on terrorism. This is a personal war. As Captain Couch has often said, "al-Qaeda doesn't have submarines or combat aircraft." To understand the military aspects of this war, you have to be with the troops on the ground. Opportunities to adopt this viewpoint are rare. This book offers one because SEAL missions, by definition, involve close contact. They are at the opposite end of the spectrum from missiles fired from a distance and impersonally destroying everything within a range of where they land. When al-Qaeda hides in Afghanistan's Zhawar Kili Valley, it is the SEALs who go in to discover and dismember the world's largest complex of caves populated with terrorists and their munitions. Couch takes you there with them in chapter 4. In Iraqi cities like Baghdad and Mosul, Dick Couch follows the SEALs as they undertake missions in urban terrain. Chapter 6 takes you along.

Finally, though, this book can be read as a case study in the motivation, organization, and conduct of operations—operations of any kind. Viewed narrowly, these are war stories. But at a deeper level, they are object lessons in how to do things that are difficult and dangerous. Why, it may reasonably be asked, is America so successful in its military, but not in its school systems, its health care, its gathering of intelligence, its stewardship of the environment? One reason—I think the dominant reason—is that we invest systematically, persistently, and richly in our military. This book shows how SEALs are chosen with great care and then tested and screened afresh so that only the mentally and physically strongest are finally selected. We may not be able to afford that in all contexts. But beyond this, we organize them in hierarchies; we recognize and celebrate their achievements; we demand qualities of character as well as skill; we train, we train, we train; we define tasks as "missions" and demand preparation; we build teams whose watchword is *trust;* we design equipment to maximize efficacy and minimize risk.

These characteristics are sadly lacking in other domains, even national security domains. In our new Department of Homeland Security, for example, the occasional one- and two-day crisis training exercises compare badly with the SEALs' years of preparation; our ad hoc procedures in domestic crises reflect too little of the learning from SEAL mission planning; our blurred civilian hierarchies and changing teams contradict the lessons in these pages; our only incidental references to character and commitment contrast with the position of these virtues at the core of the activities described in this book. And if these criticisms are true for our domestic security programs, how much more valid are they for our teachers, our hospital workers, and others who work with inadequate resources, largely in isolation, often with indifference to each other?

This book can be read as a record of success in far-off places with operations often conducted in secrecy. But you also can read these accounts as models of what can be done when we care enough to get things right. If you approach this book in this manner, you will be left at the end asking yourself: Why don't we do more things this way?

Richard Danzig
Senior Fellow, Center for Naval Analyses
Secretary of the Navy (1998–2001)

DOWN RANGE

INTRODUCTION

SEALS of my generation seldom used the term "Vietnam" and never "Nam." We said we were "In Country." Laos and Cambodia were "Up Country." Everything above the DMZ was "the North." The SEALs in Afghanistan and Iraq, the guns in this current fight, simply say they are going downrange—or back downrange. *Down Range* is the story of Navy SEAL operations in the current war on terrorism. For the SEALs in this fight, "down range" could take a number of different forms. It could be a strategic reconnaissance mission along some remote mountain trail in Afghanistan, tracking roving bands of al-Qaeda on the move. Or it could mean taking down a safe house outside Tikrit, where hard-core Baathists from Saddam's regime have taken refuge. It might be interdicting insurgents smuggling car-bomb explosives across the Iraqi-Syrian border or preventing Sunni radicals from bombing an Iraqi police station. For a Navy SEAL, down range might be silently boarding a freighter on the high seas at night, looking for weapons of mass destruction in a warehouse in Samarra, or taking down a member of Osama bin Laden's inner circle in a crowded marketplace. It could be going to the rescue of a brother warrior who is engaged in a desperate fight. The list goes on—down range could be anywhere, anytime.

Most of the SEAL operations you will read about in *Down Range* took place following the attacks on American soil on 11 September 2001, but not all. Navy SEALs were downrange well before the 9/11 strikes. As we will see, terrorists have been at war with us much longer than most of us have known we were at war with them, and SEALs have been engaged in this war for some time. Navy SEALs are highly trained warriors; they have performed some incredible acts of professional competence and personal courage in this war. Their commitment to the battle continues as I write this book, for this conflict is far from over. Most accounts in the following chapters have never been made public. Others, while they may have been mentioned on the evening news or been the subject of a newspaper article, have never received the in-depth coverage afforded in this text. Certainly, no journalist has been allowed to interview the SEAL operators to the extent that I have. There are reasons for this: SEALs prefer to remain in the shadows; they take pride in being known as quiet professionals. Often, SEAL commanders are reluctant to make public their operational successes, as the enemy may still not know just who those guys were who came in the middle of the night or how they got there. Few embedded reporters go downrange with Navy SEALs.

I enjoy a special relationship with the Navy and the SEAL community, one that goes back close to four decades. While on active duty in the late 1960s and early 1970s, when "down range" meant Vietnam, I made operational deployments with the UDT and SEAL teams, so I'm a member of this club. In 1997, I retired from the Naval Reserve as the senior SEAL reservist, having commanded three SEAL reserve units. Six years ago I rejoined the teams, in a manner of speaking. In the summer of 1999, I received permission from Naval Special Warfare Command to write a book on Basic Underwater Demolition/SEAL (BUD/S) Training. It was in October of that year I mustered with BUD/S Class 228, my second time through the BUD/S course. I graduated with Class 45 in March 1969 and served with Underwater Demolition Team 22 and SEAL Team One. But thirty years later, with Class 228, I was only auditing the course, running along with a notebook and camera behind the real trainees. In November 2001, a month after the terrorist attacks of 11 September, *The Warrior Elite: The Forging of SEAL Class 228* was published. By that time, the first SEAL elements were already in Afghanistan performing direct-action and strategic-reconnaissance missions. As America reeled with the shock and fear, and groped to come to terms with this unprecedented attack, these warriors were already at work. SEAL elements were forward-deployed, in theater, and ready for operational tasking. When it was determined that the forces who attacked America were under the protection of the Taliban, Navy SEALs had boots on the ground in Afghanistan, taking the fight to the enemy on their home turf; they were downrange. For the fledgling warriors of Class 228 who were just beginning their journey to become fully trained and qualified Navy SEALs, the prospect that their first SEAL deployment would be a combat deployment rose dramatically. Today, all of the men from Class 228 have now been deployed in harm's way, several returning downrange for their third combat tour.

I learned a great deal about the training of modern Navy SEALs in my research for *The Warrior Elite*. I learned even more during my research for *The Finishing School: Earning the Navy SEAL Trident*, which was published in March 2004. That book takes the reader through SEAL Qualification Training and into the SEAL platoons as they prepare for operational deployment. Some of those same SEALs who prepared for war in *The Finishing School* appear in the pages of this book. SEALs in training and those preparing for operational deployment spend a lot of time away from home, as did I in following along as they went about the serious business of preparing for war. With these two books behind me, I felt that I was now ready to tell the operational story of the Navy SEALs. They have done some exciting and important work since the attacks of 11 September, and their work is ongoing. But telling the story of warriors who are at war—currently engaged with a vicious enemy—is far different from documenting SEAL training. These are my guys, men I call brother warriors, though a generation or two removed. As you read of their exploits, there are Navy SEALs on deployment in dangerous environments, very much in harm's way. I have a moral and personal obligation not to impede the serious, ongoing work of these dedicated warriors, nor to put them at additional risk.

When writers and journalists write about secret organizations, like our special operations forces, or SOF as they are called, they have two options. The first is that they can approach their topic as an investigative reporter—circling their subject, probing for information, gathering a bit of data here, a fact or two there. These often turn into an adversarial relationship between the reporter and the subject. There are official reports and press releases promulgated by the military public-relations staffs, but these are generic pieces, carefully crafted to provide little or no tactical or operational detail and to protect personal identities. So the writer/reporter must prowl the fringes of the SOF community, looking for interesting scraps of information and often trying to get a SOF operator to speak about his work when he should not.

It is not that SOF do not want their story told—far from it. Most senior commanders welcome the opportunity to tell the American people about the sacrifice and contributions of their forces; they are immensely proud of them. I'm immensely proud of them. But these men who work so hard and risk so much simply require a great deal of privacy, even anonymity, to do their job. We are at war. Our SOF capability is a very important weapon in this current fight; some would say the single most important. The less our enemies know about their method—TTPs, as they are called: tactics, techniques, and procedures—the more effective our special warriors will be in defending us against the dark forces of bin Laden and others like him who wish to destroy us and would like to bring their fight to our shores.

But there is a second option. A writer or journalist can get official access and permission. During Operation Iraqi Freedom, we saw journalists embedded with our forces. They brought us breakthrough stories—stories that would have been impossible without official cooperation. Early last year, I met with Rear Admiral Bert Calland, then Commander, Naval Special Warfare Command. I told him I wanted to tell the SEAL operational story. I explained that I wanted to take a number of actual SEAL missions—those daring raids that made headlines, as well as those still unreported—and tell America about our SEAL warriors. He agreed. "Dick," he added, "the value you provide to the Naval Special Warfare community cannot be overstated. We trust you. Please don't hesitate to call on me if I can help in any way." Admiral Calland's support was only part of the equation. The Naval Special Warfare Command—or WARCOM, as the SEALs call their senior command—falls under their parent command, the United States Special Operations Command, or SOCOM. Permission to tell this story had to come from SOCOM as well and its commander, General Doug Brown. My thanks to the general, and the admiral, for allowing me the opportunity to tell the SEAL operational story.

With official permission comes access to privileged command and operational information. This demands trust on the part of all concerned. Official access and cooperation also come with official oversight and editorial review. I understand and appreciate this. I've been in special operations and I've been in the intelligence business, and I have held the highest-level security clearances. This background and experience serves as a guide in deciding what information should not be in print, as it may put those in harm's way at more risk. As for the scrutiny by the SEAL operational commanders and units, I welcomed it. There is an upside to this official supervision. In my books on SEAL training, I might have missed an incorrect technical detail that also might have escaped most readers, but not the guys preparing for the fight. They don't miss it, even something as trivial as the exact weight of a weapon or the muzzle velocity of a particular round. And for want of a better term, there is the slang—the working terms that SEALs use have changed since my days in the teams. Operationally, the SEAL task unit and task group commanders helped me work with the command-and-control aspects of SEAL operations without compromising sensitive information. On many different levels, official review of *Down Range* has provided me with a work that is much more technically and tactically sound.

There is also the matter of operational accuracy—getting it right when there is opportunity for ambiguity. When it comes to combat operations, all information is secondhand. Two men on the same mission or engagement may witness the action in two entirely different ways; it's a story told from their perspective—from their side of the ridgeline or their side of the skirmish line. In some cases, their side of the oil platform or building. I happen to know something about firefights, firsthand. They can be confusing, violent affairs, often difficult to unravel. I know the questions to ask, and in each of the SEAL missions described in the following chapters, I sought information from as many SEALs as possible about a specific engagement. One of my most important tasks was to show a piece of text to one of the SEALs who was on the operation and ask, "Does this *feel* right to you? Am I *seeing* this the way you saw it?" Candidly, not all the SEALs I wished to speak with would talk to me. For some, the action was too recent and too painful; they had teammates who were killed or wounded. I understand this; I've put friends and teammates in body bags. It leaves a mark on your soul. For others recently back from the fight, they are simply private men, quiet professionals who choose to remain silent. Others, especially those who have been decorated for valor, are just modest. So be it. But many were willing to talk about their operations—to discuss what happened, and how they felt about what happened. These were sometimes intense, emotional interviews; sometimes they took me back to another war and another place, a long time ago.

These SEALs talk with me for two reasons. First of all, I'm one of them, and we speak the same operational language. We can jump into the middle of an account of a PLO (a Patrol Leader Order) or a VBSS (a shipboard visit, board, search, and seizure) with no preliminaries. I've been there and done that, and I've got the T-shirt (it's a plain, olive-drab T-shirt without macho words or slogans). The second and very crucial reason is that they have been cleared to speak to me by their chain of command. This is on the record—subject, of course, to official review. Whether it's a military special operations unit or a special police unit, you can usually find someone who will speak off the record about what they do. Those willing to do this are breaking faith with their brother warriors. Often, those who talk out of school have their own agenda, and it has been my experience that few journalists have the ability to separate fact from their source's fiction. It has also been my experience that real warriors will not violate security regulations and speak about their activities unless they have official permission to do so. When I was at CIA, an old case officer told me, "Always remember that the people from whom you want information are traitors; they have broken faith with their service and their country, and you can never completely trust them." It's the same with military special operators; the good ones will only speak with official approval from their chain of command.

Down Range details Navy SEAL operations as they relate to the global war on terrorism. Since 11 September, SEALs have begun to work more closely with other SOF components and with conventional military units. Our SOF components have unique and distinct mission capabilities, but there can be some overlap. When there is, they work together. SEALs speak about Army and Air Force SOF units with a great deal of respect. The same is true of most foreign military SOF components. In Afghanistan and Iraq, SEALs often worked closely with conventional Marine Corps units. I heard nothing but praise for our U.S. Marines from the SEALs in this fight. Some writers and some books would have you believe that there exists a great deal of animosity between SOF and conventional military units. This has not been my experience. Conventional armored columns were terribly inappropriate in Afghanistan, a lesson the Russians never learned in a decade of bloody occupation. The Northern Alliance and Afghan irregulars, with direction from our Army Special Forces and support from the U.S. Air Force, toppled the regime in Kabul in a matter of months. Yet it was our conventional armored columns, supported by SOF, that routed the Iraqi army and took Baghdad in a matter of weeks. General Tommy Franks certainly had a clear understanding of what SOF can and cannot do—where it can assist our conventional military forces and when SOF must take center stage and, in turn, be supported by conventional forces.

There is also the relationship between SOF components—Special Forces, SEALs, Rangers, Air Force Special Tactics, and others. Who are the most elite? Who are the toughest? Who are the most secret? It seems that every time I pick up a current book on one of these SOF units, the writer champions one of these units by denigrating all the others. This is not the SOF world I know, but then these books are seldom written by authors who have gone downrange for real, let alone come from a SOF background. I often lecture at our Army, Navy, and Air Force special operations commands. They speak of the other service components as their SOF brothers. Professionally competitive, yes, but not professionally jealous or acrimonious. More to the point, each of them has an expertise that, while perhaps not unique to that component, is something they do better than anyone else. So as far as who is the toughest unit, I'll answer that now: on any given day or any given mission, any one of them.

SOF components seldom train together, but they often operate together. I spoke about this with a Navy SEAL, one of "my guys" from BUD/S Class 228. He was just back from Afghanistan. I asked him if he operated with other SOF units.

"All the time. They want their guns in this fight just as bad as we do. We were often out with the Army SF guys—some of them, some of us."

"Work together okay?"

"It was fine. We have a little more time on our guns, so I think we shoot a little better than they do. But they know the land and the people a lot better than we do. Several of them could speak Pashto. They were great to work with."

"How about the Combat Control Teams?"

"The Air Force CCT guys? Never leave the base camp without one. They're great to have along in the squad file, especially if you're down-range in a remote area, like central Afghanistan. If we saw the bad guys first, and we usually did, they got a two-thousand-pound JDAM [Joint Direct Attack Munition—a smart bomb] long before we, or they, got within rifle range. Why get into a firefight when your combat controller can erase them with a JDAM?"

Each of the various SOF components has its primary area of expertise, a mission or missions within the special operations continuum that is its strong suit. Army Rangers are perhaps the finest light infantry in the world. They specialize in airborne assault and long-range patrol. Special Forces, or Green Berets, are the unconventional warfare specialists and excel at foreign internal defense. They are the cross-culture experts. They can fight other people's wars, but, more important, they have the ability to teach the locals to fight their own war. Their war is in developing a "by, with, and through" capability in working with others, and their value in this current conflict cannot be understated. The Air Force Special Tactics Teams specialize in combat air support, landing zone preparation for conventional forces, and the recovery of downed pilots. There are Army SOF units that conduct psychological operations and civil affairs units that go to the aid of populations during that dangerous twilight period between war and peace. These units are ready and able to put their guns in the fight, but their missions often call on them for important and highly technical noncombat special operations.

But special operations disciplines do overlap, and often it's a matter of which SOF component is available for the job. Army Special Forces are certainly capable of direct-action missions and SEALs can conduct foreign internal defense, but those are not their strong suits. SOF and theater commanders usually try to meet their mission taskings with the best available talent. Sometimes it's a question of regional availability or, if the mission is time sensitive, who can get there first. But if it's to be a raid or a difficult reconnaissance mission, with a high probability

of a gunfight, that special operations task force commander will usually send his Navy SEALs.

Prior to 11 September, Navy SEALs were viewed as the SOF maritime proponent; their unique role was special operations conducted in
and from the sea. They still do this, but in the current war on terrorism, they have been called on to do so much more. Since 11 September,
Navy SEALs have come ashore, much as they did in Vietnam. All of
their work in Afghanistan and most of that in Iraq have been land operations. In this war, SEALs routinely go well beyond the water's edge
to conduct direct-action and strategic-reconnaissance missions—DA
and SR. This has been driven by need and technology. In Afghanistan,
while the Army Special Forces, the Northern Alliance, and American
airpower was driving the Taliban from power, SEALs were tasked with
the targeting of roving bands of al-Qaeda and terrorist training camps.
These were target individuals or fixed-ground targets. With real-time
imagery from satellites and Predator drones, the time between target
acquisition and target engagement shrunk dramatically. This kind of
real-time, actionable intelligence is perishable. SEALs, with their highly
trained, disciplined strike teams, quickly became the force of choice for
rapid-response direct-action missions. These direct-action SEAL units
could saddle up and be on the insertion helos in a matter of minutes.
Team leaders would often brief their men en route—on the way to the
target. They quickly became adept at hitting the ground running and
shooting. SEALs carried this strike-quick, strike-hard legacy into the
Iraqi campaign, swooping into presidential palaces and pouncing on
senior Baathist cadre when they showed themselves or when the gath-
erers of intelligence found their hiding places. They became adept at
reacting to intelligence developed by the OGAs—other governmental
agencies. This emerging role of Navy SEALs as the premier SOF direct-
action strike force is well documented in *Down Range*.

Much of what SEALs were asked to do in Afghanistan and Iraq was
not new, but it was a new focus for them and required the development
of new tactics and procedures. Much of it was on-the-job training—

improvising while carrying out the mission. Lessons learned had to be quickly refined and implemented for the next mission. Lives depended on it. But Navy SEALs are masters when it comes to innovation and tactical evolution. They are not slaves to doctrine. They are quick to use what works and discard what doesn't. *Down Range* details this new war and the way these warriors fight. As this book goes to press, deployed Navy SEALs and the SEAL training cadres continue to develop and refine methods and tactics to make their guns in this fight that much better. I honestly have to say that what you are about to read may, in many cases, be old business. The Navy SEALs have again evolved, taken their game to a new and different level.

All U.S. military units in the field operate under rules of engagement, and so do Navy SEALs. The ROEs will vary depending on the mission, the target, and the proximity of civilians and noncombatants in and around the target. I, too, have ROEs; let me tell you about mine. The men you will be reading about are real; only their names have been changed. A part of my agreement with the Navy, with few exceptions, is that I will reveal no personal identities. Nor can I identify specific teams or units by name. Certain SEAL and Naval Special Warfare components have designated capabilities or specialities. I can, in certain cases, talk about what they do, or may have done on a given operation, but I cannot identify them by name or their physical unit location. It's a privacy issue, as well as a security issue. The men in these pages will be in and out of this fight for many years to come. When they are back in their communities with their families, they want none of their deployment activity to follow them home, at least not publicly. These men are warriors, 24/7, but they draw distinct and necessary lines between their personal and operational lives.

Before we go into the mechanics of how SEALs prepare for deployment, and how they are being used in this current conflict, I have an apology to make. The subtitle to this work, *Navy SEALs in the War on Terrorism,* is not entirely accurate. To be frank, it is even misleading. In my opinion, we are in a war against Islamic fundamentalists—

the Islamists. There are many who feel we are at war with *all* of Islam. I shudder to think of this; only time will tell. Nonetheless, talking about a war on terrorism is much more politically correct than a war against Islam, fundamentalist or not. Terror, along with the indiscriminate killing of whoever opposes them, is their weapon—their chosen field tactic. The roots of this enemy are in the Islamic Wahhabite sect, which came into bloom on the Arabian Peninsula in the 1930s. Much of the money, support, and recruits for al-Qaeda come from the Wahhabis and the corrosive teaching of hatred in their madrassa, or schools. Osama bin Laden, and the Saudi nationals who commandeered the planes on 11 September, were Wahhabis. Wahhabite doctrine calls for a strict adherence to the teachings of Islam and the destruction of all else, which includes the West, Western values, and even moderate Muslims who do not share their strict creed. What do they want, besides killing Americans and other infidels? What were the attacks of 11 September all about? Again, in my opinion, the goal of these Islamists is the domination of the world's 300 million Muslims and the resources of the Middle East oil fields—75 percent of all known reserves—to further their fanatical view of Islam. So while we in the West, and I in this book, often refer to the war on terrorism, there is a great deal more on the table. We may be experiencing a clash of civilizations, as Samuel Huntington predicted in his notable work. It's a question of whether we in the West want our grandchildren and great-grandchildren to live in a world where the immense resources of the Middle East are in the hands of the bin Ladens and al-Zarqawis of the world—men who believe, or at least want their followers to believe, that paradise is granted to those who die while trying to kill non-Muslims. This is an extremely deadly and serious business.

Oddly enough, the "terrorists" have been at war with us much longer than most Americans think; it did not just start with the attacks of 11 September. The year 1983 saw the bombing of the Marine barracks in Lebanon that killed 241 U.S. Marines and the bombing of two U.S. embassies. In June 1985, there was the hijacking of TWA Flight

847, along with the beating and brutal death of Navy Petty Officer Robert Stethem. Nineteen U.S. servicemen were killed in the bombing of the Khobar Towers in Saudi Arabia in June 1996. And there was the crude attack on the World Trade Center in 1993. I have often felt that when Osama bin Laden saw the panic and the media coverage generated by that aborted attack, he began planning for the strikes of 11 September 2001.

How long will our adversary in this struggle continue this fight? How soon can we "win" this war, declare victory, and get on with our pursuit of happiness? The short answer is, not soon. We face an enemy with fanatical beliefs, suicidal tactics, and a covert infrastructure. The terrorists are very committed and many see their struggle continuing well past their lifetimes. It will take a great deal of resolve on our part, for an extended time, to prevail. This may be a struggle that is not resolved in our own lifetimes. And it is, and will continue to be, a domestic political issue. It pains me to see our major political parties vying to seek political advantage with an issue so central to the welfare of the American people. It determined the 2004 presidential election, and it may well be a factor in 2008. And that election could pit a candidate with a war plan against a candidate with an exit strategy. That's modern American presidential politics. Still, it would be hard to imagine Thomas Dewey taking Franklin Roosevelt to task in the 1944 presidential election by saying, "Wrong war, wrong time." But then it would be hard to imagine a commission similar to the 9/11 Commission holding hearings in 1943 on the events that led to the attack on Pearl Harbor.

As for the guns in this fight, specifically the Navy SEALs I speak with, they see this enemy in very narrow terms. They have a sworn duty to protect and defend the nation and to obey the orders of those appointed over them. Some of them are well aware of the religious and political underpinnings of this conflict. More than a few understand that this is indeed a clash of cultures, and they study their enemy—his history, his religion, and his culture. But Navy SEALs are not clerics or politicians—they are warriors. The level to which they have taken the practice of their chosen profession requires a laserlike focus on the business of combat special operations. They are the tip of the spear, and for them, doing their job well is measured in mission success or failure—life and death. It takes a very special man to do this.

I'd like to thank the Honorable Richard Danzig for his kind foreword, and more specifically for his perception of SEAL combat missions as "a case study in the motivation, organization, and conduct of operations." The commitment to excellence found in SEAL evolutions, and within the broader scope of Naval Special Warfare, is indeed characterized by a commitment to professional excellence. Navy SEALs are very bright people who have many options in modern America—they could have chosen to be executives, corporate attorneys, or business owners. But they didn't; they chose to become warriors. They elected to take their considerable talent, personal motivation, and courage into a very dangerous line of work. We hear a great deal about the impressive salaries offered to former military special operatives in overseas corporate security positions. What is not so widely known is that former special operators earn generous salaries in the domestic corporate world. Business, like special operations, is a competitive enterprise. In a sales call or a business proposal, as in a firefight, there are winners and losers. Corporations want people who will not settle for second place—people who know how to win. Mr. Danzig offers an interesting perspective on why this commitment to excellence is not more prevalent in our schools, health care system, environmental stewardship, and other areas of commerce and government service. Perhaps Americans working in and out of government can take a lesson from the Navy SEALs. Certainly the lessons of the warrior have applications in many more disciplines than the narrow field of combat special operations.

Down Range will take you inside actual SEAL missions and combat operations—the mission taskings, the planning, the briefings, the successes, and the failures. These are the personal stories of the very special men who willingly took their guns to this fight and, in most cases, are still in it. What goes through their mind just before they leap from the insertion helo into an al-Qaeda stronghold? How do warriors, who put a premium on life, fight an enemy who may be on a suicide mission? How do they make split-second, life-and-death decisions when this enemy hides among innocent noncombatants? How do they cope when a teammate with whom they've trained for years is killed or wounded? You will also meet the talented operators from other SOF components and from the CIA Special Activities Division (SAD). You're going to learn something about the heart of these warriors who volunteer to take this war over there—down range—so the terrorists don't bring their violence to American soil. It is a high honor to tell their operational story.

CHAPTER 1

THE WARRIORS

Basic and Advanced Skills

Navy SEALs are a curious breed of warriors. They are special, but what makes them so? How do they get that way? Before delving into the specifics of SEAL operations, we need to look at the organization that projects this force and puts them in the fight—how they are organized and trained, and how they are deployed around the world for operational taskings. Because the battle is different today than in the past, the lengthy process that prepares SEALs for battle dramatically changed in the last few years.

If you have read my prior works on the Navy SEALs, *The Warrior Elite* and *The Finishing School*, you already have a good idea of how SEALs are made. You have to understand the animal and his training before you can understand how he hunts and moves in a hostile environment. SEAL training today is the culmination of an ongoing, evolutionary process of testing and training that in the end produces a unique warrior, one who can trace his roots to the Navy frogmen in World War II. Those hastily trained volunteers went ashore in Sicily, Normandy, and the beaches of the western Pacific Ocean ahead of the

Tom Norris, Medal of Honor recipient. Graduating from BUD/S is a milestone in a young man's journey to becoming a Navy SEAL. Here Norris, BUD/S Class 45, addresses the graduates of BUD/S Class 245. *Courtesy of the U.S. Navy (Eric Logsdon)*

amphibious landing forces. On Omaha Beach alone, more than half of the men who preceded the invasion force were killed or wounded. Two key philosophies have endured from the days of making Navy frogmen to the current practice in the making of Navy SEALs—doctrines that are unique in military training and other special operations training.

The first is a philosophy of selection. Those aspiring to become Navy SEALs are put through a harsh and efficient process that quickly reveals the right kind of men for this work—men who would rather die than quit. In the early days, volunteers were immediately thrust into a week of intense physical hardship and virtually denied any sleep. Those who survived were trained in demolitions and hydrographics, formed into teams, and sent ashore to recon and clear the landing beaches. This philosophy of "train the best, discard the rest" became the cornerstone of Navy frogman training, and, later, SEAL training. This Indoctrination Week quickly became known as Hell Week, or, during times of political correctness, Motivation Week. It survives in much of its original format to this day. The frogmen who trained for clearing beaches at Saipan and Iwo Jima can swap similar Hell Week stories with SEALs coming back from Iraq and Afghanistan. In many ways, it is a rite of passage. Early in SEAL training, candidates must not only survive, but also perform continuously as a team, for five days with no more than *five hours of sleep*. During these brutal five days, they are cold, wet, and sandy the *entire* time. Most who begin this challenging week do not finish it. They simply quit. Those who do make it through are candidates to become Navy SEALs.

The second legacy from the frogman days of World War II is the belief that officers and enlisted men should train side by side. The pain, cold water, and lack of sleep are shared equally. The only distinction is that officers and senior enlisted petty officers are held to a higher standard of leadership.

While there is a sense of continuity between those first frogmen and today's SEALs, there are also some key differences between modern

SEALs and their predecessors. One difference in the making of a modern SEAL is the length of time in training. During World War II, men were trained in a matter of a few months and rushed off to combat. Immediately following their Hell Week, they were given basic demolition training and deployed overseas. During Vietnam, training consisted of the basic training course, which had by then become BUD/S (Basic Underwater Demolition/SEAL) Training. BUD/S was then a four-month course. The advanced training that a young warrior would need to survive in combat was conducted at his SEAL team by returning team veterans. In less than a year, a young sailor or newly commissioned officer could be on patrol in the Mekong Delta. Today, few SEALs deploy without *three years* of training. They are now trained to a professional standard that is rigorous and exacting. I'm often asked if training is harder today than in my time—when being a SEAL guaranteed you were going to Vietnam. In deference to the SEALs of my era, I'll not surrender any of the ground we might claim in the "tough" category, but I can say this without reservation: Those of us from previous generations would have to take our game to a much higher professional level to meet current Navy SEAL standards. To take an analogy from professional basketball, could Jerry West or Bob Cousy guard Michael Jordan or Kobe Bryant? I don't think so. They, like the SEALs of my generation, were perhaps the best of their era. However, the bar has been raised. This is a new game with new standards of excellence and professionalism. One thing that is unchanged in the experience of frogmen of World War II, the Vietnam-era SEALs of my generation, and the SEALs on deployment today is this: If you are a Navy SEAL, with some exceptions, you will go in harm's way; your deployments will be combat deployments. If you are a Navy SEAL today, you will literally be putting your gun in the fight. When I was the OIC (officer in charge) of Whiskey Platoon, SEAL Team One in 1970, I distinctly remember telling my platoon SEALs, "This will be an active combat deployment. You're all volunteers. If anyone doesn't *want* to do this, come see me later, and I'll see that you get a set of orders to another duty station." They all chose to go with me on deployment because they wanted their gun in the fight, and I brought them all home. It was an achievement in which I still take a great deal of pride. The credit, however, goes to the professionalism of my SEALs and the enlisted leadership of my platoon.

The making of a Navy SEAL today is the construction of a triangle. This triangle is sketched or lightly drawn during basic SEAL training. The lines of the triangle are more firmly outlined during advanced training, and still more deeply etched during predeployment training. The life of a Navy SEAL is a life of training—the tracing and retracing of this triangle. One side of the triangle is conditioning—physical and mental. SEALs live with a diet of running, swimming, and constant physical training. This physical dimension and shared experience of Hell Week serve to build a mental reservoir against the times when conditions are unbearably harsh and day upon day might pass without sleep. A Navy SEAL knows he's been there before; he must always maintain the physical and mental conditioning to be able to go there again—any time and without advanced warning. You often hear a SEAL describe a difficult operation down range as "It was hard and we were cold, but it wasn't Hell Week cold." The second side of the triangle is professionalism. Training and learning are never over. Throughout his career, a SEAL must continue to refine and upgrade his professional skill set. The skills learned during basic and advanced training are not good enough for operational deployment. The skill level of a SEAL on his first deployment is less than what is expected of him on his third deployment. The life of a SEAL is one of professional evolution—a continuous cultivation of a special operations skill set. Many things remain the same and must be practiced again, but new skills have to be learned to meet emerging enemy capabilities. The final part of the triangle is the base, which represents character. To be a fully formed SEAL warrior, a man must develop a firm moral platform from which to project his power. The Navy core values of honor, courage, and commitment are part of the equation. There is also the short list of discipline, integrity, trust, and personal accountability. The development of character and the maintenance of personal honor are as important as the physical and professional components in creating a Navy SEAL.

Now let's talk about the mechanics of training Navy SEALs. The first challenge that an aspiring sailor or young officer must face is Basic Underwater Demolition/SEAL Training—BUD/S. It is the BUD/S experience that defines the SEAL culture and forms the glue that binds all SEALs together, from seaman to admiral. It is a thirty-week course that separates those who think they want to become a Navy SEAL from those who are willing to pay the price to achieve that goal. There has always been a debate about BUD/S: Is it training—a course of instruction—or simply a testing or screening process? From my close observation of BUD/S Class 228, which was featured in *The Warrior Elite*, and subsequent BUD/S training, I believe it is both. Skills learned during BUD/S provide the foundation for the diverse warrior skill set that all SEALs must develop. These skills are mixed in with a daunting physical regime throughout the BUD/S curriculum. The seven-and-a-half month BUD/S course is conducted at the Naval Special Warfare Center at Coronado, California.

BUD/S is conducted in three separate and distinct phases preceded by a four-to-six-week Indoctrination Course, or Indoc. This introductory period is a mix of running, swimming, and physical training, or PT. The new trainees are introduced to the obstacle course. They learn about cold water by spending extended periods in the Pacific Ocean. Few have been teeth-rattling, to-the-bone cold, but they get a taste of this in the Indoctrination Course. This course is to prepare BUD/S trainees for First Phase training. About 20 percent will voluntarily drop from training during Indoc. There are a few injuries, and some will quit from the pain of the moment—but most quit because they now understand that the long, tiring days and the cold water will go on for months and months. Indeed, long days and physical hardship are the life of a Navy SEAL. Indoc also introduces the trainees to the protocols and routines that have evolved from the early days to what is now modern BUD/S training.

First Phase is the conditioning phase; the physical regime is taken up a notch or two from Indoc. First Phase trainees do PT with sections of telephone poles to build strength and teamwork. They begin surf-passage drills in rubber boats. They learn the concept of "it pays to be a winner." Those who come in first get a brief rest. Those that don't are rewarded with a trip to the surf and a roll in the sand. First Phase is all about teamwork, desire, stress, and the management of physical pain—pain that is not unbearable, but which becomes a daily burden. First Phase is also about Hell Week, which is scheduled two to four weeks after this phase begins. Twenty to 40 percent of a class will quit prior to Hell Week. Of those who remain, some half or more will quit during Hell Week. For all their physical trials, First Phase and Hell Week are primarily a mental game. Many quit prior to Hell Week because they know what is ahead; the trainees now understand what it is to be tired and cold all the time. Just thinking about being tired, cold, *and* denied sleep causes them to quit. During Hell Week, 90 percent of the trainees quit during the first day. Why is this? Certainly the first day of this five-day ordeal should be the most bearable. But many quit because they say to themselves, "One day and I'm really hurting—I can't do this for *four more days.*" The ones who do make it are thinking, "One day and I'm really hurting—but I'll hang in there for *one more day.*" The actual teaching that is done in BUD/S really begins after Hell Week. As the survivors heal from their brutal week, they begin to learn about the basics of hydrographic reconnaissance, cartography, and small-boat navigation.

Second Phase is the dive phase. There is a saying in the teams that you can't be a SEAL unless you first become a frogman. Throughout Indoc and First Phase, the BUD/S trainees have been challenged by cold water and long swims. They were also made to perform skills like tying knots underwater at fifteen feet while they hold their breath. They had to master a technique called "drown proofing," where they must survive and perform tasks while their feet are bound and their hands are tied behind their backs. All this is to get them comfortable and confident in the water. During Second Phase, they learn to dive. After classroom work in diving physics and physiology, they take to the pool. They not only learn to dive, they learn to dive under stress and harassment while performing specific tasks underwater. After a brief introduction to an open-circuit scuba, the trainees begin diving with the rig used in the teams, the Draeger LAR (lung-activated re-breather) V scuba. Within a matter of days of their first underwater experience, the apprentice frogmen are boring holes in San Diego Bay on a compass heading—at night. In Second Phase, they will learn the basics of underwater navigation, pace count (estimating distance traveled while swimming underwater), maintenance of their tactical scubas, and diving safety—the foundation for their journey to becoming proficient combat swimmers. In the SEAL teams, they think of themselves as combat swimmers, rather than as divers.

Third Phase is the Demolitions and Tactics Phase. In the past it has been called Land-Warfare Phase. It is in Third Phase that these sailors learn the basics of soldiering. They are introduced to combat demolitions and a variety of weapons. They learn the basics of small-unit tactics and land navigation. Their primary weapon, as it will be in the teams, is the M4 rifle. They carry it everywhere. Much of BUD/S Third Phase is conducted on San Clemente Island off the California coast, where there are shooting, grenade, and heavy demolition ranges. And, of course, water. Tactical training problems usually involve coming from the water to complete a mission on land and returning to the water. Third Phase also introduces the new men to the methodology and mechanics of mission planning. From the senior class officer to the junior enlisted man, they work as a team to plan, prepare for, and execute a special operation. It is basic and highly formatted, but this fully integrated team planning process is the baby step that will lead to the flexibility and rapid-response capability that has been the hallmark of current SEAL operations in Afghanistan and Iraq. It all begins at BUD/S during Third Phase.

Roughly one man in five who reports for Indoc will graduate from BUD/S. It is an accomplishment and milestone in their journey to becoming a Navy SEAL. It was a milestone for me when I graduated from BUD/S with Class 45 in 1969. And it was yet another milestone when I was allowed to follow Class 228 through training and document modern BUD/S training in 1999–2000 for *The Warrior Elite: The Forging of SEAL Class 228*. BUD/S graduates rightly feel a sense of great accomplishment. Even at this stage of their training, they are very special. Yet for those who do make it, BUD/S is but thirty weeks in a three-year journey to becoming an operationally qualified, deployable member of a SEAL platoon that will go to war. Completion of BUD/S serves only one purpose: It is an admission slip to SEAL Qualification Training (SQT), where the serious business of skill building takes place. Prior to beginning the all-important qualification course, the BUD/S graduates will attend airborne training and various leadership and supervisory schools.

SEAL Qualification Training is an eighteen-week course that qualifies BUD/S graduates as Navy SEALs. SQT graduates become Navy SEALs—apprentice SEALs to be sure, but SQT awards the Trident, the gold Navy SEAL emblem that has become a symbol of the warrior elite. SQT is considered the premier training course in Naval Special Warfare. More time, money, resources, and cadre talent go into this course than any other course at the Naval Special Warfare Center. It is high-speed, difficult, and dangerous work, and it goes on 24/7. At SQT, BUD/S graduates must demonstrate maturity and master to standard the minimal skill set of a Navy SEAL. Most of them do, but not all. There was no such thing as SQT when I was in the teams. Veterans returning to the teams from deployment in Vietnam taught new men what they would need to survive in jungle combat. It was informal, but effective within the narrow operational limits of that war. Today, SQT addresses current operations in Afghanistan and Iraq, as well as the extended skill set that SEALs take with them on deployment. It is an impressive period in a young man's journey to becoming a SEAL warrior. Highly qualified, experienced veterans work long and hard to train, mentor, and challenge their students in a most rigorous and demanding environment. I was privileged to follow SQT Class 2-02 through those eighteen weeks. That experience became *The Finishing School: Earning the Navy SEAL Trident.*

SQT is different from BUD/S in that it is far more of a teaching environment than one of testing. There is more of a premium on judgment, maturity, and attention to detail. There are still those competitive physical training events that are physical contests in which it pays to be a winner, but SQT is more about preparing for action—SQT students learn the skills they will need to effectively put their guns in the fight. In SQT, the instructors talk more about *when* you get to the teams than *if* you get to the teams. SQT students hear things like "There is no second place in a gunfight" and "Train like you fight; fight like you train."

A great deal is crammed into those eighteen weeks. It is prep school for duty in a SEAL platoon. The course is broken down into blocks of training. There is a week of combat first aid, during which SQT students are introduced to tactical combat casualty care—TCCC. They learn about trauma management and the hard decisions that may have to be made when a brother SEAL becomes a casualty in battle. It is during SQT that the students learn the basics of Close Quarter Defense, or CQD. CQD is becoming a key combat skill that SEALs now use routinely on operational deployment. It is a core SEAL skill that allows the operator to project the appropriate level of force in a number of situations. CQD will be covered later in some detail and in actual mission scenarios. During BUD/S, the aspiring SEALs learned diving and basic underwater navigation with the LAR V scuba. During the three-week SQT Combat Swimmer Course, they will learn to penetrate harbors underwater, to attack moored vessels with limpet mines, and to perform underwater reconnaissance missions.

SQT will take their shooting skills to the next level. The student will fire all the weapons in the SEAL team inventory. During the weeklong combat pistol and combat rifle courses, each will put several thousand training rounds downrange. Attention is given to precision shooting because all SEALs are expected to be expert marksmen, but most of it is combat shooting—shooting that has to be done fast and accurately in different tactical situations. There is a week of demolitions, building on the basics learned at BUD/S but taking various explosives into the tactical arena. SQT training also includes several weeks of small-craft handling and navigation with the SEAL CRRC, or Combat Rubber Raiding Craft. These tactical Zodiac-type boats with outboards will be important in a range of SEAL maritime missions. The CRRC work also includes advanced training in over-the-beach operations. SEALs are expected to perform a number of littoral tasks and, as in BUD/S, these soon-to-be SEALs will come from the sea to the land and return to the sea, again and again. It is a core skill of the maritime special operator.

From the students' point of view, the most exciting block of SQT happens at Camp Billy Machen, the SEAL desert training facility located some 140 miles east of San Diego. Camp Billy Machen (Petty Officer Billy Machen was the first SEAL to die in combat in Vietnam) is a modern training base in a desolate, arid setting that is not unlike central Afghanistan or western Iraq. Here SEALs, and SQT students, can conduct live-fire training in miles of uninhabited desert. It is one of the few facilities in the country where warriors in training can fire 360 degrees. Here the students plan and conduct land-warfare training exercises using small arms, shoulder-fired rockets, and demolitions. Some of the missions are strategic-reconnaissance operations—long nighttime patrols on which they are graded on gathering intelligence and remaining hidden. Others are direct-action strikes that emphasize the two imperatives of the raider: the element of surprise and violence of action. It's at Camp Billy Machen that the students must pass the final gut check of the SEAL basic and advanced training curriculums. It's simply called the Ruck Run. The SQT students at Camp Billy Machen muster for the Ruck Run attired for combat patrol—boots, camouflage uniform, weapons, ammunition, water, and a field pack. They carry about sixty-five pounds of equipment and *run* a half marathon. They must run these thirteen miles pausing only for graded evolutions on a shooting or a grenade range. It's a race and a matter of pride, but they must meet a minimum standard or they will not graduate from SQT. The benchmark for being cold, miserable, and functioning without sleep is Hell Week. For those carrying a combat load into the fight, whether it is running through a compound in Baghdad or a mountain pass in Afghanistan, it is the Ruck Run at SQT.

Recently, a two-week course at the SEAL winter training facility at Kodiak Island has been added to the SQT training syllabus. It is a reminder of the range of conditions in which SEALs may be asked to operate. One week they are in the California desert, where the temperatures routinely range over a hundred degrees. The next week they find themselves in Alaska, patrolling across a glacier or rappelling over a rocky cliff into near-freezing water. Versatility is key to the Naval Special Warfare skill set. At the completion of SEAL Qualification Training, these new warriors are awarded their Tridents. There is still much to do and learn, but they have earned the right to wear the emblem of the Navy SEALs.

The newly minted SEALs leave SQT and report to their teams, ready for the serious training that will make them combat-ready, deployable members of a SEAL platoon. Most will report to one of the eight commissioned SEAL (sea, land, and air) teams, but a few will be assigned to one of the two SDV teams. The SDV teams operate small minisubmarines called SEAL delivery vehicles. Due to the missions and capabilities of the SEAL SDVs, many of which are classified, the training and missions of the SDV teams will only be touched on in this book. We will, however, learn how they were used on one occasion to contribute to the operational success of a classic SEAL mission in Iraq.

New SEALs reporting to one of the numbered SEAL teams—Team One, Team Two, and so on—will immediately be assigned to a platoon that is beginning its workup for operational deployment.

BUD/S selects men for heart, and SQT provides them with the basic tools to become a SEAL operator. But it is at the team, in a SEAL platoon preparing for operational deployment, that a new man learns to become a warrior and function as a member of a warrior team. This is not a book on SEAL training. I investigated the training of these warriors in some detail in *The Warrior Elite* and *The Finishing School*. But it may be helpful, before we talk about SEAL operations in this war on terrorism, to address the training and preparation that takes place before the SEAL team becomes a SEAL squadron and, with its platoons and associated special operations support components, goes into harm's way.

For the new SEAL, as for the veteran SEAL on his fourth deployment, the predeployment workup is a time to refresh basic disciplines and acquire new skills and tactics, to bring the platoon up to current operational standards, and to integrate the SEAL platoon with other squadron components. For the veterans, very little is new, but there are SEAL disciplines that they may not have used on their last deployment. These skills need to be dusted off. And in today's dynamic operational environment, there is continuous feedback from the deployed SEALs regarding the current enemy and how to fight him. There is always something new to learn. For the new men fresh from SQT, many of their skills, recently learned and perfected, may in fact be superior to their veteran platoon mates. However, a great deal of what the first-tour SEALs will be doing in a platoon workup will be new, and their existing skill level will be greatly accelerated. For these new SEALs, the learning curve is still very steep. They are like rookies on a professional sports team. They are untested, but they have demonstrated the ability to perform at this level. It's big-boy time, as they say in the platoons, with big-boy rules and big-boy standards. It's been my observation that the new men are treated with respect and as equals, because the veterans know the new men are the future of the teams. But the platoon veterans expect the rookies to listen, learn, and work hard. In

BUD/S and SQT, teamwork is important, but the basic trainees and SQT students do not train for any length of time as a dedicated team. The "team" they have known so far is usually five to fifteen men organized into a squad or a boat crew for training purposes. These teams were changed or reconfigured to meet different training venues and scenarios, and to adjust to the attrition that goes with early SEAL training. In the numbered SEAL teams, the basic combat team or element is the SEAL platoon. The platoon has many variations of tactical employment, but it is the SEAL platoon that lives and trains as a unit. More than that, it's an operational family unit. In many ways, the platoon culture *is* the SEAL culture.

The operational workup for the deployment of a SEAL squadron (the squadron concept will be explained shortly) and its SEAL platoons is eighteen months in duration. This preparation is reasonably well formatted and, for the platoons, conducted in three distinct six-month phases. The first of those phases is professional development, or PRODEV. It is followed by Unit Level Training—ULT, or simply platoon training—and finally Squadron Integration Training, or SIT. That said, operational imperatives drive the training and deployment of all Naval Special Warfare assets. The programmed "train for eighteen months, deploy overseas for six" rotation is the ideal, but may be modified to respond to operational taskings. SEALs and Naval Special Warfare assets can and will be surged to meet operational imperatives. Before examining the PRODEV-ULT-SIT process, it might be helpful to look at how SEALs are organized and trained for operational combat. The deployment organization of SEALs and all Naval Special Warfare assets was changed dramatically just as the war on terrorism unfolded.

The SEAL Squadron

Prior to January 2002, there were six numbered SEAL teams: Teams Two, Four, and Eight on the East Coast and Teams One, Three, and Five on the West Coast. SEAL Team Six was disestablished several years ago. The Naval Special Warfare Command, or WARCOM, carries the responsibility for keeping twelve combat-ready, operational SEAL platoons forward-deployed and at the disposal of the theater commanders. There are other NSW assets available and in place for theater commanders, but the central standing requirement is twelve operational SEAL platoons. This load was shared equally by both coasts with each team equipping, training, and deploying two freshly trained platoons every six months. This kept six platoons from each coast overseas, in theater, and on the job. This is why there were combat-ready SEAL platoons in Central Command and the Arabian Sea, ready for operational tasking, on 11 September. These forward-deployed platoons were in Afghanistan within weeks of the al-Qaeda strikes in New York and Washington, D.C. The platoon SEALs conducted strategic-reconnaissance missions and sent back critical intelligence to assist the forces that would soon arrive to vanquish the Taliban.

So prior to January 2002, Naval Special Warfare deployed SEAL platoons with minimal command-and-control support. Under this arrangement, the team commanding officer had no operational or tactical responsibility. Basically, his obligation ended with the deployment of his platoons and their assignment to the theater commander. Team commanding officers were, in many respects, senior training officers, and much of the team command structure, a training cadre. This all changed with the advent of the Naval Special Warfare 21 concept.

NSW 21 is built around an enhanced SEAL team or SEAL squadron. The squadron is a six-platoon SEAL organization that has a reinforced command-and-control structure and is assigned an expanded complement of NSW small craft, SDVs, and supporting NSW and non-NSW elements. After a period of interoperability training with this expanded force structure, the squadron deploys as a unit. The SEALs have their personal weapons and personal gear, but much of their operational equipment remains forward-deployed. Going forward, there will also be enhanced NSW Group–driven intelligence and mission-support capabilities at the disposal of the deployed squadrons. Basically, we are now deploying teams of SEALs—or, more accurately, SEAL squadrons—not just individual platoons. The deployed squadrons still report to the theater commanders for fleet and special operations tasking, but there is now a trained, integrated NSW support organization to extend the reach of the operational SEAL platoons. And there is a dedicated, forward-deployed SEAL squadron command structure to help the theater commanders—commander in chiefs, or CINCs—better use their SEALs.

The most visible change of NSW 21 is that there are now two new SEAL teams on each coast—Team Seven in Coronado and Team Ten in Little Creek, Virginia. The number of deployed operational platoons has remained unchanged, although there are two additional SEAL teams on the horizon. What is not so visible is the consolidation of team administrative, logistical, and training functions under the Naval Special Warfare Groups—NSW Group One in Coronado and NSW Group Two in Norfolk, Virginia. Change is always hard. The transition from six to eight SEAL teams and the team-to-squadron evolution was not without its growing pains. But the benefits to the men and the SEAL mission have been significant.

Professional Development

Basic and advanced training of Navy SEALs continues to evolve and improve to meet the changing conditions and requirements of Naval Special Warfare. When our new SEAL arrives at his team from SQT, he is assigned to a SEAL platoon. As a "new guy," as the recent Trident holders are called, he will face up to eighteen months of rigorous training at his first operational command before he deploys overseas. Again, there are three well-defined, six-month phases of training that prepare SEALs and SEAL platoons for deployment with their SEAL squadron.

The first of these three phases is the professional development period, or PRODEV. For the veterans returning from overseas, it's a chance to see their families and take some of the leave that has been accumulating on the books since their last predeployment workup and overseas deployment. For the new men fresh from the training command, the new guys, it's a chance to get acquainted with their new team and their first platoon, and to get some specialized schooling.

Each deploying SEAL platoon requires a mix of skills: communicators, snipers, breachers, linguists, tactical air controllers, and a host of training and operational supervisory qualifications. These schools lead to required qualifications and designations that collectively allow the platoon to safely train and to perform as an operational combat team. Many of these qualifications are mission- and theater-specific for certain special operations and maritime requirements. When a platoon returns from the fight, one or two of its members may be leaving the teams, their service and service obligation over. A few may transfer to a shore assignment—like instructor duty, for example—but the core of the platoon usually remains intact. New men from SQT will fill in and be sent to certain schools to round out the collective platoon requirements. The same may occur for veteran SEALs that may be coming to the platoon from instructor duty or another operational command. During the platoon reconstitution that goes on at the beginning of PRODEV, there is a great deal of logrolling and behind-the-scenes dealing on the part of the platoon officers and senior petty officers to get the best men for their platoon and to get their platoon SEALs to the right schools. Since the game is now training for future combat, it still pays to be a winner.

Unit Level Training

Individual SEALs will leave PRODEV as a platoon for Unit Level Training. Currently, ULT is conducted by the Training Detachments

(TRADETs) of the Naval Special Warfare Groups on each coast. The TRADETs have a big responsibility: They have to train SEAL platoons for war. Their job is to take the laundry list of SEAL capabilities— maritime operations, diving, land warfare, air operations, mission planning, and so on—and make sure that each deploying platoon is ready as a combat team to use those skills to meet the current threat and to conduct combat operations in that environment. On paper, that means they must be trained to perform certain tasks under certain conditions and to a certain standard. There are no free passes. Platoons experiencing trouble are candidates for leadership changes. For the TRADET cadre, it goes well past requirements and standards. They are training their brother SEALs for combat. Their success in doing that is not simply a completed checklist; it is the performance of those platoons when they get to the fight. True success means that they can carry out their mission taskings and that they all come back in one piece. The training cadres take these duties very seriously. This process goes on for six months, often for seven days a week, and it takes a great deal out of both the trainers and those being trained. For the most part, the SEAL operators and the SEAL trainers feel the platoons that complete ULT are ready for combat. All wish they had a little more time to train or that they had demonstrated more skill or professionalism in one training evolution or another, but that is the price of excellence. A SEAL or SEAL platoon can never be satisfied; they always know they can achieve more—that given time and opportunity, they can be a little more ready for the fight.

Squadron Integration Training

Twelve months into the predeployment workup, the SEAL team becomes a SEAL squadron. The commanding officer of a SEAL team takes on the larger role of a SEAL squadron commander. The SEAL squadron is the primary vehicle for force projection in Naval Special Warfare.

The current manning of a SEAL team is in the order of 130 individuals. Of that number, some 84 are platoon SEALs—in the vernacular of the teams, pure shooters. Another 12 to 14 members of the team are SEALs that serve in nonplatoon roles. These SEALs include the senior leadership—commanding officer, executive officer, operations officer, command master chief. They will serve as task unit commanders or in other deployed leadership positions. The other qualified SEALs, including new SEAL ensigns fresh from the finishing school, will serve in the task units or in liaison positions, or with the squadron's Special Boat Team assets. These new SEAL officers are called Smees—subject-matter experts. They will take on an assigned special operations discipline and become the team authority on the subject. Under certain conditions, these nonplatoon SEALs, including the Smees, may go into the field, either with the platoons or with other NSW elements that support the platoons. The team rosters may contain as many as thirty non-SEAL teammates. These are intelligence specialists, communicators, logisticians, and administrative personnel. While the operational end of the SEAL business is a guy thing, there are females among these non-SEAL teammates. Why are there no female SEALs or "GI Janes"? Two reasons: The first is that there is a congressional ban on women assuming direct ground combat roles. The second is that few women have the upper-body strength to weather SEAL training. Yet without these non-SEAL support personnel, the teams and the squadrons could not function.

Six months prior to operational deployment, D-180, the SEAL team "pluses up" to become a SEAL squadron. This means that the SEAL team acquires additional personnel to fully configure the SEAL squadron. At this time, the new squadron begins six months of Squadron Integration Training (SIT). When a team commanding officer puts on his hat as the squadron commander, he will ultimately be responsible for up to 220 souls and take them in harm's way. This number is a moving target, as the role of the squadrons expand and are redefined by deployment experience and operational requirements.

Soon after D-180, a number of units will change operational control, or "chop," to the squadron.

The new SEAL squadron will acquire a navy of sorts—its SEAL combatant craft. The platoons own and operate their Zodiac-like CRRCs and outboards, but the larger craft that SEALs often need to get to the job site are the province of the NSW Special Boat Teams. The largest of the SEAL squadron craft are operated by the squadron Mk V detachment. The Mk V Det consists of one officer, fifteen enlisted men, and two Mk V Special Operations Craft. The Mk V is an eighty-two-foot boat that can carry a platoon of SEALs and is armed with heavy machine guns and grenade launchers. It is powered by two turbo-charged MTU diesels rated at over 2,200 horsepower each. It's a scalded dog; the Mk V can run in a light sea state at more than fifty knots. Carrying SEALs is just one of its special operations taskings. The Mk V is fast, agile, and, with its pump-jet engines, draws only five feet of water, so it is an excellent light maritime interdiction and surveillance platform.

The squadron will also take on four detachments of rigid-hull inflatable boats, or RHIBs. Each detachment has up to eight men and two boats, officially designated as the eleven-meter NSW RHIB. These versatile boats are the squadron workhorses. Each RHIB is powered by two turbocharged Caterpillar in-line, six-cylinder diesels with jet-pump drives and can carry a SEAL squad–size element at close to forty knots. Like the Mk Vs, the RHIBs carry machine guns and grenade launchers, and they can do something that a larger boat cannot do—they can be parachuted. When needed, SEAL squadrons will deploy with an MCADS (maritime craft, air deployable system) RHIB detachment. The MCADS detachment gives a deployed SEAL squadron a unique capability. It can drop an eleven-meter RHIB, a crew of three, and a squad of SEALs from a C-130 aircraft into the water. This blend of SEALs and Special Boat Team combatant-craft crewmen allow SEALs to come from the air to the sea, and, from the sea, over the horizon to the land to conduct a land attack or maritime mission.

The combat crewmen who maintain and drive the Mk Vs and RHIBs are special in their own right. The Special Warfare Combatant Craft (SWCC) crewmen are sailors who have been carefully selected and highly trained. SWCC personnel are multitasked in the conduct of their trade; they must be proficient in navigation, communications, engineering, seamanship, and weapons. There are a number of NSW taskings and missions that require the smooth integration of SEALs and SWCC crews. Since the first SEAL teams were commissioned, the SEALs and the boat support crews have been brothers-in-arms. The SWCC crews often take the same risks in combat as SEALs and can be tasked independently for maritime special operations. The professional respect that SEALs have for the boat guys is deep and long-standing. A great many SEALs owe their lives to the courage of these special sailors. Indeed, I am one of them. During my last SEAL deployment in Vietnam, there were more Purple Hearts awarded in my special boat detachment than in my SEAL platoon.

SEAL squadrons also deploy with the ability to conduct special operations from SEAL delivery vehicles. Up to two platoons of SDV SEALs will chop to the squadron during SIT. SDV SEALs, as we will later see in an operational context, are specially trained in the navigation, operation, and maritime application of these unique submersibles. They also come to the squadron with a number of talented technicians to keep these sophisticated craft maintained and operable. Much of what SEALs currently do falls under the heading of direct action and special reconnaissance, and the same can be said of SDV operations. Much of the capability and reach of the SDV SEALs is beyond the scope of this book and, in some cases, beyond the security boundaries established for this work. SDVs allow SEALs to travel a considerable distance underwater and come from under the sea.

Other Naval Special Warfare personnel assigned to the squadron include members of the NSW mobile communications teams, or MCTs. The squadron will pick up four or five of these special communicators and perhaps additional MCT forward-deployed personnel when the squadron arrives in theater. These communicators do not typically operate with the SEALs or aboard Special Warfare Combatant Craft, but serve to support and maintain the command-and-control links of the deployed operational elements. The squadron will also pick up additional NSW intelligence personnel to augment the management of tactical intelligence and assist with mission-planning support.

The SEAL squadron also acquires non-NSW assets and personnel for operational deployment. One of these, which can and will accompany SEALs and NSW combatant craft on combat operations, is the squadron's explosive ordnance disposal detachment. The EOD Det will normally consist of one officer and six enlisted EOD technicians. These men are trained in the render-safe procedures and disposal of military and improvised explosives. Depending on the requirements of the mission, EOD personnel will accompany SEAL squads and platoons in the field and may be embarked on squadron small craft as well.

Other non-NSW personnel assigned to the squadron include linguists, cryptologists, theater-specific intelligence personnel, and special communications technicians. There may be others, depending on the ever-changing squadron taskings. In the past, squadrons have deployed with a sizable Marine Corps detachment. And the deployed squadrons may be joined by detachments or individuals from other SOF components, such as Army Special Forces or the Air Force Combat Control Teams.

While the basic components of the squadron are somewhat fixed, each squadron will be a little different when it deploys than the previous one. A deployed squadron commander will speak almost daily to the squadron commander who will relieve him. Shortcomings and lessons learned are immediately applied to the ongoing Squadron Integration Training. This allows the squadron commander to use his six-month SIT period to build and configure his squadron assets to meet the most current deployment needs. Just as SEAL training must reflect changing mission demands, so must the SEAL squadron evolve to meet emerging special operations taskings and theater requirements. During this final six months of training, the squadron commander will look for every opportunity, either in-house or during scheduled exercises with other naval or military units, to exercise his squadron. He has to keep his SEAL platoons sharp and ensure that all squadron components—operational, staff, and support—function as an integrated team.

Not accounting for the deployment of special NSW units for specific tasking or the ability to surge forces to meet an urgent contingency, the Naval Special Warfare Command keeps two squadrons and twelve regular SEAL platoons forward-deployed at all times. With the current focus on counterterrorism operations in the Middle East or the Central Command (CENTCOM) theater, up to half of the deployed SEAL squadron's assets, or more, are operating in CENTCOM at any given time. Those not in CENTCOM are engaged around the world training with allied forces or to meet treaty obligations. Since terrorism is a global issue, they may become engaged in this fight anytime, anywhere.

Operational Deployment

Before going into SEAL operations, it may be helpful to take a moment and learn just *how* SEALs and other SOF components are engaged while on deployment. This refers to the command-and-control structure that directs their activities while the operators are downrange. The squadron deployment concept is relatively new, and so is the command structure that puts them in the fight. First, we'll look at the way that it used to be.

During my time in Vietnam and long after, SEAL platoons and SEAL support assets were trained by the parent team and sent overseas to work for a deployed command, usually an Army or Marine ground force commander or for an at-sea naval task force commander. SEAL platoons were *attached* units, and for the most part, they *supported* conventional forces. Now, under NSW Force 21, squadrons deploy with an embedded command-and-control structure. When General Tommy Franks, the CENTCOM commander, sent SEALs and other SOF assets to war, they were sent on missions, controlled while in the field, and supported by their own command structure.

We will now explore this down at the working level. Deployed SEAL platoons, along with a blend of other squadron assets, usually find themselves under the direct control of a Naval Special Warfare Task Unit, or NSWTU. The task unit (TU) may have a single platoon or several platoons, perhaps a boat detachment, a small intelligence staff, communicators, or other squadron components. The task unit commander could be the squadron commander, the executive officer, the operations officer, or some other experienced SEAL officer. A deployed squadron may break down its operational and staff assets to form one to four task units. Task units respond to operational taskings from higher authority or develop taskings in their assigned area or sector. The idea here is that SEALs and other Naval Special Warfare assets go to war with command, control, communication, and coordination (C4) provided by internal squadron personnel. Our task unit may have Army or Air Force SOF elements assigned, in which case it becomes a *joint* task unit. If there are SOF forces of other nations attached, like the Polish special operators that work closely with SEALs, our task unit becomes a *combined* task unit. The designation of a Naval Special Warfare task unit (usually with a SEAL command and control) that has assigned Air Force combat controllers, a Marine Force Recon unit, and a British Special Air Service component is a NSW *joint combined* task unit, or NSWJCTU. The role of a deployed task unit commander, along with his staff and support personnel, is to oversee his SEAL and NSW assets while they are in the field. In most cases, this activity is controlled and coordinated from a command center we call the TOC—tactical operations center.

One more command-and-control issue before we follow our SEALs into combat. The operations of task units are usually coordinated, and some times directed, by higher authority in the form of a special operations task *group* (TG). This task group commander will be a senior officer, and often a senior SEAL officer. During the Afghan campaign and in Iraq, that officer was usually the commander of Naval Special Warfare Group One in Coronado or Group Two in Norfolk. These commanders deployed to Afghanistan and Iraq in the role of operational task group commanders. Quite often these task groups were joint task groups or joint combined task groups. In this context, our senior SEAL officers found themselves commanding a task group with SEALs, NSW squadron assets, other service's SOF components, and foreign SOF components. If you followed all this, you are now qualified to stand watch in a TOC and deploy with a SEAL Squadron.

This forward-deployed structure of task groups and task units is not a new concept. Task groups and their subordinate task units have performed the command and control of SEAL operational components for several decades, but their usage has been restricted to military exercise play—war games. Afghanistan and Iraq were the first venues where the TGs and TUs were employed in combat for extended periods of time. This is also the first time team (now squadron) and group commanders have forward-deployed to fill these roles. This command-and-control structure has proved highly effective, primarily due to the experience and initiative of the SEAL task group and task unit commanders. They understand the business as only SOF operators can, and have been able to effectively direct their SEAL and SOF components because of their SOF history and background. Because of the SOF-centric nature of the current conflict, we often see senior Navy SEAL officers in the key roles of task group commanders, so the system has worked well in the current conflict. While the task group/task unit currently supports and directs SOF operations in Iraq, new changes are in the works.

Traditionally, SOF components have reported to and worked for task force commanders and theater commanders who were responsible for the conduct of wars or theater actions that were conventional in nature. SOF, and the SOF subset called Navy SEALS, were *supporting* forces. A part of the current Department of Defense reorganization will have, as theater warfare plans dictate, special operations task forces that have theater-wide responsibilities. These SOF forces will have theater command responsibilities and may be *supported* commands. In general terms, an SOF commander may be tasked with the conduct of a war and have conventional Army, Navy, Air Force, and Marine Corps forces supporting him in the conduct of the war. But that's in the future and way up the chain of command. For now, let's concentrate on SEAL operations in the war on terrorism, and the guns in the fight.

CHAPTER 2

AT CLOSE QUARTERS

It was just a few hours before dawn when the two helos caught up with the *Saddam Maru*. This was not the real name of the ship, but until they boarded and were able to make a closer inspection, it would do. The Iraqi tanker was well south of the naval task group's normal patrol area, almost into the Strait of Hormuz. Twice the two H-60 Blackhawks had dropped onto Navy ships in the Gulf to refuel, and twice they had lifted off in pursuit of their quarry. Now the two helos and their complement of SEALs approached dead astern to keep in the tanker's baffles, just in case the vessel carried an air search radar. There was no moon, and the *Saddam Maru* was running completely blacked out. Inside the lead helo, the rope master tossed out two hundred feet of fast rope, a thick feltlike line that served as a fireman's pole for getting SEALs quickly from a hovering helo to their objective. The rope master's job was to get his SEALs from the helo to the deck of the tanker, then follow them down. With his night-vision goggles, or NVGs, he could see the bitter end of his fast rope canting down to the deck, dancing on the amidships hatch covers. Up in the cockpit, the Navy pilots, also wearing NVGs, deftly matched the speed of the

VBSS—visit, board, search, and seizure. SEALs form up on deck at the end of the fast rope and begin their assault of the ship on an offshore platform. *Courtesy of the U.S. Navy (George Kushner)*

tanker and rode their radar altimeter to keep the Blackhawk in a hover over the deck. These were fleet pilots, adept at over-water flying and hovering above underway vessels. Still, it was a neat piece of airmanship that called on all their skill and experience. But it was the rope master's show.

"Can you hold it there, sir?" he said in his boom mike.

"We'll do our best," the pilot's voice replied in his earpiece.

"Roger that. First man is on the way."

The rope master tapped the thigh of the SEAL seated on the metal deck with his legs hanging out. Without hesitating, he popped from the door of the helo and dropped into space. Another SEAL took his place and vaulted into the void. Then another. Due to the restricted field of vision and their bulky nature, SEALs usually fast-roped without the night-vision goggles. That meant they were plunging through the dark space of night, waiting for their boots to make contact with an unseen, hostile metal deck. Their only reference was the fast rope slipping through their gloved hands. Men cannot do this without a great deal of confidence and professionalism, not to mention trust in their talented Navy pilots.

It was a tough boarding. At one point, a gust of wind pushed the helo above its hover point and two of the SEALs ran out of fast rope before their boots hit the deck. One tucked and rolled, but another was knocked unconscious. When the second helo came in with its load of SEALs, the fast rope became entangled in a boat davit and one of the SEALs came perilously close to going over the side. He managed to "chicken-wing" the guardrail and scramble back onto the deck of the tanker. With the platoon corpsman tending to the downed SEAL, the team gathered itself on the long, open foredeck and began to move across the darkened ship to the aft superstructure. It was a big ship, close to a thousand feet in length. For the SEALs, it was yet another tanker in the grand cat-and-mouse game of Saddam's oil-smuggling operation. This was not a part of the sanctioned-but-corrupt oil-for-food program that began under UN directives in 1996. This particular load of oil was being smuggled out to fund Saddam's weapons and palace-maintenance coffers. But unknown to the SEALs who now moved like shadows across the metal decking, and the U.S. Navy, which was tasked with stopping these oil-smuggling operations, this was the tanker boarding that ended the game in America's favor. This was certainly unknown to the crew of the tanker. They thought they had beaten the U.S. Navy; they assumed they had clear sailing through the strait and on to a friendly unloading terminal in Yemen. As it was, they didn't even know they had been boarded by SEALs, but that was understandable. The *Saddam Maru* was sealed and welded shut; the crew thought themselves safe from such boardings. But the SEALs in this platoon were about to beat the Iraqis at their own game.

There were many players in the game other than SEALs. There were the deployed warships of the U.S. Navy, along with Canadian, British, and allied counterparts who enforced the embargo on Iraq. There were the seamen, coastguardsmen, and marines who boarded outbound and inbound shipping to ensure compliance with UN sanctions. Small amounts of contraband can be hidden in the bowels of a merchant-man, but it was the blockade-running tankers that provided Saddam with lucrative foreign currency. A load of oil like that carried by the *Saddam Maru* meant $10 million or more in Saddam's pocket. It was a combined effort that finally put Saddam out of the illegal oil business, at least the non-UN-sanctioned illegal oil business. Yet a single Navy SEAL was to have a significant impact on the outcome. His name was Lieutenant (junior grade) Sean Yarrow. His particular contribution became known in the teams as the Yarrow Entry.

The two topics in this chapter—VBSS (which stands for visit, board, search, and seizure) and CQD (Close Quarter Defense)—may seem unrelated. But, in fact, the development and refinement of both of these disciplines paralleled each other. First, a discussion of VBSS.

VBSS, like an underwater attack on shipping, submerged harbor penetration, and over-the-beach operations, is a core SEAL maritime skill. During SEAL Qualification Training, the new men are introduced to this skill, usually with the pierside boarding of a derelict ship, moored at a deserted dock for training purposes. During the SEAL squadron predeployment training, this evolution moves up a notch or two. VBSS drills are scheduled aboard naval vessels, in port and under way, and on offshore oil platforms. When possible, these exercises are conducted with noncompliant role players, usually at night. Moving as a team through the target platform or ship in the dark requires the highest order of discipline and professionalism—and many hours of practice. Team commanding officers and squadron commanders are always looking for opportunities aboard naval vessels, merchantmen, and oil rigs where their SEALs can practice these skills. Naval task force commanders at sea off San Diego and Norfolk are constantly pestered by SEALs preparing for deployment; they especially want to train against ships under way at sea. Since the attack on the USS *Cole,* those afloat commanders have been a great deal more responsive to these requests. They have to train their crews in counterboarding measures, so it's been a win-win situation.

There are any number of ways SEALs can board a ship, oil platform, or harbor installation. They're SEALs; they can come by sea, air, or land. If the target is a ship and the ship is under way, it reduces the options to sea or air. Past that, the SEALs like to keep their tactics and techniques confidential. It is, however, safe to say that they prefer to come at night, but they can conduct VBSS operations anytime and under almost any conditions. Surprise may be achieved during stormy weather or on a mild, cloudless day. Once aboard, they move like an offensive football team breaking from the line of scrimmage. But the basics still apply. The element of surprise, hopefully; violence of action, always.

After the first Gulf war in 1991, the United Nations imposed economic and military sanctions on Iraq, and barred Saddam from selling oil or buying certain materials on the world market. To encourage compliance, the UN imposed no-fly zones over certain parts of Iraq and authorized a naval presence in the Persian Gulf to enforce these sanctions. Once the bulk of the allied forces withdrew from the region in 1993, these restrictions went into place—along with Saddam's attempts to evade them. Over the no-fly zones, allied planes, mostly American and British, began flirting with Saddam's air defense radars and SAM sites. At sea, allied ships, again mostly American and British, began to patrol Iraqi shipping lanes. The assigned naval task force began to conduct what is known as MIOs—maritime interception operations. They began to board ships bound to and from Iraq to look for contraband. This contraband consisted of war-related materials coming into Iraq and oil coming out of Iraq, the sole exception being the UN oil-for-food program that began in 1996. U.S. marines, sailors, and coastguardsmen began boarding ships at sea bound to and from Iraq. Boardings were also conducted by inspection teams from other allied nations. SEALs participated in these boardings, but were often held back and used for those boardings where active resistance might be encountered. The fact that SEALs took on the potentially tough boardings does not mean that inspections undertaken by other service components did not involve professionalism and some risk to the boarding parties. The Iraqi economy collapsed under these sanctions. It wasn't long before Saddam began smuggling oil out of Iraq for cash to keep himself in power—hard currency to maintain his army and his lifestyle. Oil went overland to Jordan and Syria, but not in the quantities he needed. In the absence of pipelines, you can only move a serious amount of oil by tanker. Saddam then began sneaking contraband oil out in tankers, and the at-sea games began in earnest.

As with all nation-to-nation contests, there are rules of engagement, or ROEs. American or allied ships could not enter the territorial waters of Iraq or other Gulf states. So as long as the tankers leaving Iraq, Iraqi-flagged or otherwise, remained in friendly-to-Iraq territorial waters, the rules said we couldn't touch them. In order to leave the Gulf to reach a friendly port where they could off-load their contraband oil, they did occasionally have to enter international waters, where they became fair game for boarding. But if they were able to duck back into territorial waters of a nation unfriendly to the United States—Iran, for instance—then the tanker was again safe. And if by chance a boarding party was aboard when the tanker turned and ran for a safe haven, the boarding party had to be off the vessel before it left international waters. An armed force entering the territorial waters of another nation is considered a hostile act. In these encounters, there was no allowance for hot pursuit. An Iraqi tanker entering friendly waters was safe, or as the SEALs would say, "ali ali in free." It was under these conditions that these boarding operations were played out.

After the attacks of 11 September 2001, this at-sea game took on a new dimension. The United States began boarding vessels looking for other game—al-Qaeda operatives fleeing Afghanistan by way of Iran or Pakistan. This activity became known as LIOs—leadership interdiction operations. With both MIO and LIO activity, a great number of ships in the Persian Gulf and the Arabian Sea were being inspected. With the prospect of trying to collar fleeing members of al-Qaeda, Navy SEALs were to become more involved in these boardings.

As Saddam's financial situation worsened, he became more dependent on smuggled oil. With the approach of the coalition invasion of Iraq, the game took on a spy-versus-spy tone, with moves and counter-moves on either side. The Iraqi tanker crews took a number of measures to oppose the boarding parties. One of the most successful was welding up entryway hatches and porthole windows to deny boarders access to the interior of the ship. Since the oil smugglers operated close to Iraqi-friendly shores, they only had to delay their attackers until they could make a run for a safe haven. Stopping these tankers became a breaking-and-entering drill—could the SEALs get inside and take control of the ship before these armored tankers could turn and make a dash for friendly territorial waters? And, of course, there were restrictions on the SEALs trying to make these entries, restrictions imposed by the UN sanctions and by accepted international maritime law. One of them was that they couldn't use explosive breaching charges. A breaching charge is a small explosive charge that blows in a locked door. In talking with the SEALs who had to play the game, they naturally thought the rules were silly, because given a free hand, they would have put an end to Saddam's tanker-smuggling operation in short order. So explosive entries were out. As it was, thanks in part to the Yarrow Entry, they eventually won and still played by the rules. We'll get to this novel tanker-busting technique later; first, let's talk about CQD.

Close Quarter Defense, or CQD, became the favored technique for measured force projection in the early and mid-1990s, and was formally adopted for SEAL training by the Naval Special Warfare Center in 1996. Prior to CQD, there had been a number of hand-to-hand techniques and martial disciplines used by SEALs, but none were wholly satisfactory. The SEALs needed a skill set that was versatile and effective, and could be mastered in a reasonably short period of time. Given all that SEALs must learn and do, they really don't have the time for extensive training in martial arts; they needed tools that are combat focused and efficient. This skill set also had to be adaptable to heavily armed men working as a team in a dynamic environment and in a range of operational environments—aboard ship, in buildings, in caves, and in open country. And, finally, it had to be suitable in a threat environment that could range from compliant noncombatants to armed opposition—individually or in a crowd. The answer became CQD.

Close Quarter Defense is difficult to describe. In many ways, it is a blend of martial artistry, commando-style fighting, and the spiritual demands of a warrior. That said, it is much more than that. The word "defense" in the name is misleading; in reality, it is more of an offensive skill set. CQD is the vision and life's work of Duane Dieter. Duane and his Close Quarters Defense School in Easton, Maryland, has worked with Navy SEALs for more than fifteen years. SEALs now deploy in harm's way well drilled in CQD techniques and discipline.

SEALs continue to train at Duane's CQD school in Maryland, but most of the training is exported to the teams and conducted at the SEAL facilities in San Diego and Norfolk.

The training incorporates Duane's philosophy of "Full Circle Readiness," a concept that asks a warrior to engage mind, body, and spirit in the projection of force. It is a philosophy that is in keeping with the humanitarian concerns and responsibility that go with the business of SEAL special operations down range. Its foundation is a simple mantra, "to fight is to risk death," along with what is known as the "three-way test," three questions that every practitioner of CQD must ask in any confrontation:

1. What is the level of my skill?
2. What is the capability of my enemy?
3. What is the situation or environment?

An essential aspect of CQD is the notion or concept of the Inner Warrior and the belief that a warrior must at all times dominate his space. This means he must never allow an adversary to marginalize him or control the situation. Externally, CQD skills are a system of team-based moves, strikes, bars, or holds, and the tactical communications necessary to manage different levels of violence and force projection. CQD is a "behind-the-gun" tactic in that the practitioner maintains the ability to use his weapon. As a defined skill set, the mechanics are well beyond the scope of this book. Accompanying the offensive nature of CQD is the *internal* preparation of a warrior to project force. The Inner Warrior holds that a SEAL must have a moral foundation from which to project his power. In this way, he is capable of the highest level of aggression in mortal combat while maintaining the inner stability to control the level of violence in nonlethal situations. This same inner capability equates to a warrior who lives ethically and morally—one who succeeds in battle as well as in his personal life.

This combination of physical strength, technical skill, and moral authority allows a SEAL warrior a range of options in a given situation. He can be explosively violent in the projection of lethal force, or he can "dial it down" to a lesser force to deal with a lesser threat. This ability to dial it up or dial it down in a dynamic situation is the essence of CQD and the Inner Warrior. From this flows the notion of "earned" treatment. I have heard many a SEAL say, "They get what they deserve." In an opposed situation, or even an ambiguous one, a compliant or nonthreatening individual is engaged much differently than an armed individual. One has earned safety, even protection, while the other may have earned himself a bullet. "It's their choice," the CQD practitioner will say. "They get what they deserve, no more and no less." It requires the highest order of focus, training, and moral authority on the part of the SEAL warrior to make these decisions—to hurt, maim, or kill, or to protect and safeguard. These disciplines can be applied in a range of situations—in a crowd or in a highly confined environment like a small room. In the course of taking down a ship or a building, a SEAL operator may make a dozen or more lethal/nonlethal decisions in a matter of minutes.

"My CQD training saved my life on more than one occasion," a veteran SEAL, who had just returned from urban operations in Iraq, told me. "I've been in this business for about twelve years, and it's the most valuable skill set I take on deployment. We use it almost every time we're on an operation. One night we were taking down a house on the outskirts of Baghdad, and we knew a really bad guy was in the building. Myself and another SEAL were setting a breaching charge on the front door when the door swings open, and this Iraqi dude comes charging out. He was on me before I could react, and we were on the ground rolling around when the breaching charge goes off. The rest of the guys poured into the house just like they were supposed to. My brother SEAL was stunned and couldn't help me, so I had to deal with this dude myself. It was all instinct; I gave him a rapid series of hand strikes, then brought my weapon around for a barrel strike. I had him on his belly, cuffed and searched, in no time at all. As it turned out, he was just some guy who was scared and tried to run. He fought me because I would not let him run. I could have shot him, but he didn't deserve a bullet. Now if he had pulled a knife or a gun, well, that would have been different. Sometimes when you come through a scrap and *don't* have to kill someone, you feel pretty good about it. Does that make sense?"

"You have to understand how fast we move when we're clearing a house," another SEAL told me. "Speed is everything, but we have to move safely. And we have to move as a team. We're always ready to shoot, but we very seldom need to. The objective during the takedown of a house or residence is usually an individual and, occasionally, the house itself—a bomb factory or a weapons cache. So when we encounter someone, we have to quickly judge if that person poses a threat and meet that threat with the proper amount of force. Every situation is different. I've been on operations that involved clearing a large home and a lot of different things are going on. On the first floor, two of the guys have just disarmed a bodyguard and taken him down hard—hard enough that he needs help from the platoon corpsman. On the second floor, another two guys are trying to soothe a grandmother who thinks the world is coming to an end. And up on the third floor, one of the guys is cuffing and searching the bad guy we came to get while his brother SEAL is trying to calm down the guy's wife. We've been known to crank that dial all the way to the left and all the way to the right on the same operation."

"What is left and what is right?" I asked him.

"Full right is a bullet, and full left is handing out a candy bar," he replied. Then he added with a grin, "Or is it the other way around? Either way, we have to get it right."

Currently, CQD training in the teams is taught at three levels. Level One, as discussed in some detail in *The Finishing School,* is usually reserved for SQT. During this weeklong course, the apprentice SEALs learn the basic strikes and a team-centric approach to force projection in compliant and noncompliant situations. There is some classroom instruction, but most of the teaching is contact work. The students are either applying force or serving as role players who provide carefully choreographed resistance. Blows are delivered and, depending on the protective equipment worn by the training partners, blows are taken. CQD is serious business, and both students and instructors routinely absorb a ration of welts and bruises during this training. It is full-contact training and an important part of learning the craft of the SEAL warrior.

"We want to make it as real as possible," one of the CQD instructors told me. CQD instructors are SEALs selected for their technical ability as well as their character—warriors worthy to teach other warriors. "So that means we play the game full speed when we can and in as many different adversarial situations as possible. Professionally, it's rewarding for all concerned and sometimes even fun. But don't take that the wrong way. We all understand that this is serious life-and-death business."

Few SEALs have not had at least Level One CQD, and are now ready for sustained training at Level Two. Level Two CQD training is done at the platoon level, usually during the professional development and occasionally during Unit Level Training of a SEAL platoon's predeployment workup. Level Two takes the operators into formations and movement in the clearing of rooms and deals with tactical flow, movement, and response. During Level Two training, there is an emphasis on shooting/nonshooting situations. The SEALs learn to apply CQD techniques in crowded environments and in situations of low-light visibility. As in Level One, the training is full-contact work, with platoon SEALs and designated role players serving as training partners. Often these training partners wear headgear and body armor to absorb hand and weapon strikes. In shooting situations, they make liberal use of Simunitions, paint bullets that have the same short-range ballistics and cyclic rates of fire as live ammunition. Simunitions—or Sims, as the SEALs call them—allow for gunfights without

the lethality. The idea is to repeatedly put the operator or several operators working as a team in confrontational situations. Most often this
is done with Hooded Box Drills.

Duane Dieter developed the Hooded Box Drill to simulate the intensity of the fight and as a method to validate the skills of the operator.
The box is a "space" delineated by tape on the mat or floor that the
operator or team of operators must defend or control. The hood is a
curtain that drops about their faces to block their vision while a confrontational situation is arranged in front of them. When the curtain is
raised, the operator or team of operators is confronted with a tactical
situation. They must react, sometimes with lethal force—often with
nonlethal force. Role players confront and challenge the SEALs with
situations that demand immediate action. The SEAL operational team
may face a man with a gun in his hand but with his hands over his
head. There may be three men dressed in Arab headgear advancing on
them but with no weapons in sight. The SEALs must react, communicate, disarm, and dominate their adversaries with the appropriate
amount of force. There are an endless variety of confrontational situations that can be played out in the Hooded Box Drills. Many of them
draw on real events that have taken place in Afghanistan, Iraq, and
elsewhere.

"There's a lot of shouting and adrenaline pumping during these
drills," says Chief Ray Dalton. Dalton heads up the West Coast CQD
training. "It's very emotional for the operators, for the role players,
and for my instructors. Sometimes the instructors serve as role players.
This can get very physical. We wear protection, but it's still a fight, and
we want our CQD students not to hold back. But we only let it go on
just so long. Then the instructor in charge of the drill will call 'Endex'
[end exercise], and we settle everybody down. After the drill, we talk
about what was done correctly and where there needs to be improvement; or if not improvement, other ways that the situation could have
been handled or force could have been applied. The idea is that when
the guys are deployed and they play it out for real, to some extent it's

just another training exercise. They react almost without thinking, because there is no time to think, and that reaction has to be the correct one. Lives depend on it."

"You learn a great deal in Level Two CQD," one of the platoon SEALs coming off deployment said. "And those lessons are put to use daily. One of the things we learn is to engage the most deadly threat first. This means you could have a guy coming at you who is unarmed, while some dude across the room has a rifle or a pistol. You learn to develop a situational awareness—to take in the whole situation at a glance, then take the best course of action. It takes practice, and the box drills do that for you.

"In Baghdad, we were taking down a house where one of Saddam's thugs was holed up. I came through the door into a room and this Iraqi, one of the target's bodyguards, came at me with a knife. Now, under normal conditions, that knife would have earned him a bullet. You never let a guy get close to you with a lethal weapon—if you can help it. But, at a glance, I saw a woman and some kids behind him. We have to be careful shooting in houses, even when there are people in the next room. The rounds from an M4 can go through a man or through a wall, and still have enough power to kill. So I let this Iraqi come at me and took him out with a barrel strike. He went down like a sack of cement. We moved on through the house and found the guy we came to get. The bodyguard with the knife was still out cold when we hustled the target out of there.

"With the CQD training behind me, it was all instinct, and yet it was almost in slow motion. It was like 'Okay, he's earned a bullet, shoot him—oops, can't shoot him—Mom and kids behind him—barrel strike to the head.' It was a chain of decisions, but they happened instantly. And I'll tell you something else. It really feels good to have done the right thing—to have made a good call. If I hadn't had the ability to recognize the potential harm to noncombatants *and* the ability to take him down without lethal force, I'd have had no choice but to shoot him and risk the others. I wouldn't have minded shooting him, but my training gave me a better option—certainly better for the noncombatants and, as it turned out, better for him."

Level Three training, taught personally by Duane Dieter, expands and builds on Level Two disciplines. It builds on the tactical awareness and sensory skill development, like that described above. Level Three expands into specialized weapons, team formations, vehicle take-downs, counterassault tactics, high-value prisoner snatches, friendly personnel recoveries, and a range of emergency and improvised tactics. Level Three includes Hooded Box Drills with live ammunition and advanced work in tactical "kill houses"—special structures designed for multiple room-clearing training with live fire. This is high-speed, expensive training using as many as a hundred trained role players.

Level Three CQD training usually takes place during Squadron Integration Training. As a squadron commander readies his forces for deployment, he will look for ways to better prepare his squadron components for the operational theater. This often means he will send as many of his SEAL platoons to Level Three CQD training as he can. He will also arrange for some of his non-SEAL assets, specifically his small-boat crews and his explosive ordnance disposal technicians, to get Level One training. While these squadron units may not be in the van of a SEAL assault element, they may have to help with the controlling and marshaling of prisoners on a combat operation.

The SEALs boarding the *Saddam Maru* knew it was going to be a challenge, so they came aboard with a full platoon. The previous day, a Canadian special operations team had boarded this same tanker. They had worked on it for close to forty-five minutes, but they could not crack the armadillo-like deckhouse that had been welded tight and was further strengthened with double-reinforced steel at the normal entry points. This vessel had additional steel plating on various portions of the deck housing, so that no single cut into the bulkheads of the pilot-house could provide an access. The tanker's crew, on later questioning, felt that they were invulnerable—that the counterboarding and entry-denial measures recently installed on the vessel had made them safe from the allied boarding parties. But they had failed to take into account the Yarrow Entry.

Lieutenant (junior grade) Sean Yarrow was on his first SEAL deployment. He was large for a Navy SEAL—six-two and two hundred pounds. Yarrow grew up in Pittsburgh and graduated from the Naval Academy in June 1998. He went through BUD/S with Class 222. In June 2001, he found himself deployed with a SEAL platoon in an ARG—an Amphibious Ready Group—on patrol in the Persian Gulf. The ARG was fully engaged in MIO and anti-oil-smuggling operations, and his platoon was doing its share of the boardings. The idea that an organization called al-Qaeda could and would conduct such devastating attacks were, at that time, quite far removed from most of America's thinking, and certainly from Sean Yarrow's. He was a newly minted SEAL officer trying to contribute to the operations of his platoon. Sean, like the other members of his platoon, had Level One training in CQD.

The oil-smuggling game was being played with some intensity during the summer of 2001, and at that time the Iraqis had the upper hand. SEAL boarding parties would swoop down upon a tanker carrying contraband oil. The Iraqi master would turn his vessel for the safe haven of friendly territorial waters and the race was on. Could the SEALs crack the steel nut of the tanker pilothouse before the ship made it from international waters to a safe haven? At that stage, the SEALs method of cracking the secure deckhouse of a tanker was to find a convenient weather-deck hatch and begin cutting. Usually, they went for one of the pilothouse hatches, which were the closest to the ship control station. No sense in cracking a lower-deck hatch and finding an internal passageway hatch welded shut. After getting aboard and setting external security, the SEAL breaching team fired up its Quicksaw, a gas-driven rotary saw with an eighteen-inch diamond-tipped blade for cutting metal, and went to work. As the boarded tanker put its rudder over to run for freedom, the scream of a saw blade biting into metal echoed across the weather decks and into the night. That summer, the Iraqis began welding a secondary level of three-eighths-inch steel and I-beam spacers, which slowed the cutting-and-entering process considerably. This double-steel reinforcement took too long to breach, and the boarding SEALs simply couldn't get through in the allotted time. Things were leaning in the Iraqis' favor.

Sean Yarrow's role in the platoon at that time was that of the assigned third officer, or third-O. He had limited tactical duties in the platoon and some administrative responsibilities, but his primary job as a new first-tour officer was to watch and learn. He was a platoon SEAL and not technically a Smee, but his leadership duties in the platoon were limited. He was a new guy—a new officer. When the platoon boarded a tanker and set up its security and entry teams, his job was to roam the decks of the ship with a hooligan, a crowbarlike lever arm, and look for an easier way. While his platoon mates attacked a pilothouse door, Sean poked and pried at other hatches and portholes, trying to force one of them open. In the course of his duties, he noticed that the center forward-facing window to the pilothouse was not welded shut, as were the others. This single window had to be kept free so that the helmsman could see to steer the ship and was perhaps the only source of ventilation in the pilothouse. However, the window was all but inaccessible. All the forward-facing pilothouse windows were on a sheer metal face that comprised the forward bulkhead of the ship's superstructure. In fact, due to tanker design, these windows were often set in a reverse slope to provide for easier viewing of the forward decking and to assist in conning the ship during docking operations. But Yarrow had an idea. After an unsuccessful attempt to cut into a tanker before it passed into Iranian territorial waters, he vowed to give his idea a try the next time out.

"Yarrow had a good idea to come in through the front bridge windows," said Chief Don Latham, the platoon chief petty officer, "but getting over the pilothouse to the front window, often at night, when you don't have a lot of time, is tricky work. It's like being a window washer on a high-rise building in a combat situation. And those tankers, even when they're loaded, can pitch and roll.

"We boarded a lot of tankers that summer," Latham continued, "and they became more and more difficult. The ones we did stop would be taken to a holding area down near Bahrain, where they were held in an offshore penalty box of sorts until their owners paid the fine and got their tankers back. Then they would be back trying to smuggle oil. One of them—it had a long Spanish-sounding name—we called the *Dirty Taco*. It was a filthy ship. We boarded it three times; our platoon stopped it twice. Toward the end, most of the tankers were getting through because they were welded up tight, and we simply didn't have the time to crack them."

Aboard their aircraft carrier, the SEALs set up a practice area on the hangar deck. "There was a mezzanine deck above the hangar deck where we could work with the ropes," one of the platoon SEALs recalled. "The drill was to do it quickly and safely. That meant we had to have the ropes and harnesses set up ahead of time and we had to practice. The idea was to get two SEALs quickly over the pilothouse, one to make the entry and the other to give him security. We set up a rope course on the hanger deck of the carrier. Soon we had the chief and Mister Yarrow dangling over the mezzanine deck, rappelling down to the hangar deck. The speed came when we practiced it over and over."

"A few days later we intercepted an Iraqi tanker in international waters," said Yarrow. "As always, the master refused to heave to, so we boarded her. While the guys began to grind away at the pilothouse door, I rappelled over the pilothouse and down to the open center window. The guy at the helm took off when he saw me. I entered through the open window and the chief came in behind me. I put the helm over, while the chief covered me. We then began working on the outside door from the inside. With the tanker headed out to sea, we had time to crack the doors and clear the ship. Chalk one up for the good guys."

The SEALs had gained an advantage, but the cat-and-mouse game wasn't over—not yet. The Iraqis began welding rebar, then hinged plates, across the window in front of the helm; but in the absence of a periscope, they needed to see out from somewhere in the pilothouse. Basically, there was no way they could weld double plating to a window that they needed to have open at least part of the time. But Sean Yarrow was ready for them. Now when the platoon boarded a ship, both Yarrow and his chief were in rappelling harnesses with two men assigned to belay them. They had worked out a system of ropes and belay points. While the breaching team began cutting at one of the hatches, Yarrow, armed with a Quicksaw, would swing down to the vulnerable window and begin to cut at the rebar or the single sheet of steel plating.

"I would sling my weapon and fire up the saw," Yarrow said. "Chief Latham would be there with his weapon to give security while I did the cutting. We were like a couple of spiders swaying in the wind, but we got the system down so that we always beat the breaching team into the pilothouse. We'd found a way in, and unless the Iraqis came up with something new, we could now win the race. Usually, it took us no more than ten minutes to get inside and take control of a ship."

"Good young officer," Chief Don Latham said of Yarrow. "Smart young officer. Like the rest of the platoon, I wasn't so sure about Yarrow's idea—it seemed a little harebrained when he proposed going in over the front of the pilothouse. But it worked, and it worked every time."

"Why didn't the Iraqis put armed men aboard these tankers?" I asked. "Wouldn't that have changed things?"

"I think they knew their best chance was to play it unarmed. If they had fired on a boarding party, then all bets were off. They could no longer claim to be unarmed merchantmen. We would have then broken out the explosive breaching charges and taken out a bulkhead or two. I don't think they wanted to get in a firefight with us. No one wants to get in a firefight with us."

But Saddam wanted the money from his smuggled oil and the *Saddam Maru* was one of his last gambits. The pilothouse windows of the

Saddam Maru had a decidedly reverse slope, so Yarrow and Latham had to work at a difficult angle. The vessel also had both rebar and a single hinged plate on the front pilothouse window. When the crewmen on watch heard the SEALs clamoring on the roof of the pilothouse, they immediately bolted the window. The tanker turned and made for the nearest Gulf state's territorial waters; the clock was ticking. The two SEALs gripped themselves in close to the face of the superstructure and broke out their tools. By this time, Yarrow could hear the whine of the gas engine from the Quicksaw of the SEAL breaching team at the pilothouse door. Soon the sound of his own saw joined it. For those inside, it must have sounded like dueling chain-saw engines. The scream of the saw blades biting into steel alone must have been unbearable. Clamped onto the front of the pilothouse like a couple of insects, the two SEALs worked against time. Yarrow quickly cut through the rebar and then began on the movable plate. He cut an access hole, tossed the saw inside, and then wriggled through the opening. Depending on the situation, the first man through an entry would toss in a flash-bang—a small grenade designed to temporarily blind and stun those inside. Seeing no one, Yarrow made the entry without the fanfare. Chief Latham, still outside, struggled to gain a purchase so he could follow his officer.

Yarrow moved across the deserted pilothouse to where the other SEALs were still trying to cut through the door. While the door was double plated, it was designed to be opened from the inside to provide access to the bridge wings. This access would be necessary to conn the ship in restricted waters or when mooring the ship. Yarrow was able to remove the inner plating that was clamped to the I beams on the inside of the door. The dogging—the series of clamping levers that secured the hatch to the pilothouse opening—was tied in place in a series of knots with stout line. While he was considering how to deal with this, an Iraqi crewman came into the pilothouse and approached him from behind. The crewman was too close by the time Yarrow turned around, so he couldn't bring his primary weapon up to bear. It was now CQD time. Reflexively, Yarrow gave the Iraqi a hand strike to the sternum and the man went down, conscious but stunned. Chief Latham, who was even bigger than Yarrow, was still trying to get through the opening and could not assist him. Yarrow slung his MP5 submachine gun and, with his knife, began to cut at the ropes that secured the hatch dogs. Enter a second Iraqi. Yarrow quickly drew his Sig Sauer 9mm sidearm and ordered the man to lie on the deck. He appeared to be unarmed, but he kept coming. Yarrow gave him a barrel strike with the pistol and the second Iraqi went down. He had almost cut through all the ropes at the pilothouse door and Chief Latham was almost through the window access when a third Iraqi came at him. Another barrel strike and he, too, joined his friends on the floor.

"The Iraqis do that sometimes," Yarrow said. "They have orders to fight to the death, but they really aren't going to do that. So they have to do something, show some physical resistance. If they have a gun or a knife, then they're in serious trouble. Usually, they just need to be hit and put down, and their honor is intact. Normally, we do everything in pairs or as a team, which is a lot safer. But this time I was alone. When I look back on it, it was just like a Hooded Box Drill at CQD training."

"It was a scene out of the movies," Latham said, recalling the incident. "By the time I got into the pilothouse, Mister Yarrow was standing there, pistol in one hand, knife in the other, and a pile of Iraqis on the deck. It took only a few more minutes to get the rest of the platoon in and we owned the ship."

The sortie of the *Saddam Maru* was the beginning of the end of the Iraqi oil-smuggling operations. The route their tankers had to follow required that they be in international waters for at least part of the journey. With the Yarrow Entry, the SEALs were now consistently boarding and stopping these tankers. The Yarrow Entry was passed down to new platoons coming into theater and became part of SEAL platoon predeployment training. Following the attacks of 11 September, more warships took up station in the Persian Gulf and the northern Arabian Sea, but few tankers ventured out with contraband oil.

Within weeks of those attacks, additional SEAL platoons deployed to the region, along with units of the fleet. The boardings continued, but now they were looking for al-Qaeda leaders trying to leave the region by sea, work that in many ways was more dangerous than stopping the flow of illegal oil.

The escalating conflict between Saddam and the U.S. Navy in the late 1990s and through the summer of 2001 was a critical point in time. Of course, today, in the aftermath of the overthrow of Saddam Hussein's regime, armored Iraqi tankers no longer try to sneak contraband oil from Umm Qsar to neutral ports. The U.S. Navy now guards the offshore oil terminals to protect them from sabotage, and American security forces protect the oil infrastructure ashore. Some would think it ironic that Iraqi oil flowed freely to the export-loading terminals when the proceeds went into Saddam's offshore bank accounts, but now has to be guarded when the revenue is the property of the Iraqi people. In any event, the SEAL actions before the war were important, and this pre-9/11 struggle proved to be instructional in several ways.

First, there was the restraint shown by U.S. naval forces and their allies operating under the U.S. Central Command. They were unchallenged in their supremacy of the sea and could have, through action at sea or hot pursuit into friendly territorial waters, quickly ended Saddam's smuggling operations. The Navy could have sunk the whole lot. But the United States closely adhered to international law and the conventions of the sea. The Iraqi masters and the crews aboard these tankers put to sea because they dared not refuse the Iraqi dictator. But they also knew that if boarded and stopped, they would be treated humanely. They trusted the Americans not to seriously hurt them. In fact, the boarding crews quickly learned that the Iraqis often invited a token slapping or crack on the head as proof to Saddam that they had resisted the Americans. Their ships might be impounded, but the crews would be put ashore and not harmed.

The other instructional element of these operations was in the ways in which the SEAL boarding parties developed new tactics to complete their assigned mission. I know there was a certain amount of grousing among the platoons about the limitations under which they had to work, but like units of the fleet, SEALs understand rules of engagement. ROEs and the restrictions they impose are simply part of the job. SEALs know they must operate within those limitations and still accomplish the mission. They have to, as with the Yarrow Entry, find creative ways to get the job done within the boundaries established by higher authority.

The VBSS operations in the Persian Gulf and contiguous waters provided an excellent training ground. The MIO, LIO, and contraband searches validated the worth and use of the SEAL's CQD training. SEALs were put aboard ships where the likelihood of opposition was greatest. The boarding parties became practiced at quickly securing a room or compartment and moving quickly to the next. They learned to distinguish between bravado and a genuine threat. They developed techniques for marshaling prisoners in a safe-and-secure manner while they searched a vessel. All these experiences and lessons learned came back with the returning platoons and were made part of the training to prepare other platoons for future deployment. These boardings were the training wheels for what was to come. Aboard those ships, prior to 11 September, SEALs had to deal with crewmen, usually merchant seamen, who were variously compliant and who were seldom armed. But the SEALs were about to take their CQD skills ashore. Ahead were continuous operations in Afghanistan and Iraq, where the opposition would be hard-core Baathists and al-Qaeda, and where the game would be much deadlier. Soon SEALs began entering buildings where women, children, old men, and armed men would all be present. They would do this on a regular basis, and their ROEs would still bind them to humane treatment of all concerned. This work would require a continuous refinement of their tactics and CQD techniques to allow them to get the job done and yet still play the lethal game within the rules.

Lieutenant Sean Yarrow managed to stay close to the fight. He was on deployment as a SEAL AOIC (assistant officer in charge) in the spring

of 2003 and participated in one of the more significant SEAL operations of the Iraqi War. "It seemed that when I was on deployment, my
platoon was always in the middle of it. I hope it's a pattern that continues." Lieutenant Yarrow is temporarily assigned to Naval Special
Warfare Group One. He is awaiting assignment as a SEAL platoon
OIC (officer in charge) and for another deployment to the Central
Command.

After seven deployments and eighteen years of service, Chief Don
Latham is taking a break from the deployment rotation. He is currently
on assignment to Naval Special Warfare Command. Chief Latham, a
Colorado native who graduated with BUD/S Class 153, currently
works with an operational-planning cell that develops new tactics for
SEALs currently in the fight.

"We are very busy," says Duane Dieter. "Close Quarter Defense is in
high demand by any number of civilian, military, and law enforcement
agencies. But the SEALs continue to be our most active end users. We
now have SEALs taking these skills back with them on their fourth and
fifth deployment. It's a continuing validation of everything we do here
at CQD." Duane Dieter recently returned from overseas, where he operated with SEALs he had trained. "It was very satisfying," he reported,
"to see them using to good advantage the skills we taught them."

CHAPTER 3

SR AND DA: NAVY SEALS COME ASHORE

For most Americans, the war on terrorism began on 11 September 2001, the day the Islamists attacked the United States. Those in the intelligence business and those who studied terrorists prior to 9/11 knew differently. But to have a war, there must be two combatants, and prior to the attacks of 11 September, there had been only one. During the last two decades of the twentieth century, "they" killed more than 350 of our citizens in and around the Middle East *and* in the United States, even though most Americans believed we were living in a period of peace. As a result of the *first* attack in 1993 on the Twin Towers in New York City, six Americans died. Around the world, hundreds of foreign nationals also lost their lives as collateral damage, and hundreds more of our citizens were wounded. These attacks, even though they were organized, coordinated, and directed by Islamic fundamentalists, were treated as criminal acts, not acts of war. We had simply become accustomed to a periodic loss of life through terrorist activity. Our response was to try to bring these criminals to justice, so we deployed FBI agents and evidentiary teams.

Not all Americans believed that we were at peace, and among those

SEAL mobility. SEALs have adapted the standard military HMMWV, or Humvee, to the unique requirements of SEAL operations. *Courtesy of the U.S. Navy (Eric Logsdon)*

were the SEALs who regularly deployed to the Central Command. They saw the carnage at the Marine barracks in Beirut; they saw the body bags with American sailors being carried from the USS *Cole*. Many that I spoke with felt our nation was not doing enough to meet this growing threat, and more than a few thought that they were being unnecessarily restrained. For example, in late July 1996, a naval task force was hastily assembled when it was thought that Imad Mugniyah, the Hezbollah security chief, was aboard the freighter *Ibn Tufail* as it made its way around the Arabian Peninsula and into the Persian Gulf. The task force, with a complement of marines and two SEAL platoons, shadowed the *Ibn Tufail*. They were in position to seize the ship and had a plan to capture this known terrorist. The SEALs were to fast-rope onto the vessel and seize control. The marines would then come aboard and do a thorough search. Imad Mugniyah was at the time the most wanted terrorist in the world. He was the man responsible for the deaths of 241 marines and sailors in Beirut.

"We were locked and loaded, sitting aboard the helos," one of the assault leaders told me, "and the helos were turning on deck, ready for liftoff. We had the ship in international waters and we had the force in place. We even had the diagrams of the internal ship spaces. Then the word came down—'mission canceled.' We were told that there was insufficient intelligence; that he may not have been aboard. We were absolutely stunned. It really shook our marines; this guy killed over two hundred of their brothers. I still think about it. It was my platoon's one chance to make a difference, and we were stood down. If it had been after 9/11, we would have taken that ship, or any other vessel in open waters, if there was a hint that there might be a terrorist leader aboard."

There has been much subsequent debate as to whether Mugniyah was or was not aboard that ship in the Gulf in 1996. One thing, however, is clear. Prior to 11 September, we treated terrorists as criminals, but now we can treat them as combatants in a war.

On 11 September 2001, there were twelve Navy SEAL platoons deployed worldwide. Some of these platoons were aboard units of the fleet with Amphibious Ready Groups. Others were assigned to Naval Special Warfare Units, overseas shore facilities that serve as home base for deployed SEAL platoons. There were SEALs in Europe, South America, and Korea, as well as throughout the Pacific. Then, as now, Naval Special Warfare maintained a standing global deployment posture. At that time there was an emphasis on placing NSW assets in the Middle East, but there was no concentration of those forces. Those platoons assigned to CENTCOM were engaged in readiness and training exercises with Gulf state allies and enforcing the United Nations embargo on Iraq. One platoon was usually with the task force patrolling the Gulf. Lieutenant (junior grade) Sean Yarrow and Chief Petty Officer Don Latham were in one such platoon. Prior to 11 September, they were engaged in MIO duties—maritime interception operations largely associated with the Iraqi embargo. Another platoon was shore based at the Naval Special Warfare Unit in Bahrain and assigned to training duties in Kuwait. Both platoons were assets of the Central Command.

"When we got word of the attack on America, we couldn't believe it," Chief Randy Lowery said. He was the platoon chief of the CENTCOM platoon in Bahrain. "We were shocked, angry, and we wanted to get our guns into the fight. But where and who? That took a while to sort out. The only thing we knew was that the training exercises were over; from now on it was going to be real world. Half the platoon was in Kuwait and the other half was in Bahrain. The first thing we did was get the guys back from Kuwait and get our gear together. That didn't take long, as we pretty much keep up to speed while on deployment, but there's always something to do. Now there was a clear reason to do it. For those first few days we sat at the unit in Bahrain, checked our gear, and watched those Twin Towers come down again and again on the TV replays."

It took a few weeks to bring the who and the where into focus. When it became known that the prime suspect was Osama bin Laden and that his base of operations was Afghanistan, under the protection of the Taliban, General Tommy Franks and his war planners went to work. They began with a strategy that clearly would not work—a massive conventional ground operation. That had been tried by the Russian army for a decade, and it had failed. Franks and his staff then came up with a two-pronged approach for the Afghan campaign. Army Special Forces were sent into northern Afghanistan to work with the entrenched Taliban opposition, the Northern Alliance—a loose confederation of clans that opposed the government in Kabul. The southern component of this double-pronged approach was to be a conventional ground force and coalition special operations components operating in the south. But the major effort was to be delivered by the Army Special Forces and the Northern Alliance backed by American airpower. Two days before the attacks on America, 9 September, bin Laden and the Taliban managed to assassinate General Ahmed Shah Massoud, the charismatic leader of the Northern Alliance. It didn't matter. In a classic unconventional warfare campaign, the Army Special Forces quickly regrouped the Northern Alliance clans and turned them south. The Afghan campaign was on.

Looking back through the prism of Iraq, it is easy to forget that conventional wisdom of the time held that we would be bogged down for months, even years, digging the redoubtable Afghan mountain fighters out of their caves. The doubters predicted quagmire and stalemate. When the campaign seemed stalled, congressional leaders pressed General Franks to think about more troops and a more conventional approach to the war. Franks would have none of it. The leaders of the Northern Alliance urged their men forward, but as they pushed south, those leaders were never too far from a Special Forces team sergeant and his radio—the radio that linked the ground forces to American air strikes.

In the south, there was the question of how to introduce an expeditionary force on the ground in a landlocked, hostile nation. The U.S. Marines would make up that force, but the question was how to get them into Afghanistan without the convenience of an ocean and a beach landing site. Surveys were made of the nearest beaches in Pakistan, but there were logistic and political obstacles that eliminated them from consideration. The only solution was a massive long-range airborne assault. The marines and their equipment would fly into Afghanistan. An insertion site was selected in the central Afghan plain, but a lot of questions about the site had to be answered before that many marines would be airlifted into this hostile environment. In preparation for the Marine Corps insertion, the SEAL platoon in Bahrain was moved to a forward operating base on Masirah Island, off the coast of Oman. No specific orders had been given, but the platoon was told to prepare for strategic reconnaissance—an SR mission. Along with the platoon, other Naval Special Warfare assets under what was soon to become Task Force K-Bar began to assemble on Masirah.

While the SEALs and marines gathered offshore and at hastily prepared regional bases, and the Special Forces organized their indigenous fighters in the north, another SOF force made a bold assault south of the southern city of Kandahar. On the night of 20 October, barely five weeks after America was attacked, a hundred Rangers made an airborne assault on a compound thought to be frequented by Taliban leader Mullah Muhammad Omar. The Rangers did not get Omar, but they came up with several weapons caches and some valuable documents. This did little material damage to the Taliban, or al-Qaeda, but spoke volumes in terms of SOF capability. It told the Taliban and those under their protection that anytime, anywhere, American airborne infantry can drop from the sky. It sent the message that American SOF forces can go where they want and when they want. After the Rangers jumped into Afghanistan near Kandahar, those responsible for the 11 September attacks slept a little less often and a little less soundly. And they seldom slept two nights in succession in the same place.

The movement of SEALs and SEAL support assets from Bahrain to Masirah required planning and time. Central Afghanistan was not only more than a thousand miles from friendly bases in Bahrain and Kuwait, but any direct air route would take them into Iranian airspace for much of their journey. Masirah was no closer than Bahrain to Afghanistan, but coalition forces could get there without having to overfly Iran. At sea, assigned warships of the Navy's 7th Fleet began to make their way from the Persian Gulf and the Pacific toward the northern Arabian Sea. In addition to basing arrangements in Oman, there was an air base west of Karachi, Pakistan, a temporary arrangement that allowed for the staging of forces and for the landing of allied military aircraft to refuel. These sites were located in Muslim nations, so Western military activity had to be kept very low key. For the marines of the 15th Marine Expeditionary Unit (MEU), it was "haze gray, under way." They would wait for the call to action aboard warships at sea. The SEALs would make their preparations on Masirah.

The platoon arrived on the island in mid-October and waited for further orders. They set up temporary quarters in air-conditioned tents along the edge of the airfield. They lived well enough, but they had to contend with constantly blowing sand. All they were told was that planning was under way to get a U.S. presence in Afghanistan as quickly as possible. Lieutenant Steve Autry, the platoon's OIC, was told little, other than his platoon would probably be tasked with a reconnaissance mission that might include a mobility requirement. "Mobility" is a euphemism for motorized travel. SEALs had long trained with and developed mobility tactics for their desert patrol vehicles, or DPVs, but this training did not extend to all deployed platoons. DPVs were armed vehicles, similar to dune buggies, that carried a crew of three and could be fitted with a stretcher to recover a downed pilot. During the Gulf War, they had been used for combat search and rescue (CSAR). These nimble vehicles could be carried by CH-53 helicopters and quickly unloaded in the desert with the idea that they could dash in to pick up an aviator on the ground. But the platoon in Oman had no DPVs—and if they had, they would have found the vehicles ill-suited to carry armed SEALs for a motorized reconnaissance patrol.

"We were initially given four Humvees that were set up for desert patrol—perfect for our mobility needs," Chief Petty Officer Will Gates recalled. The Humvee, or Hummer, is the conventional name for the versatile HMMWV (high-mobility multipurpose wheeled vehicle). "But, as it turned out, they weren't to be our vehicles. *They* belonged to the Army. Another requirement came along and those vehicles were taken from us. We were once again without any mobility. No vehicles, no mission. Then the Special Boat Team assigned to a nearby shore facility came to our rescue. They had four new standard-issue Army Humvees, but they were stock vehicles—no ring turret in the top for a mounted machine gun or anything. Basically, they were pickup trucks. They were vehicles used for pulling boats and for general utility work."

Gates was the platoon leading petty officer and the only one in the platoon with mobility experience. He is a short, barrel-chested man with regular features, soft brown eyes, and an easy grin. While he was the platoon LPO he was also a chief petty officer, having been promoted to chief while on this deployment. Chief Gates is from Ohio and graduated with BUD/S Class 170.

"We got right to work on them," he recalled, "especially when we found out about the mission parameters and where we were going. It was going to be a race: Could we get the vehicles ready in time to do the mission?"

The area chosen for landing the marines in Afghanistan was an old dirt airstrip and compound that had been used by wealthy Arabs for bird hunting, but there had been little sport hunting allowed under the austere regime of the Taliban. While the site appeared deserted, it did not necessarily mean that it was totally abandoned. The Taliban was well armed and, after the Rangers' visit to the compound of their leader, they were on high alert. Taliban irregulars and Arabs with al-Qaeda connections could be tenacious fighters, and they still had a quantity of U.S.-made shoulder-fired Stinger antiaircraft missiles. These missiles were deadly against helicopters and low-flying troop transports. We had provided the Afghans with the missiles and trained them in their use. It was the introduction of Stingers that tipped the balance in the Afghans' favor during the long Russian occupation.

The mission handed to the SEAL platoon was to quietly slip into the area and observe the old airstrip to ensure that it was suitable and secure. They were then to prepare the site for the arrival of the marines and guide them in. This meant that they had to make their approach at night, without alerting the enemy that this was to be the primary invasion site in southern Afghanistan.

"We found a dry lake bed some ten miles from the target and built our plan around the ability to land there and make our way to the landing site," Lieutenant Autry recalled. "Since we had to get on the ground, travel to the site, and go to ground in a single night, this meant we couldn't hump it, not with the gear we had to carry. That's when we began to give a lot of attention to the Humvees. Fortunately, we had Chief Gates and Dan Lloyd."

Dan Lloyd's job in the platoon was that of first lieutenant, a shipboard term for the person in charge of the small craft and deck seamanship. In a SEAL platoon, the first lieutenant's duties include CRRCs, outboard motors, vehicles, and all things mechanical. He was a guy who also loved tinkering with cars. His attention and talent were now directed at the four Humvees that had to be made ready for the mission. Gates and Lloyd were given the responsibility for converting the Humvee pickup trucks into Humvees suitable for armed reconnaissance.

"Given all the vehicles we have now," Gates said, "and the mobility training that we routinely give the platoons in predeployment workup, it's hard to imagine all that we did at Masirah to get ready, and the short time we had to do it. It was an amazing experience. We were getting about four hours sleep a night, then we launched into Afghanistan. No one worked harder than Danny Lloyd. The guy never slept.

"Once we had the new vehicles, we began to strip them down," Gates recalled. "Like I said, these were stock vehicles and we had to convert them for combat use. We cut holes in the tops to mount a heavy machine gun and removed the doors so those inside had good fields of fire. We found some office swivel chairs, modified them, and welded them in the vehicles. There was a junkyard nearby where we could scrounge for parts. We'd take a Quicksaw and cut the top off a wrecked vehicle and weld it on top of one of ours. But we couldn't have done it without the Air Force. We had nothing—no tools and no place to work. They had a garage with tools, work bays, and lifts. We started working there at night when they weren't busy, but Dan and I had no chance of doing this by ourselves. I went to the lead Air Force mechanic and said, 'We're getting ready to launch into Afghanistan on an important mission. Can you give us a hand?' They jumped right in and helped us during their off-duty hours. Some of those Air Force mechanics worked their job in the daytime and helped us at night. We set up a Humvee modification operation. There was a plumbing shop on the base where we scrounged some PVC and metal piping. As soon as we got them modified, we had to repaint them all in desert camouflage."

"They didn't look all that pretty," Dan Lloyd recalled. "As a matter of fact, they looked like jalopies, but mechanically they were sound. The Air Force techs had all the diagnostic test equipment for Humvees, and they gave them a thorough going-over. We didn't have any back-ups, so all these vehicles had to run reliably and quietly."

"We had to get those vehicles ready in a hurry," Chief Gates continued, "and we worked around the clock to make it happen. Given the mission profile, those Hummers *were* the operation. Then there were the tactics associated with a mobility operation. The platoon didn't have much training in vehicles, so in the few days allowed, I had to get them up to speed on a mobility patrol."

As Gates explained it, a mounted patrol is much like a foot patrol. There has to be good communication along the file, and if there is trouble, certain actions have to be instinctual. As with a foot patrol, there are certain procedures for halts, danger-crossing points, sighting of the enemy, and especially for enemy contact. And because they are relying on vehicles, they had to be prepared for any mechanical problems that might arise—minor repairs or a flat tire. At the edge of the airfield in Oman, Gates gave his platoon a quick course in mobility operations.

"We were a West Coast platoon, and no one but myself had any mobility training. Fortunately, we had two SEALs from the East Coast assigned to our platoon, and they had worked with Hummers. They helped with the training and became two of our drivers."

Since there is plenty of uninhabited desert on Masirah, there was ample space, if only a limited time, for the SEALs to rehearse for the operation. When they were not modifying the Humvees, they were out rehearsing mobility patrol procedures. And when they weren't doing that, they were reviewing imagery of the target area and planning the operation. When the target window came, the platoon was as ready as it could be in the time allowed. The SEALs were to be inserted on the darkest night of the month.

"Our plan called for four Humvees to be put down about ten miles from the target site on the dry lake bed," Chief Lowery recalled. "We had to fly in, land, make our way to the target, and go to ground, and we had to do this in about eleven hours of darkness. If we couldn't do it without being compromised, then the whole operation was at risk. Looking back on it, the hardest part was just getting on the ground without raising the alarm."

For close to a week, the SEALs stood ready. When time allowed, they continued to tweak the vehicles and conducted more rehearsals. The operation was a go, then a no-go, and back to a go. This often happens in a complex SR operation. The delay wasn't due to indecision at the command level, but because of logistical problems encountered by the Marine Corps. There are many moving parts that accompany the long-range airborne infiltration of a Marine Expeditionary Unit. There was the preparation of marines who were gathered and waiting offshore, the staging of aircraft—both rotary and fixed wing—that were to fly the marines in, and the logistic train that had to follow and support the marines once they were on the ground. All these considerations had to be addressed to ensure success. Failure was not an option. This was to be the first sustained American ground effort in the war on terrorism. For it to begin well, the strategic reconnaissance assigned to the SEALs was critical. On the afternoon of 20 November, the word came down—again: It was a go.

"We'd grown accustomed to saddling up and standing down," Lieutenant Steve Autry recalled. "It was irritating, but it's part of the job. We had to be professionals and handle it. Check the equipment, check the radios, check the vehicles, take a piss, break out an MRE, and stand by. It's part of the game. When the 'go' came on the twentieth, it was like all the others. But this time we pulled up the ramp and the 130s took off." The mission called for two aircraft, each carrying two Humvees. "At the time, we knew that we could be recalled at any time, but at least we were in the air. The guys were good about it. I told them that if we had a hundred false alarms and never did the mission, we'd play each one like it was the real thing, and they did. That's what being a pro is all about—making yourself good to go and staying good to go."

"The insertion site was a little over eight hundred miles from our base," Chief Lowery said of the run to the target, "about a three-hour flight. We didn't come down to the deck until we got close to Afghan airspace, where the terrain was flat. Then the pilots took it down to a few hundred feet. At that height, the MC-130s fly themselves with their terrain-following radar, and if the ground is hilly, it can get really rough in the back. Fortunately, we didn't have to fly low level over Pakistan or in a mountainous part of Afghanistan, so the ride in wasn't too bad. I can't say enough about our special operations pilots; they made a straight pass in and dropped us right onto the insertion point."

The MC-130J special operations Combat Talon is a sophisticated insertion platform with a very capable electronics suite. It is a sixty-ton, four-engine aircraft that can do a lot of things. An MC-130J can do what a human cannot—react quickly enough to fly at two hundred feet at three hundred knots—but it takes a talented pilot with a good pair of night-vision goggles to land that much airplane in the middle of nowhere at night on a dry lake bed. The two aircraft dropped to the hard-packed sand within seconds of each other and began their roll-out, the big turbofan engines reversing thrust to bring them to a stop. As soon as the wheels kissed Afghan soil, the SEALs were at work. They had rehearsed this many times in the premission workup. Their first order of business was to get the Humvees unchained and ready to off-load. Every man aboard had a duty and a place to be in preparing to exit the aircraft. As soon as the tail ramp was lowered, SEALs rushed from darkened cargo bays and set up a security perimeter. The Humvees followed them down the ramp. The two 130s pirouetted neatly and roared back into the sky in the direction from which they had come. As the roar of the engines faded, silence returned to the dry lake bed. For close to a half hour, the men on the ground waited, watching and listening. They heard nothing and saw nothing, yet they waited in the dark silence.

In some ways, this was as it had been for myself and my brother SEALs in Vietnam so many years ago. The SEAL support craft would nose into the bank of a Mekong river, and we would swarm ashore in a security perimeter. The boat would leave, then we would wait in the mud and the mangroves listening for enemy movement before we continued with the patrol. Often, the boat would ground itself several places along the river, so the Vietcong would not know exactly where we inserted.

On this night, intelligence and imagery held that their insertion point was deserted, so the Combat Talons made only the one landing. Still, the men on the ground waited and listened, and probed the darkness with their night-vision goggles. Finally, the word was passed over their squad radios: Get ready to move out.

"When the word came to move out," Will Gates told me, "we came off the perimeter and found our assigned vehicle and assigned place in the vehicle—four Humvees, five guys in each Hummer. It was more than dark. Without NVGs, we could see nothing. You could literally hold your hand in front of your face and not see it. Again, it was just like we rehearsed it—no talking, everyone found their place. The drivers started their engines and took their station behind the lead vehicle. After all the prep and the practice, it was satisfying for me to see everything go as planned. Well, almost as planned. There were pockets of deep sand that we had to avoid, and at one point we started down a steep wadi or ravine that turned into a dead end. We had to turn around and drive back out. But the drivers kept proper spacing and the guys kept good 360-degree security. Using GPS navigation, we finally found the dirt road that led from the insertion point to the target area and headed out. We moved slowly, about fifteen or twenty miles an hour. There was a lot of drifting sand, and we'd have had a tough go of it if we hadn't had the road. Actually, it wasn't so much of a road as it was two ruts in the sand. It was good to be moving on the ground. It had been ten years since the Gulf War, since SEALs were out in bad-guy land on a mission, at least a mission that I can talk about."

"It was eerie," one of the platoon SEALs told me, "rolling across that flat, desolate land and watching it slip by in the green glow of my night-vision goggles. Thank God for the NVGs; I've never been out on a night that dark. This was my first platoon and my first operation. My country had been attacked, and I had the privilege of being one of the first guys on the ground. What a thrill!"

"We had a lot to do before the sun came up," Chief Lowery explained. "There were eighteen SEALs and two Air Force combat controllers. The two CCT guys and their gear were there to help with the landing zone survey and preparation. We landed about eleven p.m. and arrived at our layup position, or LUP, about two-thirty in the morning. Then the work began. We knew from the imagery that there was only one place for an LUP and one place for the OP—an observation post. There was this knoll about a half mile from the abandoned strip; the rest of the ground was dead flat in every direction. We dug the Humvees in behind the knoll and covered them with camouflage netting. We dug an OP at the top of the knoll where we could put eyes on the target and remain concealed. When the sun came up, we were in place and had good commo with the task unit back at the base. Then we began the wait. We rotated four guys at a time through the OP while the rest of us hunkered down in the LUP. During the day, we were on the binoculars; at night, it was NVGs."

"Did you approach the airstrip and compound at all?" I asked.

"The plan was for us to make a search of the compound right before the marines were to arrive, the idea being that the less we moved about, the better chance we had of observing someone in the area without anyone seeing us. And according to plan, the marines were due to arrive in two days, so that gave us almost two full day-night cycles with eyes on before they got there. Then the operation got delayed twenty-four hours. On the third day, we got yet another twenty-four-hour delay."

"So what did you do?"

"What we get paid to do. Watch and wait. The days got up into the mid-sixties, but the nights were in the low twenties, so we got a little cold. Not Hell Week cold, but it was chilly. We had to ration our water and MREs to make them go the distance. If we'd had to stay another forty-eight hours, we would have needed a resupply, at least for water." Lowery grinned. "It wasn't so bad. We all brought along a turkey MRE for Thanksgiving dinner. And believe me, we were all very thankful. We were on the ground, and even though it was strictly an SR mission, we were ready to put our guns in the fight. We were downrange and everyone felt good about it."

"On the afternoon of the fourth day," Lieutenant Autry said, "we got word that the marines would be coming in that night, so we began to prepare for their arrival. During the previous days and nights we had seen nothing—no people, no animals, no dogs, nothing. We were pretty sure we had exactly what we wanted, an empty piece of desert. But we had to be certain, and on the last night we did just that. After dark, half of us with the two Air Force CCTs made a foot patrol down the airstrip. We quickly searched the buildings in the compound to ensure that they were deserted. The initial wave of marines would be coming in by helo—CH-53s—which are vulnerable to ground fire. We wanted to make sure there were no bad guys hiding out in the compound. We held security while the combat controllers did their job. They set out beacons around the perimeter of the landing zone that would guide the Marine helos in. Once they had done that, we called in that the LZ was secure and hurried back away from the airstrip perimeter to watch the fun. In they came, one CH-53 after another, dumping off combat-loaded marines, and lifting back off. Given the distance from the staging area in southern Pakistan, they must have had to refuel on the way in or out, or maybe both ways. We watched as they set up a security perimeter around the strip and took over the compound."

"When did you link up with them?" I asked.

"We didn't so much as link up with them as they came out to get us. No matter how good the communications, we're always worried about friendly fire—a blue-on-blue exchange—so they sent a patrol out for us. We exchanged recognition signals, and they brought us back in through their perimeter. The ground force commander thanked us for freezing our butts off for them, and that was it. A few hours later, they were landing C-130s and we caught one out. By noon the next day, we were back at the base enjoying a hot shower and a hot meal. We didn't fire a shot and we saw no one, but we did our job." Autry chuckled. "This was not the first time a bunch of sailors reconned a piece of sand so the Marines could land. In World War II, the Navy frogmen did it all across the Pacific. We even made the Air Force guys honorary frogmen, and we were honored to have them along with us."

"What happened to your vehicles?" I asked. "Did you turn them over to the marines?"

"No way," Chief Gates told me. "We brought them out with us. There were plenty of empty C-130s coming out of Camp Rhino, the name the marines gave their base, so we took them back with us. As it worked out, those vehicles became prototypes for SEAL mobility requirements. When we got back to Bahrain, we built another eight of them from stock Humvees. They were a little different from those original four, but not much. And those vehicles stayed in the fight. They were airlifted up to Kandahar when we moved the task force up there. When I went back for a tour in Iraq, I saw one of them in Baghdad. Of course, we have much better Humvees now, and our SR ground mobility capabilities have evolved well beyond what we did in those early days in Afghanistan, but it did my heart good to see those early Humvee conversions on the ground in Iraq, still carrying SEALs to the fight."

Not long after the marines landed at Camp Rhino, the Taliban abandoned Kandahar. The marines quickly secured the Kandahar airport, and a special operations task force was set up there to conduct and support operations against Taliban and al-Qaeda targets throughout central and southern Afghanistan. This SEAL-centric task force became known as Task Force K-Bar. It grew in size and scope to become a Joint Combined Special Operations Task Force (JCSOTF) with SEALs, Army Special Forces, Rangers, Air Force Special Tactics Teams, and SOF components from Australia, Denmark, Germany, Norway, and Turkey. When it was in full bloom, Task Force K-Bar had close to three thousand special operators and SOF support personnel. During the first six months of the Afghan campaign, over seventy-five special operations were mounted from the task force, nearly all of them SR or DA missions. For its contribution to the Afghan campaign, Task Force K-Bar was awarded the Presidential Unit Citation. The last time SEALs were awarded a PUC was when SEAL Team One earned one during the Vietnam War.

"It was at K-Bar that Navy SEALs set the tempo for strategic reconnaissance and direct actions in the war on terrorism," a SEAL planner told me. "At K-Bar, we developed the doctrine and made it happen. In special operations, we like to think of ourselves as unconventional warriors—highly adaptive fighters. But we began operations out of K-Bar with a great deal of inflexibility and an antiquated approach to operations in this new environment. All of us had a highly formatted methodology to the business of SR and DA. We were used to receiving mission tasking from a higher headquarters. Then we would begin a methodical mission analysis prior to the mission execution. It involved developing alternative courses of action, requests for additional intelligence, course-of-action selection, planning and more planning, briefings, and rehearsals. In Afghanistan, the nature of the enemy and the speed of technology did not allow for this leisurely preparation. Word would come from a source or a technical collector that an enemy truck with a suspected al-Qaeda leader was moving on a road toward the Pakistani border. He would reach the border crossing in less than an hour. So we either launched right then or let him go. Of course, the option was always there to kill him with a smart bomb, but who was *really* in the truck? Were there documents or information that could be gained if we could take him alive?"

"Initially, SEALs were the only force with the ability to move quickly," one of the platoon officers at K-Bar told me. "There were several reasons for this. One was that all Navy SEALs, since their BUD/S training days, have been involved in mission planning. So when the planning and briefing windows were shortened or all but eliminated, everyone in the platoon understood why this was being done and adjusted accordingly. Another reason is that much of what we do is governed by SOPs—standard operating procedures: how we get on or off a helo, how we set security, how we patrol at night or in the daytime. We've been together for a long time, in some cases for several years, and we know what to expect from each other in a fast-moving or ambiguous situation. During our predeployment training, we worked day after day on immediate-action drills and rapid response to different simulated tactical situations. During the platoon workup, the training cadres were constantly challenging us, throwing tactical wrinkles into the operation to force us to adapt and overcome obstacles. We trained in a very dynamic environment, and it paid off in Afghanistan.

"We also had the advantage of a command structure that had a distinct Naval Special Warfare flavor. We didn't have to go past our task force commander, who was a SEAL, for mission approval or mission authorization. Many of the non-U.S. SOF components hadn't our ability or the training to adapt to the shortened mission-preparation cycle. And, for a time, they were held on a short leash by their national command authorities. They had to get permission from back home or some general in the coalition hierarchy before they could jump on a mission. By then the opportunity was lost or the tasking had been given to us and we were out the door. If you were a Navy SEAL in 2002, operational happiness was to be in a platoon at Task Force K-Bar in Kandahar. We operated all the time."

SEALs conducted a number of successful SR and DA missions from K-Bar. One was an SR mission to keep watch on a compound that belonged to Osama bin Laden's physician. It was in the mountains at close to nine thousand feet near Shkin. In Afghanistan, SEALs conducted operations as high as thirteen thousand feet. Bin Laden was thought to be a kidney dialysis patient, and a team was sent in to keep the doctor's compound under surveillance. Both SEALs and Army Special Forces participated in this SR. It was not known whether the doctor or even bin Laden might be there, so they kept the compound under observation for several days, enduring long nights of snow and freezing rain. One night, a vehicle came out and flashed its lights several times. Then several more vehicles came into the compound from the direction of the Pakistani border. There was talk of immediately assaulting the compound with the SR team or simply destroying it with JDAMs—Joint Direct Attack Munitions, or smart bombs. The SEALs had radioed back the GPS coordinates and the facility had top priority on the target list.

"But we didn't feel right about it," one of the SR SEALs told me. "We knew there were people inside, but only a few vehicles came and went. We could kill them all with a few JDAMs, but who were we killing? Finally, we got permission for a DA—to make the assault. We went in slowly and carefully, ready to back out and call in an air strike if we met serious resistance. But we didn't. We found nothing but a few old men and lots of women and kids hiding inside. And a cache of weapons and explosives. If we'd just gone with the air strike, we'd have killed a lot of noncombatants and destroyed the documents that we managed to take out of the compound. Y'see, we have a lot of technology at our disposal, but sometimes there is nothing like eyes on a target. We felt good about doing our job and not getting the civilians hurt."

Many of the operations carried out under the direction of Task Force K-Bar were SR missions that could require an immediate or delayed direct-action follow-on operation. Occasionally, a target presented itself for a pure DA effort. One of those DA operations led to the capture of a senior Taliban leader. The capture of Mullah Khairullah Kahirkhawa, or Mullah K, was a classic marriage of American technology and SOF quick-strike capability.

In early 2002, a Predator UAV, or unmanned aerial vehicle, was on patrol in Afghanistan's rugged Paktia Province. The Predator had a building under surveillance that was thought to be one of the hiding places of Mullah K. Those manning the UAV's sensors saw men leaving the building and alerted the special operators at Task Force K-Bar. "Mullah K has left the building," they reported. "He's on the move." In less than a half hour, a plan was put together, followed by a hasty operational briefing. Then thirty SEALs and Danish special operators boarded Army and special operations helos for the assault. A Navy P-3 manned patrol aircraft relieved the Predator on station and directed the assault helos to their targets. One element took the building, and another swooped down on the convoy. The Taliban leader was captured along with his entourage. The whole operation, from alert to mission completion, took a little over an hour.

"There are always glitches and problems along the way," one of the SEALs on the operation told me. "The speed with which we were able to solve the problems and deconflict issues with friendly forces and the locals in the area pretty much dictated our success at K-Bar. We worked well with other coalition SOF units when they finally learned how to get out the door quickly and when they were allowed to operate under the control of our task force commander. Don't get me wrong; they were good guys. But it seemed like we were always waiting for them. In the case of Mullah K, the Danes were able to get out the door with us and we nailed him."

"Who were the best of the other SOF forces?" I asked him.

"Each of them brought something to the table—some mission or aspect of special operations that they were particularly good at. The Polish GROM [Grupa Reagowania Operacyjno Mobilnego] were the best, but they weren't there in the early days at K-Bar. The German KSK [Kommando Spezialkrafte] were very good. Their specialty is personal security and force protection, but they had a pretty good range of professional SOF skills.

"On one operation, we inserted with the KSK to check out a mountain cave complex. We were into waist-deep snow, so everyone was on snowshoes. They were very good in the snow. The objective was to check out some caves in this mountain stronghold that was being used by the bad guys. We inserted together by helo on the side of the mountain. The SEALs went around the mountain one way and the KSK went the other. We approached the caves carefully, but they were all abandoned. So we mapped the GPS coordinates of the cave mouths for future air strikes in case the enemy returned to them. The SEALs and KSK linked up on the other side of the mountain and extracted together. Some of the KSK were veterans of the East German army, and they weren't too keen on Americans. Most were from the West German military, and they kept their former Communist brothers in line. I mention that because it was a historical first. It was the first time an American unit and a German unit went into harm's way on the same side. Think about it—the first time *ever*. The KSK had only been around for about ten years, but their special operators were very professional. The former East Germans were a little surly at first, but we treated them with respect. Eventually, they came around. After all, we're all SOF brothers."

Not every SR or DA operation was a success. And not every operation that was a success is suitable for me to put in print, especially
those operations where SEALs and other SOF components took life.
Often, it is better for the enemy to wonder what happened to an
al-Qaeda fighter or insurgent leader. Why did he disappear? Was he
killed or did he abandon the cause? Or did he defect? Due to faulty intelligence or slow reaction time, sometimes a SEAL DA team arrived
and the target was gone or simply not there—never had been. The
SEALs call a mission like this a dry hole—operations that are unsuccessful. There were more than a few dry holes in Afghanistan, especially in the early days. One operation that was not a dry hole was the
operation in the Zhawar Kili Valley. It was one of the most notable
SEAL operations of the Afghan campaign, and is the subject of the next
chapter.

Lieutenant Steve Autry served as operations officer for a SEAL team
and saw further action in Afghanistan and Iraq. He is currently serving
with a SOF special missions unit.

Chief Randy Lowery, now Senior Chief Lowery, also returned on deployment to Iraq as a task unit operations chief. He is currently a
member of the Naval Special Warfare Parachute Demonstration Team.

Chief Will Gates was tasked with building the first generation of
SEAL Humvees for mobile SR operations. He returned to Iraq for an
operational tour as a SEAL platoon chief. He is currently attached to
Naval Special Warfare Command, where he oversees the procurement
and outfitting of Humvees for the Naval Special Warfare community
at large.

Petty Officer Dan Lloyd returned to Afghanistan for another SEAL deployment and is currently in Iraq on his third combat tour of duty.

CHAPTER 4

THE CAVES OF ZHAWAR KILI

Lieutenant Charlie Moncsko was still trying to get himself and his platoon settled into the new compound. The platoon had inserted into Camp Rhino and waited for the Taliban irregulars to abandon Kandahar ahead of the advance of the Northern Alliance. Along with an advance party of U.S. Marines, they had moved into a crumbling, deserted military complex near the airport. Kandahar International, he mused. What a joke. The cracked and chipped concrete runways were the work of the Russians who expanded the strip to handle military transports in the mid-1980s. So were the cinder-block and corrugated-roof buildings that abutted the tarmac. The archways that graced the entrance gave the civilian terminal a modern look, but everything was dirty and in disrepair. It had been nearly a decade since the Russians had left. Now foreign troops were again in Kandahar. When they arrived at the compound on New Year's Day, a little more than sixteen weeks after the attacks on New York and Washington, Moncsko wondered if the Russians were the last to take a broom to the buildings they now occupied. Between missions, his SEALs had cleaned and swept their new quarters. They still slept on the floor and the

SEALs in the mountains. Two SEALs watch their Marine Corps helo struggle from the insertion site some twelve thousand feet high in the Afghan mountains. Note the ski poles on the SEAL pack. *Courtesy of the U.S. Navy* concrete was still grimy, but their quarters had now assumed a tattered orderliness. Things would get better as the American presence in Kandahar grew, but in those early days, the SEALs at their airport compound had to make do with very little.

The mission taskings had begun immediately. Moncsko's platoon had been out three times in as many days, checking suspected Taliban activity or al-Qaeda training camps, but these were little more than break-in operations to get the feel for the area. Successful missions are built on good intelligence, and the intelligence production at K-Bar was just getting started. So far they had found deserted facilities with little or nothing of material or intelligence value. All that was about to change.

All SEALs are unique, but Moncsko is a little more unique than others. He was close to six-two and solidly built, but his lean, boyish face made him seem thinner than he was. He grew up in York, Maine, a down east community of ten thousand that lies just where the Maine coast gives way to New Hampshire. He graduated from the Naval Academy in 1993 and from BUD/S Class 193. Between Annapolis and beginning his SEAL training, he acquired a master's degree in robotics at MIT. Nine years out of the Academy, he was on his third SEAL deployment and at the top of his game. He was the officer in charge, or OIC, of a SEAL platoon on deployment in harm's way.

"Timing is everything, I suppose," Moncsko recalled of deployment and his time in Kandahar. "No one wanted what happened on 11 September, but it did happen. For thirteen years, ever since I entered the Naval Academy, I'd been working and training to do this job—to be a SEAL OIC on deployment. Before 9/11, I thought I'd spend my deployment cooling my heels in Bahrain, running training exercises and trying to keep my guys sharp *just in case*. Suddenly it was all real world. Every guy in the platoon had worked hard to get ready for this deployment. We trained like we were going to fight, and we got the chance to fight like we trained. When our nation needed us, we were good to go. I can't say enough about the guys in my platoon. They were terrific."

In addition to the filth, the platoon spaces in their makeshift quarters at Kandahar were cramped and very hot. Moncsko, sweaty and unshaven, was setting up his operational gear. It had been close to a week since he'd had a shower. When SEALs come in from a mission, they clean weapons, rearm, and prepare their personal equipment for the next operation. Only then do they tend to personal hygiene. At Kandahar, this amounted to brushing your teeth and wiping yourself down with a damp washcloth—one you'd used yesterday and the day before. Most of them had already expended their supply of Handi Wipes. His canvas equipment vest and body armor were soiled and sweat-stained, but his weapon glistened under a light coat of oil. The squad radio and everything metal on his operational harness had been wiped clean and thoroughly checked. Anything that was worn or shiny was sprayed with flat-black paint. This ritual of readying your operational gear to go right back out is a legacy from the SEALs of the Vietnam era. A SEAL must be able to jock up and be ready for combat on a moment's notice. His gear set up and good to go, Moncsko had just spread his poncho liner on the floor and was looking forward to a nap.

"Hey, Lieutenant, the boss wants to see you."

It was Frank Moss, the platoon chief petty officer. Charlie Moncsko didn't get up, but all his senses were on alert. Moncsko was the platoon OIC, but Chief Boatswain's Mate Frank Moss was the platoon rock. He was a short, stocky man with soft, rounded features that belied a very tough and experienced Navy SEAL. Moss had grown up in Virginia Beach, the home of many SEALs in the East Coast teams. He graduated with BUD/S Class 142 and had been a Navy SEAL for more than twenty years. And he'd been here before, in harm's way, but the conditions could not have been more different. While Charlie Moncsko endured the rigors of a plebe year at the Naval Academy, Petty Officer Moss was in Panama during the hunt for Manuel Noriega. He was one of the SEAL combat swimmers at Rodman, in the Canal Zone, who placed satchel charges on the hulls of two Panamanian gunboats and blew them out of the water. So much for Central

American despots; now he was hunting terrorists in the mountains of Afghanistan. Chief Moss had seen a lot in his long Navy career. No one knew this better than Lieutenant Charlie Moncsko, who carefully noted the innocent look on Moss's face.

"What's up, Chief?"

"Dunno, sir," Moss replied. "Better ask the boss."

Yeah, right, Moncsko thought; the chiefs always know what's going on. But before he could question him further, Moss added, "He said on the double, sir. He seemed a little anxious, if you know what I mean. Could be something's up."

Moncsko started to press Moss for more information, but decided against it. He'd learn about it soon enough. He pulled on desert cammie trousers and a green T-shirt and slipped into his shower shoes, then followed Moss to the tactical operations center, or TOC. The two SEALs could have been brothers—or father and son. Moncsko was taller than Moss. Both were about 170 pounds, tanned, and unkempt, yet both had a rugged, businesslike look about them. They were warriors of the same breed.

While the Northern Alliance and their Special Forces minders completed their north-to-south sweep, the Joint Combined Special Operations Task Force South, under the command of Captain Bob Harward, set up shop in Kandahar. Called Task Force K-Bar, this component had become the tasking authority for SOF missions in central and southern Afghanistan. K-Bar, named for the military-issue knife carried by SEALs and marines, was set up and open for business by the first week of January 2002. It was a joint task force in that there were SOF and conventional elements from the Army, the Navy, and the Air Force, as well as a substantial complement of marines and personnel from other governmental agencies—the OGAs. It was a combined task force because there were SOF elements from a number of allied nations, including Germany, France, and Great Britain. Looking back through the prism of our struggle in Iraq, it seems difficult to remember that the

French and the Germans were with us in Afghanistan. Yet Task Force K-Bar had a SEAL-centric command-and-control structure and bore the imprint of its SEAL commander.

Captain Bob Harward was the fiery and emotional leader of K-Bar, a job for which he was ideally suited. When the attacks came on 11 September, Harward was Commander, Naval Special Warfare Group One in Coronado. At the time, Group One exercised administrative control of the West Coast SEAL teams, as well as other West Coast Naval Special Warfare assets. The group's primary responsibility was to deploy trained Naval Special Warfare assets to the Pacific and Central Commands—PACOM and CENTCOM. In time of regional or theater conflict, the Group One commander forward-deploys, at the theater commander's discretion and direction, to command in-theater Naval Special Warfare assets. Just as Ray Smith (Rear Admiral, now retired) commanded SEAL and special boat assets during Operation Desert Shield/Desert Storm, Bob Harward was ordered to Afghanistan shortly after the September 2001 attacks for Operation Enduring Freedom. OEF was, however, quite different from Desert Storm. For the first time, a Navy SEAL commanded a task force five hundred miles from blue water. Fortunately, this was not Bob Harward's first trip to Kandahar.

Bob went to high school in Tehran while his father served as the American naval attaché to the shah of Iran's government. Teheran, like Beirut, was at one time a safe, cosmopolitan city with a substantial Western presence. In the mountains not far from the city center, the skiing was excellent. Bob speaks Farsi and has a working command of Pashto. Prior to his attending the Naval Academy, Bob and two of his high school pals spent a summer hitchhiking in Afghanistan. This was before the Russians and well before the Taliban. Now he was back.

"We set down in a CH-53 near the airport and moved into the old Taliban military barracks," Bob told me, describing the initial setup at K-Bar. We've talked many times since his return from Afghanistan—

and from Iraq. "The marines put out a security perimeter, and we got right to the business of special operations. The place hadn't changed a bit in thirty years—except, of course, for the land mines, RPGs [rocket-propelled grenades], and an occasional sniper. There was nothing here but gutted buildings and a few scrawny dogs. The guys worked their butts off, all of them. Half of them were filling sandbags and swamping the place out while the other half were setting up comms and a tactical operations center. In two days, we had a working TOC and were ready for operational tasking."

Soon intelligence was pouring into the TOC from a number of sources—from military intelligence, from local sources, and from the CIA. Some of this intelligence came from technical sources like radio intercepts and cell phone conversations. There was imagery from satellites, Predator drones, and P-3 manned aircraft. And, finally, there was human intelligence, or HUMINT, from the now steady stream of captured enemy soldiers and detainees. Southern and central Afghanistan were divided into sectors, and the special operations teams at K-Bar, based on emerging intelligence, began conducting strategic-reconnaissance and direct-action missions into these sectors. These operations had to be coordinated with the overall conduct of the campaign to avoid any friendly fire. American and allied planes roamed the skies at will, looking for any enemy movement on the ground. The last thing a group of SEALs on the ground wanted was to be mistaken for a band of Taliban irregulars.

Well before Bob Harward and Task Force K-Bar set up in Kandahar, there was a growing body of evidence that suggested the Zhawar Kili Valley might be an important al-Qaeda stronghold. Zhawar Kili was some 150 miles northeast of Kandahar and had long been suspected of being the site of an al-Qaeda training camp. It was on the target list, but there were many other potential targets on the vast central Afghan plain and in the surrounding mountains. What made the Zhawar Kili Valley unique was its location—it opened up right onto the Afghan-Pakistani border. Plans were in the queue for a sweep into the area when fresh intelligence suggested that a number of fleeing al-Qaeda were using the valley to slip out of Afghanistan and into Pakistan. When it was thought that there was a chance this might be a possible escape route for Osama bin Laden himself, the tasking became urgent. That's when Harward sent for Lieutenant Charlie Moncsko.

"What's up, sir?" Moncsko asked as he walked into the TOC.

"Life just keeps getting better," Harward said with a grin. "Fresh intel says we may have a hot one for you. You ready to go back out?"

Moncsko knew the answer, but glanced at Chief Moss for confirmation. "The platoon's up, sir. We're always ready."

Harward looked at his watch; it was already late afternoon. "Put your platoon on alert and let's start working up the operation. We'll insert you just before daylight tomorrow morning. Tim has the details on the target along with the latest intel."

"Aye, aye, sir."

SEAL platoons typically plan their own operations. They are tasked with a mission or an objective, and plan how they are going to go about it. And they plan as a team. Each man in the platoon has a role in the mission preparation. While Moss went to alert the rest of the platoon, Moncsko found Lieutenant Commander Tim Blanchard, the TOC watch officer, to find out where they were going. It was then that Moncsko learned about the Zhawar Kili caves.

The cave complex in the Zhawar Kili Valley and its use as a Taliban and al-Qaeda stronghold were well known, even before 11 September. Oddly enough, much of this underground warren had been built with American support and American money during the decade-long Russian occupation. Millions of dollars in aid and arms had been given to the Afghan resistance. This rugged valley, within sight of the Pakistani border, was a major resupply point and haven for the mujahideen in their struggle against the Russian-backed Kabul government. When the Taliban gained control of the country, they occupied the valley and made the extensive cave complex available to their al-Qaeda allies. In 1998, President Bill Clinton sent cruise missiles into the complex in response to the bombings of our embassies in East Africa. Soon after the 11 September attacks, the Zhawar Kili Valley went back on the potential target list, but until now it had not been in the crosshairs.

In the short operational life of Task Force K-Bar, the SEALs had enjoyed the lion's share of the operational taskings. This was not by design or by favoritism on Harward's part. The special operations elements of the other allied nations at K-Bar were very capable, and Harward wanted them in the field; there was plenty of work for everyone. But early on in the Afghan campaign, the allied SOF units could not go into the field without the permission and approval of their respective national command authorities. Our allies were there, but coalition nations still retained mission approval for their forces. This might have worked in past conflicts, but not this one. Special operations taskings are often driven by perishable intelligence, which means victory belongs to the swift. In the early days of the campaign, the SEALs enjoyed a more flexible and responsive command structure than their SOF brothers from other nations. And there was another reason. Many of the allied SOF components had rigid planning protocols and mission preparation windows, some taking as long as forty-eight hours. So did Navy SEALs, but they were quick to discard them.

"In the early days at K-Bar," Charlie Moncsko recalls, "nobody could get out the door quicker than SEALs. We were very good at this. All I had to do was turn my guys out of the rack and tell them to saddle up. We'd begin the mission briefing on the helo pad and finish it on the ride to the insertion point. Nobody else could move that quickly."

This was not necessarily ad hoc mission planning on the part of the SEALs. Many of their mission profiles called for the same formatted and time-consuming planning time frames as their allied counterparts. But the SEALs were quickly able to compress this planning window when the tactical situation in Afghanistan demanded speed. Years of training, rehearsals, and refined standard operational procedures made this transition possible. A great deal of SEAL advanced and predeployment training is devoted to scenario-based training. SEALs in advanced training venues and platoon training, or Unit Level Training, are presented with series of tactical situations, then given ten or fifteen minutes to brief their team before conducting the exercise. These "brief-and-go" drills were designed to refine tactical combat skills. By minimizing the briefing and preparation, they allowed for maximum time in the field. These drills proved to be the prototype for actual combat operations in Afghanistan and later, in Iraq.

SEALs normally work in small groups and with other SEALs with whom they have trained extensively. But SEALs are highly adaptable creatures, and well aware that there are some things they do very well and that some things are done better by other military components. Charlie Moncsko and Tim Blanchard were not far into their target analysis when it became apparent that more disciplines than those executed by SEALs would be needed. And while the area had been extensively surveyed from the air, there were a lot of unknowns. Hour by hour, Zhawar Kili grew in importance and scope. The prospect of senior al-Qaeda cadres hemorrhaging from Afghanistan into Pakistan put a move into the valley on the fast track. Late that evening, Harward took Blanchard aside.

"Tim," he told him, "the Zhawar Kili Valley is starting to get a lot of attention from the higher-ups. This thing is getting bigger, and I don't want it to get out of hand. There's going to be a contingent of nonoperators along, and now the Marines want to send in a substantial security contingent. All this is going to create some command-and-control problems."

Blanchard considered this. Probably not a bad idea, he thought, to have some marines along. A few more guns wouldn't hurt if they ran into trouble.

"How substantial, sir?"

"Fifty of them with a Marine captain leading the security element."

He gave Blanchard a sly grin. Tim Blanchard met the smile of his commander with an even stare. He didn't want to get ahead of himself. There was a feeling growing in the K-Bar's tactical operations center that this could be a big one. He himself could feel it in the stale, putrid air of their makeshift command center.

Harward led him to one of the floor-to-ceiling mosaic maps of their AO, or area of operations, and they looked at the rugged terrain around the target. Blanchard's mind raced. Moncsko was a Navy lieutenant. Put him in the field with a Marine captain, an officer of equal rank, as well as the nonoperators, and there could be problems. In a special operation, there can be only one ground commander. That commander may listen to his subordinates, but final decisions have to rest with a single individual. It made sense that for an operation of this size, there should be a more senior element leader on the ground. It also made sense that he was the logical choice, but this was not a given. Blanchard did know one thing for certain, and that was that Bob Harward would want to lead it. The task force commander would like nothing better than to be on the ground in harm's way at the head of an important SOF operation. Physically, Harward was certainly capable. He had been a nationally ranked triathlete, and kept himself in top condition. He was an experienced and skilled operator, and a man who relished this kind of a challenge. The Zhawar Kili Valley had all the makings of a once-in-a-lifetime special operation—one a Navy SEAL waited for his whole professional career.

When Harward spoke, there was resignation in his voice. "Relax, Tim. You're going in; I'm going to stay here." Then he smiled broadly. "Don't think for one minute that I wouldn't go if I thought I could get away with it. My job's here in the TOC; yours is in the Zhawar Kili Valley."

Like Charlie Moncsko, Tim Blanchard is a New Englander. Tim Blanchard had grown up in Sharon, Vermont, a town of just over a thousand souls located on the White River some ten miles north of Woodstock. Blanchard wrestled and played lacrosse and soccer in high school, but his passion was skiing. At the University of Vermont, he skied competitively in both Alpine and Nordic events. He is a handsome officer, with regular features, light-brown hair, and wide-set blue eyes. But his body somehow doesn't seem to match his features. Blanchard is thick. His thighs, hips, waist, and chest seem to be of the same dimension. After graduating from Vermont, he took a year at Oxford to study Chaucer. On his return to the United States, he became a professional skier, teaching Alpine skiing and competing in cross-country and extreme backcountry Nordic events. In 1992, he joined the Navy and entered Officer Candidate School at Newport, Rhode Island. Following his OCS graduation, Ensign Blanchard joined BUD/S Class 189 on his way to becoming a Navy SEAL.

Harward called Moncsko and the task force intelligence officer over to the map and they began to talk about the expanded scope of the mission. Special operations are complex undertakings with a staggering amount of details and decisions. These can be done reasonably quickly and methodically because of the smooth working relationship between the operators who will conduct the mission and the TOC staff who support the men in the field. Some staffers in the TOC are SEALs, but many are not. It doesn't matter. They all know what's at stake— mission success and the safety of the guys going downrange. There is also an unwritten corollary: The time it takes to plan a mission is *always* just slightly less than the time it takes from mission notification to mission launch. Everyone in the process understands this, and they make it happen. They're like a group of jazz musicians coming together for a jam session. They easily and professionally fall into a rhythm and cadence, sliding into established routines and improvising where appropriate. When SEALs plan and talk, it's like they're speaking a foreign language. A great deal is communicated with a word, a nod, or an idiom. And they have to be flexible, as they were when Tim Blanchard was suddenly thrust into the role of ground commander.

"Sure, I wanted to lead it," Charlie Moncsko said of his now-subordinate role. "Heck, my chief wanted to lead it and he could have, but this made all the sense in the world. It allowed me to concentrate fully on my SEALs and their duties once we were on the ground. Tim made it easier for all of us to do our jobs."

Late on 6 January and in the early morning hours of 7 January, the Zhawar Kili Valley was raked with acronyms: TLAMs (Tomahawk

Land Attack Missiles) and JDAMs (Joint Direct Attack Munitions). Precision-guided cruise missiles and smart bombs found their way to previously plotted GPS coordinates, slamming into cave entrances, fortifications, and dwellings as part of the pre-ground-attack package. Those in the Zhawar Kili Valley did not get a good night's sleep, but then neither did the operators and planners at Task Force K-Bar. There was a lot to do. In fact, no one in the raiding party went to bed that night.

At approximately 0300 on the morning of 7 January, three large helicopters idled on the edge of the tarmac at Kandahar International. There were no lights showing, just the collective scream of jet engines. Blanchard led his seventy-five-man assault element from the task force compound to the giant whirring metal insects. They broke into three groups, twenty-five men to each bird, filing up the rear boarding ramps in good order. The planning, the preparation, and the briefings were behind them now. They were on their way down range. Blanchard was of two minds. On the one hand, he wished he'd had more time to prepare. A rehearsal would have been nice. On the other, he couldn't wait to get in the air and to the objective.

The assault element would be inserted by three Marine CH-53 Super Stallion helicopters. Normally, SEALs are transported by special operations MH-53 Pavelows, an electronically sophisticated helo, but the Pavelows have only two engines. The Marine CH-53s have three engines and are configured for heavy lift and troop movement. They were ideal for insertion work in the mountains of Afghanistan, where altitude degrades helicopter performance. Blanchard, the SEAL platoon, and assorted mission specialists were aboard the lead helo. The Marine security element was on the other two birds.

Harward followed him aboard and yelled over the turbine whine, "Kick some ass!"

"Aye, aye, sir," Blanchard shouted back. Harward shook Blanchard's gloved hand and gave him a thumbs-up, then hurried back to the exit ramp of the big helo. He quickly boarded each of the other two helos to wish the marines good hunting as well.

The crew chief of Blanchard's helo came over to him and yelled in his ear, "The other birds are loaded with a good head count, sir. Ready when you are."

Blanchard looked up at the crew chief. They were bathed in dull red light, enough to see by but not so much as to affect their night vision. Outside, the air had been cool, even comfortable, but inside the body of the Super Stallion, sweat from heavily armed men mingled with the burned-kerosene odor of jet exhaust. Blanchard gave the crew chief a single thumbs-up, then turned both thumbs out, palms up, in a jerky motion: Pull chocks; let's go. The big CH-53s lifted in turn, ran out over the length of tarmac to gain what ground speed they could within the security of the airport perimeter, and soared quickly. No sense in taking chances with ground fire at this stage of the game. Blanchard donned a headset with Mickey Mouse ears and a boom mike that was hardwired to the CH-53's internal communications.

"How we doing up there?" he asked.

"We're on course, on schedule," the Marine pilot reported as they climbed up through ten thousand feet. "Everything is a go. We're about thirty minutes from rendezvous with the tanker. I'll keep you posted."

High over the southernmost range of the Hindu Kush, the three big helos found their KC-130 tanker and topped off their fuel loads. The CH-53s hadn't the legs to make the trip unrefueled, so it was decided to make the in-flight refueling on the way in. A midair refueling between a fixed-wing aircraft and a helicopter at night calls for a great deal of airmanship. The Marine pilots pulled it off smoothly and professionally. Now they were inbound for the Zhawar Kili Valley. With the refueling behind them, Blanchard had just begun to relax a little when a voice crackled in his headset.

"Hey, Tim, we got a problem." It was Blanchard's pilot in the lead helo. "The TOC just radioed that one of the Predators has some thermal activity at the primary insertion site; looks as if there may be a few locals moving about. They recommend the secondary. How about it?"

This was not good—that there were people moving on the ground meant that they may not be able to land where they wanted to. The plan called for them to insert at the head of the valley just before dawn and sweep down the valley northwest to southeast from the highest elevation to the lowest—seventy-five hundred feet down to perhaps sixty-five hundred. The first alternate was the middle of the valley, which meant they would have to move up the valley on foot, then back down. They say a battle plan doesn't survive the first shot being fired. Hell, Blanchard thought, we're not even on the ground yet.

"What do you think, Chuck?" Blanchard said to the pilot. Normally, SEALs flew with Air Force special operations pilots who trained extensively for this kind of operation. But Blanchard and the other SEALs were coming to respect and trust the capabilities of their Marine flyers.

"We'll take you where you want to go, Tim, but if it's all the same, I'd just as soon not fly into ground fire."

And we don't want to insert into a hot LZ, thought Blanchard. "Tell the TOC we're going for the first alternate. Let me know if there's any more intel."

"Roger that, Tim."

The lead pilot gave instructions to the other helos, and Blanchard settled back to wait out the ride. He told himself not to worry about what he could not control. Easier said than done.

The insertion into the secondary site went without incident. The Marine Super Stallions, their pilots flying with night-vision goggles, swooped in and dropped to the valley floor. The three helos were on the ground no more than fifteen seconds. As they lifted back into the air, the men on the ground scrambled to form a loose perimeter— seventy-five pairs of American boots at seven thousand feet. A few minutes later, all was quiet. It would be another hour before they had good light on the valley floor, and there was a lot to do before that time. It was a clear night, with no moon and no breeze. A burned-sulfur smell still hung in the air from the JDAMs and TLAMs. Blanchard and the others were curious as to what the air and missile strikes had accomplished.

The fifty-man Marine security detachment was headed up by Captain Chris Taladega. His gunnery sergeant, Winton Robertson, had helped to liberate Kuwait City as a young lance corporal during the Gulf War. There were sixteen SEALs in the platoon, Blanchard making seventeen. In addition to SEALs and marines, there were two Air Force sergeants from the Combat Control Teams, two FBI agents, two explosive ordnance disposal (EOD) technicians, an Army chem-bio specialist, and a Navy linguist who would serve as an interpreter. One of the Bureau agents was a former Navy SEAL with experience on the FBI Hostage Rescue Team. The other was a former Marine Corps infantry officer. Both were along for evidentiary purposes, not combat duty, but either one could be a gun in the fight if it came to that. The operation itself was to be a quick in-and-out sweep of the valley. They all carried a day's ration of water and a PowerBar or two. All wore body armor, and their weapons and ammunition loads were tailored for a fast-moving assault. This was a large, heavily armed, multidimensional SWAT team. The SEALs who were to check out the caves were prepared for close-quarter battle. The marines would provide security. Their duties included setting out sniper positions for overwatch of the men working on the valley floor and to serve as a blocking force. They were also prepared for urban battle and light infantry work as needed. Close-quarter battle or close-quarter combat usually refers to fighting *inside* buildings or inside the compartments of a ship, while urban battle has to do with fighting *outside* in a city or town—street fighting.

The terrain was more than rugged. The floor of the valley was desert hardpan, very much like Camp Billy Machen, the SEAL training facility near the Chocolate Mountains in Southern California. The sides were steep, boulder strewn, and cut by deep wadis. The rim of the canyon sides averaged some fifteen hundred to a thousand feet above the valley floor, a nice perch for Taliban or al-Qaeda snipers. Blanchard spoke into the boom mike of his intersquad radio.

"Chris, you there?"

"Right here, sir." A SEAL of Taladega's rank would call a SEAL lieutenant commander by his first name, but Chris Taladega was not a SEAL; he was all marine.

"Get moving. Get your guys to the high ground as soon as you can."

"Roger that, sir. We're on it." There was a quiet rustling as Taladega's marines left the insertion perimeter and began to pick their way up the rocky slopes that led from the valley floor.

While the marines climbed, Blanchard called in to let the task force know they were proceeding as planned from the alternate landing site. The helos would have reported this, but Blanchard rightly assumed an anxious Captain Harward would be prowling the TOC, wanting to hear from his ground commander. Their radios were encrypted and secure, but at the limits of their range. After repeating himself several times, he managed to get through. Then he began working his way around the perimeter, checking on his men. The false dawn was gone, and the real thing was only minutes away.

He heard a voice in his headset: "Bulldog One in place." The Marine element on his right was in position. A few minutes later, he heard, "Bulldog Two in place." Blanchard breathed a sigh of relief; his overwatch marines were in position. He found his SEAL platoon commander.

"Okay, Charlie, take us out of here."

With a hand signal from his platoon OIC, Chief Frank Moss put the platoon of SEALs into a loose diamond formation and they began to move in a northwesterly direction up the valley. The non-SEALs arrayed themselves with Blanchard and Moncsko within the security of the moving diamond. Their mission was to sweep a three-mile section of the valley—only now their task was a more difficult one. They had to move up to the head of the valley and sweep back down. Once on the move, they began to check out the cave entrances that lined the walls of the valley floor. The TLAM and JDAM strikes had done little or nothing to the infrastructure of the caves. There were craters at many of the cave mouths, but no significant damage to any of the entrances. They reached the head of the valley an hour after they had inserted and began the process of working their way back, carefully moving into the caves as they went. These were not just holes dug into the steep valley sides; they were sophisticated, interconnected tunnel complexes reinforced with steel I beams and brickwork. The tunnels were several hundred yards deep, and there were more than seventy of them. The SEALs quickly searched caves while the marines scrambled along the rough high ground to provide security. In many ways, their job was more difficult than that of the search elements moving on the valley floor.

"We were able to do our job because those hardworking marines kept a close watch over us," Moncsko said. "It was hard and dangerous work, and they did a hell of a job."

Back on the valley floor, the search teams couldn't believe what they were finding. "It was incredible," Blanchard reported. "There were thousands of tons of ammunition and explosives—thousands of tons! There were tanks, artillery, and antiaircraft guns. There was enough weaponry to outfit an army."

Each cave had to be checked carefully, for there was the ever-present threat of an ambush or booby traps. It was tedious, time-consuming, dangerous work.

"We were on a search-and-destroy mission," Charlie Moncsko explained, "but there was no way we were going to destroy that much munitions and equipment. We were scheduled to be on the ground for twelve hours and we barely had a hundred pounds of C-4 explosive with us."

The force moved methodically down the valley, trying to get a rough inventory of what they were finding. It was hard to catalog it all; there were thousands of crates of ammunition and explosives—literally millions of pounds of ordnance. Some of the caves held classrooms and training facilities. There were jail cells and safe-house accommodations that included passports and freshly laundered clothes. The caves were wired with electric lights, but there was no power. The search teams had only their flashlights.

"This was a classic terrorist-training/terror-export operation on a scale we couldn't imagine," said Ed Boskin, one of the FBI agents. "Al-Qaeda terrorists could be trained, equipped, given false documentation, and filtered across the Pakistani border. Who knows how many terrorist bombers were trained here and sent against targets in the West? The whole complex was just one big terrorist training and logistics base."

As the teams moved from cave to cave down the valley, Taladega's marines leapfrogged along the high ground on either side to provide security. Three-quarters of the way down the valley, the teams on the valley floor came across a cemetery. They were briefed to be on the lookout for fresh graves, as it was not known yet whether bin Laden was dead or alive. Any fresh grave would have to be investigated. The contents of the caves, the tanks, and the artillery hidden in the wadis, the cemetery, the intact condition of the complex—all of this was reported back to Captain Bob Harward and Task Force K-Bar. Communications were marginal, but everyone now knew this was the biggest al-Qaeda base and terrorist training facility ever found. By late afternoon, they arrived at the extraction point near the end of the valley, just a few miles from the Pakistani border. Most of them had been up for more than thirty-six hours. They were tired and hungry, and it was getting colder.

"Camel Packer, this is K-Bar actual. You there, Tim?"

"Go, ahead, sir." Even over the encrypted transmission, Blanchard could recognize Harward's voice.

"New orders from higher command, Tim. They want you guys to stay in there for another day."

"Say again, K-Bar!" Blanchard was shouting now. His radio batteries were low, and he wanted to make sure he had understood his commander. He knew the inbound extraction helos were only five minutes out.

"I say again, we want you to stay there. Can you safely go to ground and stay overnight, over?"

"Roger, wait one."

Blanchard quickly turned to Taladega. "Chris, can we dig in here for the night and hold?"

"There's a small abandoned village on the rim of the valley. We could take shelter there and set a good defensive perimeter. But we better get on it. It'll be dark soon, and it's going to get cold."

"How're your guys holding up?" Blanchard was well aware that the marines had been through a really tough scramble across the valley walls, some of them at altitudes over eighty-five hundred feet.

"They're a pretty tired bunch, sir," Taladega reported, "but they're marines. We'll make it happen."

Blanchard glanced at the others. The SEALs were fine, but he was concerned with the others. Everyone was excited with the day's find, but they were all weary. There were seventy-four American souls in that valley beside himself, and he was responsible for them. He knew Harward would not order him to stay if he had serious concerns for the welfare of his men. On the other hand, Harward would not ask him to stay if it wasn't important. And from what they had seen today, this was very important.

"K-Bar, this is Camel Packer. Roger your last. We will move out from here to the security of the village on the east rim of the valley. Any chance of a resupply, over?"

"Negative, Camel Packer. We'll get you at first light tomorrow morning, so you'll have to make do with what you have, over."

Which is nothing, Blanchard thought. "Understood, K-Bar. We're moving to the village and will check in when we go to ground for the night."

"Good copy, Tim, and good luck. K-Bar out."

In the fading light, the small force made its way up to the little village on the rim of the valley. It was more a collection of huts than a village—one- and two-room dwellings made of stone and mud. The bombs and cruise missiles of the previous evening had done little to the cave infrastructure in the valley, but they had frightened all the locals away. They had fled, and the village was abandoned. The only inhabitants were chickens, a half-dozen goats, and two cows. Bone weary after a hurried two-mile trek from the valley floor and an elevation gain of twelve hundred feet, the assault force filed into the village for the night. There was still much to do.

Blanchard needed to get out a situation report, or SITREP, to advise Harward on the intelligence they had gathered and the condition of his force. The SEAL platoon communicator broke out his laptop computer, and Blanchard began work on his formatted SITREP. Moncsko's SEALs made a thorough search of the village, and Taladega and his marines set up a defensive perimeter and sentry rotation. Thanks to the miracle of satellite communications, Blanchard was able to get off a detailed and comprehensive report. He also wanted to make sure that the TOC at K-Bar had the exact coordinates of their position. Given the amount of ordnance that had been fired into the valley the previous night, he didn't want to risk being on the wrong end of a cruise missile or a JDAM. Or worse, a roving special operations AC-130 gunship. After he sent off the message, he huddled with his two element commanders.

"We have a good perimeter here," Taladega reported. "Sergeant Robertson has a third of my marines on guard duty and the others resting. They're pretty tired, so we'll rotate them every two hours. Either the sergeant or myself will be on the perimeter at all times."

"Thanks, Chris," Blanchard replied. "Your guys did one helluva job today. Any activity out there?"

"Nothing close by, but we can see them signaling with lights in the hills to the west and north. They know we're here, and they're talking about it."

"What'd your guys turn up, Charlie?"

"There's no food here or none that we would want to eat, but we did find some mattresses and a few blankets. We also found more clothing and some passports and false ID documents. Chief Moss stacked the blankets and clothing in one of the huts—probably enough for everyone to get on another layer for the night, so long as they don't mind the fleas. And speaking of fleas, we found one of the residents. We made him an honorary SEAL—hope you don't mind."

"You what?" Blanchard said.

"One of the guys found a stray dog. Seems like he prefers our company to the Afghans, so he's one of us now. We named him JDAM. He's a little thin, but when we get some MREs, we'll fatten him right up."

Blanchard could only shake his head. That's all he needed—a mutt, and probably a fleabag at that. Whatever. He had other things to think about.

The mud huts had fire pits inside, so he allowed his men to build small warming fires. The temperature had dropped to the mid-thirties and would probably get colder. They could cope with a few fleas, but he had to make sure they stayed warm. He was a little concerned about the Army chem-bio specialist and the Navy interpreter. The FBI guys were no strangers to a hard night in the field. The two EOD technicians had been training with the SEAL platoon for some time now. They were good to go. All the others were marines or SOF operators; being cold, tired, and short on sleep was part of being on the job site. They'd get through the night and be ready for duty tomorrow morning.

"I'm going to have a look around," Blanchard said to Moncsko and Taladega. "Let me know if you see or hear anything. I don't want any of those gomers [the name SEALs often use for al-Qaeda and Taliban fighters] slipping back in here and surprising us."

Back in the TOC at Kandahar, Bob Harward was reading Blanchard's report. Along with a narrative of the day's activities, there was a request for an early extraction or early resupply the following day. "Holy shit," he exclaimed when he got to Blanchard's estimate of the enemy stores they had found. Harward turned to Lieutenant Phil Rasmussen, his TOC watch officer. "Get Tim's report out to the SOC [Rear Admiral Bert Calland, special operations commander for General Tommy Franks's Central Command] right away." Then he slipped behind his own laptop and began to draft messages, one to Calland, requesting further direction, and another to Blanchard. It was going to be a long night for him as well, but he would be warm and there would be plenty of rations. He fully understood that was not the case with his men in the field.

After Rasmussen readdressed the message, Harward again spoke to him: "Phil, start putting together a list of things those guys might be needing if we don't pull them out tomorrow."

"Aye, aye, sir," Rasmussen replied, then set off in search of his supply petty officer.

The night passed uneventfully for the men on the edge of the Zhawar Kili Valley, but they didn't rest all that easy. All night long there were signal lights in the mountains along both sides of the valley. Most of them got at least a few hours' sleep, but it was fitful rest at best, as the temperature dipped well below freezing. The next morning, there was a message from Bob Harward at Task Force K-Bar:

RATIONS, WATER, AND BATTERIES INBOUND YOUR LOCATION BY CH-53. CONTINUE TO CATALOGUE AND DOCUMENT ZK COMPLEX PER ORIGINAL INSTRUCTIONS. UPON COMPLETION OF THIS TASK PREPARE TO BEGIN DESTRUCTION OF COMPLEX. ET FOR EXFIL UNKNOWN AT THIS TIME. PREPARE LIST OF NEEDS FOR EXTENDED STAY. REMEMBER, YOU ARE ALL VOLUNTEERS. HARWARD.

Blanchard had to grin at the last. The captain loved to kid the troops, and Tim Blanchard knew that his boss would instantly trade the meager comforts of Kandahar to be there with them if he thought he could get away with it. Blanchard called his officers and senior enlisted men in to brief them on the situation. There was some grumbling, but it was only for show. Everyone was excited about what they had seen the day before. Blanchard told them to put out security and go back to work on the caves along the valley floor. Until they could do something about their woeful lack of demolitions, it was an inventory exercise.

Word was racing through CENTCOM that the Zhawar Kili complex was by far the largest al-Qaeda arms cache and training base found to date. Predator drones and P-3 Navy surveillance aircraft now had the valley under constant surveillance. Just before first light, a Predator had spotted about twenty armed men heading toward the cluster of huts where the assault force had spent the night. They were some ten kilometers away and moving quickly. The P-3 on station called on the services of a special operations AC-130 Spectre gunship and vectored the deadly aircraft to the target. The file of men moving toward the valley under cover of darkness probably never quite knew what hit them. They may or may not have heard the engines of the 130 orbiting at eighteen thousand feet, some ten thousand feet above them, when the 40mm and 105mm cannon shells slammed into them. Just after sunrise, after the gunship pilots radioed the results of their strike, Charlie Moncsko sought out Blanchard.

"Hey, Tim. With one of my SEAL squads and the others down in the valley, we have plenty of people to work the caves. Why don't I take my other squad out and see who the AC-130 caught in the open? Maybe we can find out who was trying to get back here to attack us." Navy SEALs often work in squads, with the OIC of the SEAL platoon leading one squad while his AOIC led the other.

"Sounds right, Charlie. Put together a plan and brief me before you leave. And make sure you have good comms out and back."

"Roger that. We'll be ready to go in about thirty minutes."

Meanwhile, the marines provided security on the rim of the valley and the valley floor. They now had a pretty good lay of the land and could control the approaches to the area from several fixed overwatch positions. As the search teams on the valley floor continued to explore the caves, the marines moved protectively above them. Squads of marines ranged out several hundred yards on either side of the valley rim. Their sniper teams found perches in the rock that allowed them to cover the men below, as well as the access trails into the valley. Inside the caves, the FBI men documented the training areas with digital cameras and, with the Navy interpreter, searched among the documents for useful information. The Army chem-bio specialist, a captain, sniffed about with his metered test equipment. But the central problem of how to destroy that much material and stores remained unanswered.

"It will take us a month of Sundays to rig and blow all this crap," Blanchard said aloud as he emerged from one of the caves. "This whole valley is a friggin' ammo dump."

"Maybe there's a better way," said Senior Master Sergeant Ian Hamilton. Hamilton was the senior of the two Air Force combat controllers from the CCTs (Combat Control Teams). Both were FAA certified air traffic controllers, but their work had nothing to do with managing commercial air traffic. Their job was to manage tactical support aircraft and to make precision-guided bombs a little more precise. "I think we can do a little digging here with two-thousand-pound shovels."

Meanwhile, Lieutenant Charlie Moncsko led a squad of SEALs along with a few marines and Master Sergeant Tom Jordan, the other combat controller, over a ridge to the west of Zhawar Kili. As they moved in on the site of the AC-130 gunship attack, they spotted a group of some thirty armed men moving below them. It appeared that al-Qaeda was starting to get organized and wanted their valley back.

"They were shuffling along in a loose formation," as Petty Officer Sean Montgomery, one of the platoon SEALs, described it. Montgomery himself was a former marine. "Most of them had weapons that they carried draped over their shoulders and some had bandoliers of ammunition. They were turned out in mountain garb—robes, turbans, and sandals. We watched them with binoculars for a while before they saw us. A few of them fired at us, but we were well out of effective range. We had position on them and most of us were just itching to get a few rounds downrange. The El-Tee [short for LT, or lieutenant—in this case, Moncsko] just turns to Tom and says, 'Take care of them.' By now the gomers are only three or four hundred yards away."

SEALs are able to call in close air support as well, but they haven't the in-depth training and experience of the Air Force controllers. In addition to JDAMs from Air Force and Navy tactical aircraft, there are the special operations AC-130 Spectre gunships and the deadly Army Apache helicopters and Marine Cobra helos. A small SEAL ground force can call on some expensive, lethal, and highly sophisticated assistance, and more reliably do so with an experienced controller. The Air Force CCTs train specifically to manage and direct these airborne close-support platforms. But when they have to, the Air Force special operators can put their own guns in the fight alongside their SEAL brothers.

"So," Montgomery continued, "Master Sergeant Jordan breaks out his map, gets on the radio, and raises a section of Air Force F-15E Strike Eagles. They talk for a moment, and then he turns to the rest of us. 'It's on the way,' he says. 'Look the other way and keep your mouth open; there'll be a pretty good shock wave.' And then," Montgomery said with a grin, "Jordan deadpans, 'Gee, I sure hope I got those coordinates right.' A few seconds later, four five-hundred pounders land right in the middle of those guys. The concussions felt like someone was punching you in the kidneys. We went down to the strike area and there was nothing but sandals, body parts, and a few mangled weapons. They'd simply been erased. It was the same when we found the group hit by the AC-130. There was no intelligence to be gathered, so we left everything at both sites just as it was. Their people would find what was left of them, and they would think twice about trying to come after us in the Zhawar Kili."

Back on the valley floor, a CH-53 landed briefly and dumped off a pallet of MREs, a dozen or more cases of bottled water, and some battery packs. The assault force was in business for a while longer. Later that day, Sergeant Hamilton sought out Lieutenant Commander Blanchard. Hamilton was an eighteen-year Air Force veteran and had previously worked with SEALs on several occasions. He was a powerfully built man with thick arms and wrists. His dark hair was graying at the temples, but he had a youthful face and a mischievous grin; he loved his work. He had grown up in Southie, and had a heavy Boston accent.

"Good afternoon, Senior Master Sergeant," Blanchard said formally. They were talking outside one of the major tunnel entrances. With him was Senior Chief Petty Officer Ryan Marshall, the lead EOD technician. "And to you, Senior Chief." Marshall was smaller than Hamilton, with dark features and intelligent eyes. Both the Air Force Combat Control Teams and the Navy explosive ordnance disposal teams were small organizations with very specialized missions—one dropped ordnance and the other made unexploded ordnance safe. Blanchard looked upon these two men as his demolitions brain trust. He had a problem: What to do with hundreds of thousands of pounds of explosives, ammunition, and stores once they had completed the inventory and documentation process? They could blow only a fraction of what they had found with their meager amount of C-4. More might be obtained by resupply helos, but in truth, there was not yet that much C-4 explosive in all of Afghanistan.

"Well, gentlemen, have you figured out what we're going to do with all of this stuff?"

"Yes, sir," Hamilton replied. "We're going to set up a mining operation. What's our priority on JDAMs?"

"JDAMs?" Blanchard replied. "I'll have to check, but we can probably get all we need. What do you have in mind?"

Hamilton dropped to one knee and brushed the cobbles away from a patch of hardpan with his hand. "The valley floor runs something like this," he said, drawing in the dirt with a stick, "with the valley walls going up on either side. The caves run back into the mountain at basically a straight line from the valley walls. The depth of rock above the caves run anywhere from a few meters at the mouth to a hundred meters or more at the end of some of the deeper caves. I've already started to plot the grid coordinates of the cave entrances and take azimuths on the direction of the tunneling. Most of them run fairly straight. It'll take some calculation and little trial and error, but I think we can use two-thousand-pound JDAMs with delayed fuses. If we do it right, the bombs will penetrate the mountain and detonate among the explosive stores. It's going to take a lot of JDAMs, but I think it's the best way to do the job—maybe the only way to do the job."

Blanchard thought about this for a moment and turned to Marshall. "You buy this, Senior Chief?"

"Makes sense to me, sir," the EOD man replied. "I don't even want to think about how much C-4 we'd have to hump in there to blow this stuff. This is a big job; it'd take us weeks, maybe months."

Hamilton went on to detail his plan for using air-dropped two-thousand-pound charges to destroy the caves and their contents. With Blanchard's endorsement, they set to work. Lieutenant Eric Trumbly, the SEAL platoon's assistant officer, or AOIC, had been tasked with the inspection and documentation process. Once a cave had been searched, inventoried, and photographed, it was ready for demolition. Trumbly's search teams worked all day while Master Sergeant Hamilton made his calculations—exactly how many microseconds of delay would be required for the JDAM to punch through the varying depths of rock. A cave might require a two-microsecond delay nearer the mouth and a six-microsecond delay farther back where there was several hundred feet or more of mountain above the shaft.

"It was incredible," Blanchard said. "I wouldn't have believed it if I hadn't walked into those first caves and saw it myself. If the delay was too long, you could walk back in the cave and see where the bomb had punched in from the ceiling and continued on through the floor, leaving the shaft intact. There was no reference for this kind of work in any military demolition manual; it was all trial and error. Once we got the hang of it, we were able to put the JDAMs on target and right in the middle of those explosive stores. Sergeant Hamilton wrote the book on destroying caves with JDAMs. The guy's a first-rate mining engineer."

The task element was held over another day with the expectation that they would be there longer. At first light, another helo came in with more food, water, and batteries. Blanchard and company fell into a search-document-destroy routine. It was dirty, exhausting work. Typically, they would work all day, clear the valley floor at dusk, and bring the planes in to bomb at night.

"We had a great vantage point to watch the nighttime fireworks," Blanchard said of the air strikes. "We'd get these secondary explosions that would go on for hours, so we'd work one end of the valley one day and the other end the next. We were continually amazed at the amount of ammunition and explosives in those caves."

There was some reluctance on the part of senior commanders to believe that the SEALs could have found that quantity of stores and munitions in such a remote mountain location. There was a war on, and the stockpiles of JDAMs had been severely depleted by the drive to oust the Taliban and to bomb other al-Qaeda strongholds; there was not an endless supply of these valuable weapons. But once digital images of the stockpiles in the Zhawar Kili began arriving through the satellite communications (SATCOM) link, the upper-echelon commanders became believers. Blanchard got his JDAMs, but it was still hard for some to understand how that much ordnance could be crammed into that small valley.

"It all came through Pakistan," Blanchard explained. "We found heavy vehicle tire tracks leading from the Pakistani border into the valley. They brought it in by the semitrailer load. This stuff must have come in through the port of Karachi, then up through western Pakistan, each warlord taking his fee as it passed through his district. Borders don't mean too much here. Clan boundaries and smuggling routes do. We could see the border guards from the lower end of the valley. No one can tell me they didn't know what was going on there."

While the search crews toiled in the caves, Moncsko and his rein- forced SEAL squad continued to range out from the valley cave com- plex, looking for caches of al-Qaeda material and documents. The Air Force CCT sergeants rotated. One worked the caves while the other accompanied the SEALs on these out-of-valley sweeps. On one of these forays, they found several low stone huts with passports, phony IDs, clothing, and bags of heroin. On the third day, in response to Blan- chard's request for better mobility to search the outlying areas, a sec- ond CH-53 followed the resupply bird into the valley with two desert patrol vehicles. These particular DPVs were armed with heavy ma- chine guns and rockets. The two delivered to the Zhawar Kili came with three-man SEAL crews. At first, Blanchard and Moncsko wel- comed the vehicles. But while they were excellent in getting from one end of the valley to the other on the desert hardpan, they were ill- suited for duty in the canyons and rough wadis. The DPVs were de- signed for use at high-speeds in open desert; the area around the Zhawar Kili Valley was simply too rough, and the roads that were there were too steep or too narrow for them. But SEALs are highly skilled at finding alternative ways to do their work.

"By about the fourth day," one of the platoon SEALs told me, "we were well into going native. We had hajji robes and headgear, stubble beards, and we were all really dirty. We were even starting to smell like mountain men. Hajji," he explained, "is SEAL talk for anything local in Afghanistan. We have slang for everything. We talk about hajji gear, hajji chow—kind of like talking about Mexican food or French fash- ion. As for the al-Qaeda, we call them gomers, skinnies, terrorist dirt- bags, whatever." Here he gave me an apologetic smile. "Probably not nice on our part, but we have a great deal of contempt for this terror- ist rabble. I'm sure they call us a lot worse. Anyway, we were about ten klicks [kilometers] west of the valley and we see this Toyota coming down a wadi. Two of our SEALs step out and wave to them. Our guys are wearing robes and Afghan headgear. Well, they drive right over to us. By the time these two gomers see what's happening, it's too late. Now we have ourselves a hajji DPV. Toyota four-by-fours were built for this terrain. The next day we're out making the rounds with our new set of wheels. There are four of us, two up front and the rest in the back. About midday, we see six gomers making their way along a canyon rim. We drive right over to them like we're pals of theirs. Now, these guys are armed, but they just look at us with their weapons slung, like maybe we were coming to give them a lift. Next thing they know they're looking down the barrels of four automatic weapons. Gomers, we are not. But we did give them a lift back to our camp for interrogation. You should have seen the look on their faces; you'd think we just landed there from Mars. From their perspective, we might as well have. Now, we didn't smell all that good by then, but these guys have world-class body odor. They reeked all the way back to the compound in the valley. We couldn't wait to get 'em out of our new truck."

The work in the Zhawar Kili Valley went on. The search teams continued to document and catalog. Senior Master Sergeant Hamilton orchestrated the destruction from the air, and the SEALs ranged out to patrol the surrounding area. No decision was ever made for an extended stay at Zhawar Kili. At the end of each day, the word came down for another day's extension.

"But no one complained," Tim Blanchard said. "We knew we were putting a major hurt on al-Qaeda's ability to train and support terrorist activity. God knows how many thousands of tons of ammo and material we destroyed. Often one of the JDAMs would initiate a series of secondary explosions. One of those continued for close to two days. Through it all, the guys pulled together as a team. Everyone got along and worked together: We were from different service components, but we worked as a single unit. The only one who was a little disappointed was the Army captain who was an expert in chem-bio detection. He really wanted to at least find some chemicals, but there was nothing there. You have to understand that some of these gomers are not all that sophisticated, and I'd have been surprised if there were chemicals or biologics at this kind of complex. They knew about crashing airliners into buildings, though. There were crude drawings of passenger jets and the World Trade Center towers. It was still a rat's nest, and a big one."

By the seventh day and into the eighth, the Americans in the Zhawar Kili Valley were fully acclimatized and used to hard living—sleeping on the floor and cooking over an open fire. They couldn't get any dirtier, and all but the marines were wearing hajji gear.

"We had to be careful about entering and leaving the perimeter," Moncsko added at the mention of wearing native garb. "The marines were tasked with protecting our little compound on the rim of the valley, and they were determined that no Taliban or al-Qaeda fighter was going to slip through their line with a satchel charge. We had prearranged signals and bona fides, but we were very careful, especially coming back in after dark. We now looked like the enemy, and the marines shoot very well—too well to take any chances. You hear about rivalry between SEALs and marines, but you couldn't prove that by us. Those marines looked out for us and kept us safe. Great bunch of guys—professional bunch of guys."

"Along about the third day in the Zhawar Kili," Chief Moss recalled, "the MREs began to get old, so we roasted a goat. It was horrible; tasted like it smelled, like eating shoe leather. Then we tried the chickens. They were scrawny and quick, very hard to catch. You should have seen it—chickens racing around, squawking their heads off, with a SEAL in hot pursuit. Then, when we did catch one, we had a fight on our hands to get its neck wrung. About that time, the SEALs working on the valley floor climbed up to our camp on the rim of the valley. Sam Bowden, one of the platoon SEALs working the caves, was a farm boy from Oklahoma. He watched this circus for a few minutes, then says, 'Jeez, what in the hell do you city boys think you're doing?' Then he went to work. He walked quietly up to one of the chickens, making little clucking sounds, then quick as a snake he has it by the neck. And then, and you won't believe this, he folds the chicken's head under its wing and holds it there while slowly moving the chicken in a big circular motion. After some fifteen revolutions, the chicken is asleep. Bowden snaps its head off, plucks it, and has it on a spit over the fire, all in about five minutes. A half hour later, there are four birds turning over the coals. Someone comes up with a couple of MRE-size bottles of Tabasco sauce for marinade and we were in business. My mouth's watering just thinking about it. It was marvelous. We sat out there on the rim of that valley, eating roasted chicken, watching the JDAMs slam into the caves, and listening for the roar of secondary explosions. It doesn't get any better than that for a Navy SEAL."

On the seventh day, Harward informed them they would be pulled out the following day and told them to make all preparations for leaving the Zhawar Kili Valley and redeploying back to Task Force K-Bar at Kandahar. That afternoon, the SEALs and EOD technicians set out to blow the last cave the old-fashioned way—with C-4. They had found barrels of diesel oil and a small quantity of gasoline in this cave. They divided their C-4 into three charges and primed them with time fuse and blasting caps. The first two charges detonated with little or no effect, and seemed like firecrackers compared to the two-thousand-pound JDAMs. When the third charge went, the ground began to move and kept moving. It seems that there were fuel and ammunition stores buried well inside the cave, munitions they hadn't found—until now. All night long the rumbling continued as more cached stores and fuel fed the ongoing explosion. With this final demolition, all the caves in the Zhawar Kili Valley had been demolished or collapsed, and the weaponry hid in the wadis and ravines destroyed.

"We all left that valley ten or fifteen pounds lighter than we entered it," Tim Blanchard reported. "I'd say we worked twenty hours a day and never slept for more than a two-hour stretch. We were dirty, hungry, cold, or hot most of our waking hours. It was wonderful. Had they taken us from the Zhawar Kili Valley and dropped us into another valley, we were good to go. There is absolutely nothing like being given an important and difficult mission and seeing your men accomplish that mission. Ninety-nine point nine of what was there is no longer available to al-Qaeda. It must have taken them years to gather that much equipment and ammunition. Who knows how long it took them just to dig those caves. We destroyed it all in a week."

On the morning of 14 January, two Marine MH-60s landed to collect the DPVs and a third of Blanchard's force. That afternoon they returned to collect the last of the SEALs and the marines, and one well-fed and totally rehabilitated Afghan dog. Before they left, Hamilton plotted the grid coordinates at the mouths of the major caves and approaches to the valley. There is always the possibility that the al-Qaeda will return to try to salvage some of their stores. If they do, an airborne or implanted sensor will register their presence with a great deal of accuracy. Then a two-thousand-pound American calling card will fall from an unseen airplane or be delivered by a cruise missile well offshore in the Arabian Sea.

The SEALs' coming ashore for the strategic-reconnaissance mission at Camp Rhino was a large step for the maritime proponent of America's special operations forces. So were those initial platoon-size direct-action missions conducted by Task Force K-Bar. But the mission into the Zhawar Kili Valley was as unique as it was propitious. Never before had SEALs conducted an airborne assault that far inland. Never before had they operated in a force that large, let alone provided the command and control on the ground for such a force. Zhawar Kili laid the groundwork for the larger multiunit, multiservice operations that would attend the SEAL operations in Iraq.

"We learned a lot at Zhawar Kili," Tim Blanchard told me well after the fact. "We directed some 404,000 pounds of ordnance into that valley. Not since Vietnam have that many bombs been dropped into that small of an area, and never that much so close to friendly troops. We did it routinely. As far as I know, it was the largest ground-controlled aerial bombardment in history. This was probably the largest and most important al-Qaeda training and resupply facility in Afghanistan, bigger than Tora Bora. We closed it down barely four months after the 11 September attacks. I'm proud of the role I was able to play in this operation. What made it happen was the way the ground force worked together: the marines, the SEALs, the CCTs, the Bureau agents—all of them. Every man contributed. We sweated it out during the day and froze our butts off at night, but we made it happen."

Commander Tim Blanchard is now assigned to the Special Operations Command, Pacific—SOCPAC. His duties regularly take him back to Afghanistan and Iraq.

"When I talk to other platoon commanders, they're very jealous of those of us assigned to Task Force K-Bar," said Charlie Moncsko. "We had some good missions canceled on us and drilled a few dry holes—operations where you go in and there is nothing there. But then you get one like Zhawar Kili. It validates all your hard work and training, and you know you made a difference. I had a couple of first-tour SEALs in my platoon, and this experience alone will make them solid veterans on future deployments. We all learned a lot—the kinds of things you can't really train for. We had never trained with old Toyota pickup trucks in hajji dress, but as it turned out, that was the best way to move about the country. And the secondary explosions! They went on all night long! What a week!"

Lieutenant Commander Charlie Moncsko is now on loan from the SEAL teams to NASA. He is in the astronaut program, training as a space shuttle mission specialist.

"Dropping bombs is what I do," said Senior Master Sergeant Ian Hamilton of the experience. "Hell, it's what I've wanted to do since I was a little boy. This was not the first time I've worked with Navy

SEALs, and the Zhawar Kili operation was not the last time. It will, though, probably be the last time I ever have that many aircraft available to me or that much ordnance at my disposal. I got everything I wanted and then some. I'd been up for about two and a half days and half goofy with lack of sleep when this little-girl voice checks into the net: 'Hey, guys, where do you want me to put 'em?' It was a female F-18 pilot off the *Teddy Roosevelt* with four two-thousand-pound JDAMs. Snapped me right awake. I mean, really, is this the way to fight a war, or what?"

Senior Master Sergeant Ian Hamilton is currently an instructor at the Air Force Combat Control Teams school at Pope Air Force Base in North Carolina. He was back directing air support for special operations during the Iraqi War.

"No question about it," recalled Bob Harward, "Zhawar Kili was a turning point for us. It showed that even with a large, complex objective we could plan and execute the mission in a very narrow time window. And once on the ground, we could adapt to various contingencies as they arose. After Zhawar Kili, the joint command structure was much more willing to give us the job and tell us to simply do it, rather than having us reporting back up the chain every step of the way for direction and permission. It all seems routine now, but not back then. Think about it: SEALs in the mountains running direct-action and strategic-reconnaissance missions. No one thought we could do it, let alone do it better than anyone else. It all came down to just how quickly can you plan, jock up, and get a team onto an insertion helo. Our guys were nothing short of fantastic."

Captain Bob Harward also directed a joint combined task force during the Iraqi War. He is now Deputy Commander, Naval Special Warfare Command, and on the promotion list for rear admiral.

CHAPTER 5

NIGHT OF THE NAVY SEALS

Air Force MH-53 Pavelow Three-Four-Charlie came in as low and as fast as the two pilots up front could manage. Both were wearing NVGs during the approach and, in unison, both flipped them up some hundred meters from the target. The air strikes going in ahead of Three-Four-Charlie caused near-blinding plumes of light in the sensitive optics. In the back of the big helicopter, eighteen men couldn't wait to get off the bird. Back at Ali al-Salim Air Base in Kuwait, where they had staged for the mission, they couldn't wait to get *on* the helo. It was just before midnight on 20 March 2003—the eve of the invasion of Iraq. It was to be the largest combat operation in the forty-some years the Navy SEALs had been in existence.

"You have to go back to the invasion beaches at Normandy," a SEAL commander told me, "or some of the larger amphibious operations in the Pacific to find that many men on an operation. And even then, maybe not that many people moving at the exact same time. We've never seen the likes of this in our community, and we may never see it again."

The SEALs on Three-Four-Charlie were but one of five Naval Special

Special Boat Team eleven-meter RHIB. The RHIBs are the workhorse patrol craft of the SBTs and a key platform for SEAL maritime insertion. *Courtesy of the U.S. Navy (Eric Logsdon)*

Warfare elements in play that night. For the past day and a half at Ali al-Salim Air Base, they had been constantly harassed by incoming Iraqi Scud missiles. The Scuds had done no damage, but with the possibility of chemical warheads, an incoming missile forced everyone at the base to go through the chemical attack drill. They'd had to drop what they were doing and scramble into the cumbersome and hot MOPP (Military Operational Prevention and Protection) gear, which would protect them from possible exposure to chemical, biological, or nuclear agents or weapons. By the time they had boarded the helo less than an hour earlier, the assault element was more than harassed; they were pissed. Now they would soon be able to vent some of that anger and frustration. Yet those same feelings were tempered by the dangers ahead and the responsibilities of the mission entrusted to them. This mission was *very* important. Everyone on the Pavelow knew that. It had to be done right; there was no room for error.

Aboard Three-Four-Charlie were eight Navy SEALs, eight British Royal Marines, a Navy EOD technician, and an Air Force combat controller. The eight SEALs were relative newcomers to the region. They were from an assigned PACOM SEAL platoon that had been engaged in an exercise on Okinawa with the Japanese Self-Defense Force when the call came.

"We were ecstatic," one of the platoon SEALs recalled. "In some ways we felt we were in exile, assigned to a training mission while preparations for the real thing were under way. We all thought the war was going to be over and done with before we could get our guns into the fight. When the word came to pack up and stand by to be airlifted to Kuwait, we were very happy campers. It was a sobering and exciting time for us. I remember getting on the cell phone and calling home. About all I could say was 'Honey, I'm going forward.' "

That was three weeks earlier. When the platoon arrived at Ali al-Salim, it quickly moved into recently constructed prefab barracks and was briefed on its part of the upcoming mission. The deployed SEAL squadron had been tasked with capturing the Iraqi oil export apparatus in its entirety—intact. Initial mission planning called only for those SEAL platoons in CENTCOM to be involved. As the planners fleshed out the target package, the need for more SEALs in the assault elements grew. Two additional PACOM platoons were brought into theater—one from Guam, and this one from Okinawa. On their arrival, the Okinawa PACOM platoon was split into two squads and began to rehearse for its two respective targets—the PPL at MABOT, and the PPL at KAAOT. In the world of acronyms, MABOT stood for the Mina al-Bakr Oil Terminal. KAAOT was short for Khor al-Amaya Oil Terminal. PPL is short for petroleum pumping lock—essentially, an oil pumping station. The meaning of MABOT has met with some confusion. It was named for Saddam's Baathist predecessor—Mina al-Bakr—but the name has since been changed to simply the Basra Oil Terminal, after the city of Basra. Basra, located at the head of the al-Faw peninsula, is the largest city in southern Iraq. In this book, I will continue to use MABOT and KAAOT, as the SEALs and special boat crewmen still refer to them as such.

Because the SEAL squad on Three-Four-Charlie was relatively new to the area, they were assigned to one of the smaller targets the SEALs would hit that night. Intelligence reports held that the PPLs had few oil workers at the site and the lightest security. The plan was for the two PPL attack teams to be inserted by helo at the perimeter of the facilities, from where they could make a basic assault on the installations. The SEALs were to search and secure the structures; the Royal Marines were to provide security. Mock-ups of the PPLs had been constructed at the Udairi training range, located adjacent to the Ali al-Salim Air Base. The scale of the mock PPL stations was reduced somewhat and prefab wooden buildings took the place of bunkers, maintenance buildings, and the "pig" house at the center of each practice site. But the physical relationship and purpose of each structure was identical to the real thing. The PPLs, situated on the tip of the al-Faw peninsula, serve as spigots of a sort that send oil to the offshore loading platforms. They also serve a valve station where the pigs, or

solid pipeline parcels—sluglike projectiles—can be placed into or re-
trieved from the pipelines to monitor pressure and to clean the
pipeline. Both facilities were key components of the Iraqi oil export
structure.

Chief John Morales was the platoon's chief petty officer. His squad
was assigned to take the MABOT PPL. The eight SEALs in the platoon's other squad were assigned to the KAAOT PPL farther up the
coast. Morales was also the assistant patrol leader for the mission and,
as APL, would be the last one to leave Three-Four-Charlie when they
broke from the helo onto the target. Morales had a lot on his mind. As
one of the last platoons to be added to the target package, they did not
have as much time to rehearse and prepare for the mission. Due to a
shake-up in this platoon's leadership during the stateside predeployment workup, he had not been with this platoon as long as he would
have liked. The platoon was solid, and so was this particular squad—
his squad. Still, he would have liked to have been with them a little
longer. And then there was his officer, the platoon AOIC and squad
leader, Lieutenant (junior grade) Craig Thomas. Thomas was a good
one. In Chief John Morales's opinion, he was one of the best. And he
should know. Morales had been called away from duty at Basic Underwater Demolition/SEAL Training to take over as the platoon chief. He
had been a Third Phase instructor at the Naval Special Warfare Center.
He had put then Ensign Thomas through training. The enlisted BUD/S
instructors know they will serve with and fight alongside the men they
put through training and serve under the new officers they train. But
Chief Morales had not thought it would have happened this quickly
with Thomas. He had confidence in Thomas's ability, both as a warrior
and as a leader. Still, it was the young officer's first deployment and
first operational mission. And given the last-minute intelligence, it
would be, in all probability, a combat operation—perhaps a sticky
one. Lieutenant Thomas would not be alone in his baptism of fire;
more than half the SEALs in the squad had yet to see combat.

Initially, they thought it might be a mission with little or no con-

BUD/S First Phase training. Initial BUD/S training is about being cold and wet, and enduring physical hardship. Here, First Phase trainees push 'em out. *Courtesy of the U.S. Navy (Eric Logsdon)*

BUD/S teamwork. Basic SEAL training stresses teamwork in a challenging and difficult environment. First Phase trainees participate in log PT (physical training). *Courtesy of the U.S. Navy (Eric Logsdon)*

A BUD/S student during Hell Week in the demolition pits. Basic SEAL training is designed to condition young warriors for future combat. For BUD/S graduates, it's certain combat. *Courtesy of the U.S. Navy (Eric Logsdon)*

Before you can be a SEAL, you have to be a frogman. Basic SEAL trainees receive pool training during BUD/S Second Phase. *Courtesy of the U.S. Navy (Eric Logsdon)*

Third Phase training. BUD/S Third Phase, and much of current SEAL pre-deployment, involves weapons training. They will soon send rounds downrange for real on deployment. *Courtesy of the U.S. Navy (Eric Logsdon)*

Prep school for Afghanistan. A SEAL platoon trains in the California desert for operational deployment to Central Command. *Courtesy of the U.S. Navy (Eric Logsdon)*

Hanging over water. A SEAL making his way by fast rope from a CH-53 to the deck of a ship under way. He controls the rapid descent with hands and feet. *Courtesy of the U.S. Navy (Robert Benson)*

On the deck; race for cover. SEALs rehearse getting onto a moving ship and sprinting for cover to seize the vessel. Operationally, they do this at night. *Courtesy of the U.S. Navy (George Kusner)*

On the move for a ship takedown. SEALs set up a security perimeter after insertion by Navy H-60 helos. A second H-60 may have a protective sniper overwatch to cover their boarding. *Courtesy of the U.S. Navy (Eric Logsdon)*

Two platoon SEALS train in Close Quarter Defense (CQD) techniques, skills they will put to use in operational deployment in Iraq and Afghanistan. *Courtesy of Cliff Hollenbeck*

Tough duty. SEALs train as a team in applying CQD techniques to take down a suspect. The man on the floor is a SEAL playing the role of a noncompliant terrorist. *Courtesy of the author*

SEAL drivers and gunners put their Humvees through their paces during predeployment training at Fort A. P. Hill in Virginia. *Courtesy of the U.S. Navy (Shawn Eklund)*

Humvee training in open country. Mobility training in Humvees is part of all SEAL predeployment training. Note the tire on the rear of the vehicle—that's so a disabled Hummer can be pushed from danger. *Courtesy of the U.S. Navy (Eric Logsdon)*

One of the hastily converted Humvees that carried Navy SEALs on the strategic-reconnaissance mission to Camp Rhino in Afghanistan. *Courtesy of the U.S. Navy*

Two SEALs on an SR mission in eastern Afghanistan. Note the LAAW rocket carried by one of the SEALS. *Courtesy of the U.S. Navy (Tim Turner)*

Captain Bob Harward, the commander of Task Force K-Bar during the Afghan campaign, briefs Admiral Vern Clark, Chief of Naval Operations. *Courtesy of the U.S. Navy (Eric Logsdon)*

SEALs search just one of the many caves in Afghanistan's Zhawar Kili Valley. This sophisticated cave complex was crammed with weapons and munitions. *Courtesy of the U.S. Navy*

A SEAL element in the Zhawar Kili Valley watches as JDAMs initiate secondary explosions from al-Qaeda munitions stored in cave complexes. *Courtesy of the U.S. Navy*

A scruffy bunch, 2002. A SEAL element following an eight-day mission into the Zhawar Kili Valley. This photo was taken at a refueling stop in Bagram on the element's return to Kandahar. *Courtesy of the U.S. Navy*

A scruffy bunch, 1970. A SEAL platoon in the Mekong Delta. Vietnam-era SEALs and today's SEALs share the same fate: years of combat deployments. The author is at the center of the photo. *Courtesy of the author*

Platoon SEALs train at the Naval Special Warfare training facility near the Chocolate Mountains, under conditions not unlike those found in central Afghanistan and western Iraq. *Courtesy of the U.S. Navy (Eric Logsdon)*

Big and fast. The largest and fastest special boat in the NSW fleet, the eighty-two-foot Mk V Special Operations Craft, can make fifty knots, and carries automatic weapons and grenade launchers. *Courtesy of the U.S. Navy (Eric Logsdon)*

Boarding from the sea. SEALs practice boarding ships and oil platforms by day and then at night. Most boarding operations, like at the MABOT platform during the invasion of Iraq, take place at night. *Courtesy of the U.S. Navy (Eric Logsdon)*

Close-quarter battle at sea. Drills like these keep SEALs sharp for clearing internal spaces like those found on the offshore oil platforms at MABOT and KAAOT. *Courtesy of the U.S. Navy (Eric Logsdon)*

Move up, move fast. During drills, SEALs swarm up to take an oil platform. Drills like this led to the successful boarding of the Iraqi oil platforms. *Courtesy of the U.S. Navy (Eric Logsdon)*

Brother SOF warriors. Two Air Force combat controllers clear containers near an airfield. Air Force Combat Control Teams often accompanied SEALs on missions in Iraq and Afghanistan. *Courtesy of the U.S. Air Force (Scott Reed)*

Snipers down range. Snipers are an integral part of many SEAL missions. SEALs, both in urban and rural terrain, often work under the protection of a sniper overwatch. *Courtesy of the U.S. Navy (Eric Logsdon)*

Getting ready. SEALs prepare their Humvees for an upcoming operation on the outskirts of Baghdad. A great deal of time and preparation goes into readying these vehicles for a mission. *Courtesy of the author*

Saddle up. When the vehicles are ready, SEALs gear up with their body armor and weapons. Note the snap-tie handcuffs on the SEAL's backplate armor. *Courtesy of the author*

The mean streets. SEALs on a Humvee move through the streets of Baghdad. Even during routine movements, they are on alert and take nothing for granted. *Courtesy of the author*

Navy SEAL with "Indig," 2002. SEAL with two Afghans. SEALs often work best when they interface with the locals. This SEAL is armed with an AKM assault rifle. *Courtesy of the U.S. Navy*

Navy SEAL with "Indig," 1970. In Afghanistan and Iraq, as in Vietnam, SEALs have learned to live with and trust local allies. This is the author with a Vietnamese scout/interpreter at base camp. *Courtesy of the author*

tact—that the facility would be manned only by oil workers with but a token security force. But four hours prior to their lifting off from Ali al-Salim Air Base, a recent intelligence report indicated that additional armed personnel had been seen in the area. They had been airborne for no more than ten minutes when Lieutenant Thomas's voice crackled over the squad radio net.

"Okay, guys, intel has now put the enemy strength at a dozen or more, and they appear to be regular troops. So everybody stay sharp, okay?"

Around the red, dimly lit interior of the Pavelow, everyone gave a thumbs-up in acknowledgment. Across the cabin, Chief Morales caught his squad officer's eye. Thomas grinned and shrugged. "Whatever," he seemed to be saying. Morales, indeed all of them, had hoped for an unopposed capture of the PPL. But they had trained and rehearsed for active resistance on the part of the Iraqis. Now it looked as if that's the way it would be.

Thomas was big for an officer in the teams and big for a Navy SEAL. He was six-five and a muscular 230 pounds. He had graduated from the Naval Academy with the Class of '99 and with BUD/S Class 228 in 2000. Normally, his first deployment would have had him in a nonoperational support role with the deployed squadron. He would have been a Smee. But he, much like Chief Morales, had been elevated to the assistant officer in charge because of platoon leadership changes. Yet in his short tenure within the teams, he had demonstrated his tactical skill and leadership ability. Now it appeared both would be tested under fire.

"Ten minutes to the insertion; ten minutes." Morales was pleased that Thomas's voice was flat calm as he gave the time hack.

"Five minutes," he said. He waited. Finally, he said, "One minute."

They were all in full battle gear, Kevlar helmets, and body armor. And everyone, especially the marines, carried a generous load of ammo, grenades, rockets, and demolitions. They were all heavily loaded, but ready to leap into battle.

"Thirty seconds." Again, Morales was comforted by the conversational tone in Thomas's voice.

"Fifteen seconds—get ready." In unison, as they had in the re-hearsals, each man unclipped his seat belt and dropped one knee to the floor of the helo, holding the frame of the bench seats to steady themselves. As the helo rocked back to bleed off airspeed, the .50-caliber machine gun clamped to the Pavelow's tail ramp began to fire steady three-to-five-round bursts. Then rounds began to nick through the thin skin of the helo; they were taking ground fire.

"Stand by . . . Stand by . . . Go! Go! Go!"

The big helo squatted on the perimeter of the PPL. It was supposed to land wheels-down, but due to the shouted instructions of the crew chief it held a hover three to five feet off the ground. They were on a field of concertina—coils and coils of barbed wire. Either the intelligence reports had missed it, or the concertina had just recently been laid by the reinforced garrison. Thomas was the first to the edge of the ramp, but stood to one side as Provost Sergeant Rupert Jackson led his Royal Marines off the ramp. As the element's security or blocking force, they were first off the helo. The first two marines became tangled and went facedown in the wire. The next two, using them as stepping-stones, managed to get a few yards from the helo before they went down. The next four marines tumbled off—stepping, rolling and struggling in the concertina. The SEALs coming off behind them faired a little better, but not much.

Chief Morales immediately sensed that something was very wrong, but at this point they were committed. They were sitting ducks while the helo hovered just off the ground. The safest thing for all concerned was for them to be off the helo and for the helo to clear off. He began to shove the SEALs in front of him toward the ramp. A few seconds later, he, too, was rolling in the concertina wire. As the helo veered away from their insertion point, rounds began to flick overhead. The fire was neither concentrated nor effective, but the garrison at the PPL *was* shooting at them.

Seven miles away, at the KAAOT PPL, the other squad from Morales's platoon in yet another Air Force MH-53, along with their contingent of Royal Marines, swooped in for their attack. Thirty miles to the north, "upstream" on the pipeline river of oil that flowed down the peninsula to the Gulf, two full SEAL platoons and their support elements began their assault on the large metering and manifold station at az-Zubayr.

The SEALs and Royal Marines at the MABOT PPL worked their way clear of the concertina. The marines moved along the perimeter to their security positions while the SEALs formed up for the assault.

Twelve miles out to sea, well over the horizon from the coastal PPL stations, the vital MABOT and KAAOT tanker-loading complexes lay peacefully under a starlit sky. While their brother SEALs closed for their raids ashore, two other assault elements moved into position to attack the offshore terminals. The MABOT terminal represented the most active and important of the two oil-loading facilities. Moments before Chief Morales's SEAL squad and the Royal Marines became entangled in the concertina wire, three Special Boat Team RHIB craft idled up to a position several hundred yards from the MABOT terminal. The moon was not yet up, but the terminal was lit up like a Christmas tree; the three rigid-hulled craft were trying to stay just outside the bubble of illumination thrown out from the series of platforms that constituted the terminal. The boats were heavily laden with SEALs and their support personnel. Much like the SEALs and Royal Marines at the MABOT PPL as they hovered above the concertina wire, the embarked SEALs at the MABOT offshore platform felt very vulnerable and exposed. Two men stood close to each other at the conning station of the lead RHIB.

"We can't stay here much longer, sir," Chief Jim Collins said to Lieutenant Jan Watkins. "And if we get any closer, they're sure to see us. Hell, they may have already seen us."

This was the exact situation that Watkins had feared and tried to avoid. He glanced at his watch, distinctly feeling the element of surprise slipping away. Aboard his little fleet of three RHIBs were forty-nine souls—thirty-one SEALs, twelve Special Warfare Combatant Craft crewmen, two Navy EOD techs, two interpreters, and an Air Force combat controller. And himself. Watkins was responsible for all of them. As with Chief Morales's element moving against the MABOT PPL onshore, a great deal had happened to change the planned operation in the last forty-eight hours. And as with the PPL assault elements ashore, the situation had grown potentially more dangerous on the eve of the planned attacks. But as the SEALs were learning in this fight, assault plans have to be flexible. Had not new intelligence dictated otherwise, they would have idled right up to the terminal, and his men would have swarmed over the platforms as they had rehearsed it so many times. But with the arrival of the Republican Guard at the platform, things had changed—and that dictated a change in the tactics for the assault. Watkins took a deep breath and turned to his Special Boat Team chief.

"Let's do it, Chief. Take us in hard."

"Stand by to run in on step," Chief Collins said quietly into his lip microphone. In the other two craft, the coxswains acknowledged the order and passed a warning to those embarked in their boats. "Hang on, everybody," Collins said in a conversational tone. His RHIB carried only SEALs. To his lip mike and the other coxswains, he said, "Stand by . . . and hit it!"

There was a throaty growl as six turbocharged Caterpillar diesel engines quickly revved to full power and 2,820 horses all bellowed in unison. The three RHIBs surged forward and brought their heavy loads up on step. In a matter of seconds, all were flying across the top of the water toward the MABOT platform. Jan Watkins stood next to Collins in the coxswain's flat. He glanced around at his SEALs, crouched in two files against each of the main tubes of the RHIB, coiled and ready to move. On the bow between the two rows of SEALs, a lone SWCC gunner stood looking at MABOT over his .50-caliber machine gun, waiting for signs of resistance on the lighted platform in front of them.

Lieutenant Jan Watkins was an experienced SEAL platoon commander. He had been around the teams for a while, and then some. He was
a mustang officer, which meant he had prior enlisted experience. In
the planning for this coordinated operation—an operation to secure
the Iraqi oil export infrastructure intact—it became apparent that the
MABOT offshore facility would be the most important and perhaps
the most dangerous of the five targets. The task group commander had
wanted one of his best men on the MABOT platform. Watkins was selected to lead the SEAL force against this key installation. He was chosen for his leadership skills as well as his operational experience.

Watkins had grown up in Naples, Florida, and enlisted in the Navy
shortly after high school. After boot camp, he received orders to
BUD/S, where he graduated with Class 130 in 1984. He had two deployments as an enlisted man before being accepted into a Navy edu-
cational program that sends outstanding sailors back to college on
their way to becoming commissioned officers. It took Watkins a little
over two and a half years to complete his four-year degree—in nursing. He was commissioned as an ensign in the Navy Nurse Corps, a
former Navy SEAL in a largely female organization. For the next three
years, he attended his nursing duties at Balboa Naval Hospital. In the
early 1990s, an oversupply of Navy nurses and an exodus of officers
from the teams allowed Watkins the opportunity he had been looking
for. In 1994, he returned to the teams and began operational training
for duty as a platoon officer. This was his third deployment since his
return to the teams.

While the MABOT was a difficult and dangerous target, it was still
the kind of leadership challenge that a SEAL officer waits his whole career for. As a former enlisted man and Navy nurse, Jan Watkins had
simply waited longer than most.

The roar of the engines canceled all conversation, yet Watkins whis-
pered aloud to himself, "Oh please God, let us get on that terminal before they have time to react."

During the last forty-eight hours, the oil workers on the MABOT platform had been replaced with a Republican Guard garrison. The intelligence reports had them aboard the offshore platforms with crew-served weapons, RPGs, and crate upon crate of explosives. Watkins and every man in his element knew that at any moment their fragile boats could be ripped apart by heavy machine-gun fire or rocket-propelled grenades. Or the oil terminal could erupt in a fireball and take them with it. Or if Watkins's prayers were answered, they would get there before the Republican Guardsmen had time to react. Whatever happened, it would happen soon.

Several miles southwest, a similar element began its high-speed run into the KAAOT facility. They, too, were carried to their objective by three Special Boat Team RHIBS. There were EOD techs, translators, a combat controller, but no SEALs. This assault element consisted of the GROM—the Polish special operators. (More contributions of the GROM will be covered later in this chapter and in chapter 6.) The SEALs in Iraq looked on them, with good reason, as their SOF brothers. They were tough, competent, and very brave. Special operations components of many of the nations who had been with the SEALs in Afghanistan were gone, but the Poles did not abandon them during the Iraqi campaign.

As it was, Watkins and his RHIB-borne force were not the first SEALs to visit MABOT. Neither were the GROM the first at KAAOT. Days before the SEAL and the GROM were to attack the platforms, two SEAL delivery vehicles, or SDVs, were launched at night by special operations Mk V support craft. These minisubmersibles were the older but reliable Mk-8 Mod 1 SDVs. They are wet submersibles, unlike the newer ASDS—the Advanced SEAL Delivery System, which is a small dry submarine. The Mk-8s can carry a number of SEALs, but the two that left their Mk V mother craft that night carried two men each, a pilot and a navigator.

"This was a good operation for us," one of the SDV pilots told me. "The water depth was no more than thirty-five to forty feet, so we used Draeger LAR V scubas. We had a good GPS fix before we made our dive, and my navigator took me straight to our platform. The nav problem was very easy and straightforward," he said, avoiding the technical aspects of their navigation systems, which are classified, "so we had no problems on the run into the target. Given the complex mission profiles we train for on a regular basis, this one was a piece of cake. The water temp was sixty-one, so we were in full wet suits. The Gulf is a strange place. Three months later and the temperature there would have been in the low eighties. Cool water is better. It usually makes for better visibility. As it was that night, we could see about twenty feet. We were in the water for a little over four hours, so we were all ready for a hot cup of coffee by the time we were recovered."

The SEALs and the SDVs were from the deployed SEAL squadron's SDV platoon. The land-warfare requirements in Afghanistan and the VBSS operations in the Gulf leading up to the Iraqi invasion meant that the SDV SEALs had seen little action to date. Most deployed squadron commanders did what they could to use their SDV SEALs in non-SDV SR and DA missions, but their complex specialty required continuous training in underwater operations. This meant that they were not usually as current in their land-warfare proficiencies as their non-SDV brother SEALs. Launching and recovering an SDV from a surface craft alone requires practice and a unique skill set, not to mention the sophisticated underwater ballet that attends the launching of an SDV from a submerged nuclear submarine. In addition, there were the perishable skills of underwater navigation and rehearsals for a variety of reconnaissance and direct-action littoral missions that can only be conducted from an SDV. The SEAL delivery vehicles are a cornerstone of the Navy SEALs' ability to project clandestine, maritime force. Executing these missions requires continuous training and the highest degree of professional attention. Still, the SDV SEALs felt a little left out. While their brother SEALs were engaged in Afghanistan in real-world operations, they trained much as they did before the attacks of 11 September. Now, on the eve of war in Iraq, they were going to do it for real—or in the secret world of SDV operations, as real as this writer will be allowed to discuss about this highly technical SEAL speciality.

"There were two of us in each boat," Lieutenant Rick Cotton told me. Rick was the SDV platoon OIC. "I was on the MABOT platform, and served as the navigator for my pilot. We pulled up to the outboard loading platform pad and tied the boat off to one of the platform legs. I was glad we were on Draegers; we were on the lower end of the scuba's depth capability, but it's a smaller and simpler rig. In planning the operation, we wanted to keep things as simple as possible." Unlike other SEALS, the SDV men train with the Mk-16 scuba. The Mk-16 is a sophisticated, mixed-gas rig that can operate at deeper depths—depths that might be needed for the launch of SDVs from a submerged submarine. The LAR V Draeger is a pure-oxygen attack scuba designed for shallow-water operations.

"After we tied up the boat," Cotton said, "we came up under the platform and went to work. We took a lot of pictures and made notes about the latticework and access wells. And we listened a lot. We wanted to get an overall impression of their activity and alert status, and to see if there were any obstacles in making the platform boarding from surface craft. One of our key tasks was to validate access to the platform decking from sea level. There were four platforms associated with the complex, and they were strung out over two miles. We were able to get a look at two of them—one of the tanker loading platforms and the berthing platform. It was pretty quiet, but the platforms themselves were very well lit. We stayed in the shadows underneath; they never knew we were there.

"As SDV operations go, this was a pretty simple and straightforward mission. In retrospect, we could have done it by sneaking close in rubber boats, then made the final approach swimming on the surface with the last few hundred meters underwater on scuba. But then we didn't know for sure if they had a surface search radar capability. The SDVs allowed for a much greater standoff for the surface support boats. This was a good use of our SDVs, and the information we got helped with the assault. I know; I was on the assault element. It's not often you get to do the recon *and* the assault. The guys back at my SDV team were green with envy."

"So you've been in SDVs since you finished basic training?"

"That's right. I began with BUD/S Class 221 and graduated with Class 225 in 1999. I had a hell of a time with stress fractures." Stress fractures often plague big men in BUD/S training. Cotton is six-one and weighs close to 240. "After SQT, I went to Mk-16 and basic SDV training in Panama City, Florida. From there, I went straight to my SDV team. This was my second deployment—and let me tell you," he added with a grin, "given all the training time I've spent underwater, it was great to get to do one for real. Timing is everything."

"Naval Academy?" I asked, sensing he may be a fellow alumnus.

"No, sir," Cotton said proudly. "Air Force Academy, Class of '98."

"Really! How'd you get into this business?"

"I went to Air Force to play football. Then, while playing rugby off-season, I got a concussion. They told me it would keep me from flying. I'd always wanted to fly, but now what? Then," he went on with the same easy grin, "I read a book called *SEAL Team One*. Right then I decided that if I could manage to take my commission in the Navy, that's what I want to do, and here I am."

"No fooling," I said, trying to sound casual. *SEAL Team One* was my first novel and my first book.

As with the three land targets, the offshore terminal assault teams had a great deal of physical intelligence about their targets, including overhead imagery, and the complete construction and mechanical schematics. The elements attacking the offshore targets had additional advantages. Patrolling ships and special operations small craft passed within five miles of the platforms on a routine basis. Navy helos from HCS-4 and HCS-5 (Helicopter Combat Support Special Squadrons) had made periodic flybys of these structures. All of this activity had to be done in context of the heavy but routine surface and airborne activity off the coast of Iraq. And finally, there were eyes on by the SDV reconnaissance teams ahead of the attack. As any SEAL will tell you, there is no substitute for close-up eyes on a target. But since the operation called for five simultaneous surprise assaults, the reconnaissance effort of these targets had to be done without alerting the Iraqis manning the at-sea platforms or the onshore facilities.

The onshore targets were clearly land-attack venues—vehicular or air assault. But there was a lot to recommend sending an assault element back to MABOT and KAAOT in SDVs and have them silently steal aboard the loading terminals, to capture them or to guide in surface raiders. Yet along with the obvious advantages of preserving the element of surprise, there are a number of restrictions that attend an undersea operation. In this case, it was the issue of timing. The plan called for all five key facilities of the pipeline oil-loading infrastructure to be attacked simultaneously, because alerting one of them was the same as alerting them all. Since continuous communication among the five attacking elements was needed to ensure a coordinated effort, it was decided to board the offshore terminals by surface craft. Here the capabilities of the Polish GROM were factored in. Good as these warriors are, they are not trained in maritime and underwater operations in the manner of Navy SEALs. They simply could not have come from SDVs, so the SDVs served only as reconnaissance platforms.

At the Kuwait Naval Base (KNB), Jan Watkins's two SEAL platoons and the GROM continued to prepare for the offshore assaults. Some seventy miles of open water separated KNB from the two Iraqi oil terminals. While the SEALs and their Royal Marine blocking forces rehearsed, elements of the 5th Regimental Combat Team, 1st Marine Expeditionary Force prepared to attack the petroleum infrastructure farther north of al-Faw in the Rumaila oil fields. Specifically, they were to secure four gas and oil separation plants. These four GOSP installations, along with the five assigned SEAL targets, represented the critical nodes in the Iraqi crude oil export network. In total, these key facilities represented 85 percent of Iraq's oil export capability.

Of the two offshore platforms, MABOT was clearly the most active. Right up until the invasion began, there was a constant parade of tankers at MABOT. The facility had the capacity to load 1.6 million barrels of oil a day. In the weeks leading up to hostilities, a full complement of four tankers were often seen at MABOT, as if Saddam wanted to pump as much oil as possible before the invasion. This was the last of the corrupt UN oil-for-food program, which Saddam Hussein had managed to use to his own advantage, politically and militarily. The facility also maintained a standing volume, without augmentation from the inshore oil fields, of eight hundred thousand barrels. If this facility alone could not be taken intact, and fell victim to intentional sabotage, the environmental disaster would be twelve times that caused by the *Exxon Valdez*. On the positive side of the ledger, MABOT alone could pump close to $25 *billion* in oil revenue per year.

KAAOT was a smaller facility with less capacity. It then operated at a capacity of some two hundred thousand barrels per day. KAAOT was deliberately blown up by the Iraqis during the Iran-Iraq War at a huge environmental cost to the area. Repairs have been ongoing to this offshore terminal, but many international oil shippers still question its safety. Yet its potential economic benefit to the postwar recovery of Iraq was substantial. And like MABOT, it remained capable of an environmental disaster.

At KNB, Lieutenant Jan Watkins continued to plan, read updated intelligence reports, rehearse, and worry. The digital imagery and information brought back by the SDVs helped to assuage some of his fears, but there were still many unanswered questions.

"One of the problems was its sheer size," Watkins told me. "Picture if you can four platforms connected by a latticework highway some twelve miles out into the Persian Gulf. The first is an inboard platform used as a helo platform to off-load personnel and supplies. The second one, some three hundred meters farther out, is the first loading platform. It's as long as a football field and can handle two tankers, one on either side, for loading. The third, another loading station, is another three hundred meters out from there. Both the loading platforms are crammed with plumbing and holding tanks for servicing the tankers. The forty-eight-inch pipelines come out of the seabed and up to these platforms. The last platform, again some three hundred meters from the second refueling station, is the berthing and living quarters. Sitting on this platform is a four-story building and a holding area for containers. Equipment and supplies to support the oil transshipment operations were loaded into semitruck containers and hoisted aboard this outboard platform. It's a huge platform—the whole facility was huge. That's why we, the force who was to board the platforms, was going to be a large one—at least large for a SEAL special operation.

"We had the schematics and engineering drawings of the platforms and all kinds of overhead imagery. To get our arms around this, we laid out the dimensions of the structure with surveyors' tape at our training range just outside KNB. It took several minutes to walk from one platform to the next. We knew exactly where the oil nodes were, where the pipes came out of the seabed and onto the platforms. Our mission was to quickly get onto the platforms and secure the initial valving where those big pipelines came up out of the water. We also had to think about the terminal storage tanks and to make them safe. From the SDV recon, we were reasonably sure that no explosives had been prepositioned underwater. Our whole focus was to get aboard and secure those nodes."

I asked about making an initial probe with attack swimmers from SDVs, especially to deal with the explosives.

"We sure considered that," one of the SEAL planners with the deployed task force told me, "but one of our objectives was to take down all five facilities at the same time. Timing was only one of the reasons we decided to go with helos and surface craft. Another was that we needed to get our EOD technicians to the sites as quickly as possible. If the pipelines were loaded with explosives, the EOD techs would have to be there to safely disarm them. Otherwise, the mission goes up in smoke, literally, and so do the men in the assault element. The EOD guys were critical to the operation, and there was simply not enough time to get them up to speed on SDVs. There were a lot of moving parts to an operation this large and complex. We had to make compromises to keep it as simple and straightforward as possible."

"Intelligence reports had the platforms manned by oil workers," Watkins recalled, "so an insertion by surface craft was appropriate. During the planning and rehearsals, our total focus was getting to the pipelines and the first series of valves, clearing them of any explosives, and keeping them secure. Next, we would make sure the terminal oil storage tanks were secure. Then, and only then, we would move to the barracks platform and deal with Iraqi personnel on the rig. But even under this scenario, we needed a lot of folks. We knew it would be a pretty extensive search-and-security operation. The assault force that trained and rehearsed for the mission at KNB was composed of thirty-six men. There were thirty-one SEALS and myself—my platoon, half of another platoon, and the SDV SEALs. The two EOD guys and the combat controller could put their guns in the fight if they had to, but that was not why they were with us. The two interpreters were strictly noncombatants. That's a lot of people moving at night, but we had time to rehearse and prepare. The SDV SEALs were good to go, but they were a little rusty on their CQD skills, so we set up a mini CQD refresher course right there at KNB. And we had to work up procedures for handling prisoners. We fully expected to take prisoners unless they chose to fight it out. That would be their choice, not ours."

I was interested in the rehearsals and how they went about preparing for the platform takedown.

"We're SEALs, and we're good at improvising. We set up a string of fifty-five-gallon oil drums to simulate pipeline sections. We found a two-story building where we could conduct room-clearing drills. And there were the piers at KNB where we could conduct our boarding drills—coming from the boats up onto a structure. We found or made rehearsal venues where we could walk and run through the various segments of the whole operation. As far as the rehearsals went, we couldn't have done without the marines."

"The marines?" I asked.

"You bet. There was a U.S. Marine contingent with us at KNB. They would be the follow-on force to hold and keep the platforms secure after we made the takedown. But in any training or rehearsal situation, you're only as good as your training partner. On the piers or out on the training range or in the buildings, the marines served as Iraqi role players. Sometimes they were in character as compliant oil workers, and sometimes we asked them to take on noncompliant roles. It's no fun to be taken down hard, pushed into the deck, and cuffed. But they did it, night after night, and they didn't complain. They kept us sharp, and when the operation went down, my guys were all tuned up for what they had to do. Those marines worked hard to help us get ready—almost as hard as our boat guys. Let me tell you, nobody—but *nobody*—put in as much time and effort for this operation than the guys on our boats."

"There's no one I respect more than our SEALs," Chief Jim Collins told me, "but I'm here to tell you that the hardest working sailors in the U.S. Navy are our combatant craft crewmen." In addition to being the lead RHIB coxswain for the MABOT attack, Chief Collins was the maintenance chief assigned to the Special Boat Team that would support both oil platform operations. That meant that most nights he and his boat crews were supporting rehearsals for the SEALs preparing for MABOT or the GROM preparing for KAAOT.

"Many, many times the guys worked all night supporting rehearsals and worked all day keeping the boats up. The Gulf is a very harsh operating climate. On average, we figure an hour of maintenance for every hour under way. If there was no room in the maintenance barn, the guys would be out in the parking lot changing an engine in the hot sun. Then they would button it up and have the boat back on the water that night. Our rule was that we always, and I mean always, had that boat pierside—properly manned, fueled, and ready to perform—*before* the SEALs appeared on the dock. We wait for them; they don't wait for us."

There has always been a bond between the SEALs and the "boat guys." This goes back to when detachments from Boat Support Units One and Two, the forerunners of the current Special Boat Teams, deployed to Vietnam with SEAL Teams One and Two. They drove us to work right after dark and came back for us just before sunrise. And sometimes, when we in the SEAL squads found ourselves with more Vietcong than we had bargained for, they came in hot and took us out of harm's way. The Special Boat Teams, like the Navy SEALs, trace their lineage back to World War II and to their founder, Captain Phil Bucklew. Bucklew pioneered small-craft reconnaissance tactics when he used small boats to scout the landing beaches at Sicily, Salerno, and Normandy. For his gallantry, he was twice awarded the Navy Cross, along with a Silver Star. Throughout his distinguished career, he developed the small-craft units of Naval Special Warfare, and commanded Naval Special Warfare Group One during the Vietnam era. Today, Navy SEALs train at the Phil H. Bucklew Naval Special Warfare Center in Coronado—a fitting tribute to one of our finest warriors.

"Chief Collins was not exaggerating," Watkins told me. "They were out there every night—on time, on station. We put a lot of hours on those boats during rehearsals. And when it came time to do it for real, they put us on the platform on time and right at our insertion point."

The Special Boat Teams played an essential role in the offshore attacks. After supporting the SDV reconnaissance operations and the assault element rehearsals, they began to assemble craft for the attacks on the platforms. In all, there were eleven craft involved. The mother craft of this little battle group would be the 338-foot *Joint Venture* (HSV-X1). The *Joint Venture* is a relatively new and innovative concept in littoral force projection. It is a military adaptation of an Australian-built catamaran car ferry that can make fifty knots in open water. It is operated by a U.S. Navy crew of forty-five officers and men. The SEALs have found it exceptionally well suited as a maritime special operations support platform. It can carry large amounts of men and equipment, and can support a full range of special operations small craft, including SDVs, and can support helicopter flight operations. For the assaults on MABOT and KAAOT, it would serve as an off-shore command-and-control facility, and carry the U.S. Marine security detachments that would relieve the SEALs and the GROM after the oil terminals were seized.

Most of the SEALs and the GROM would make the run from KNB to the target area in the Mk V Special Operations Craft that would support the operation. Four loaded Mk Vs would make the transit with the assault elements and get them within five to seven miles of their targets. There, the SEALs and the GROM would transfer into the six rigid-hull inflatable boats for the final assault.

For the assault on MABOT, the entire thirty-six-man assault element would crowd onto three RHIBs. The Mk Vs would be standing off close by, ready to swoop in if their support or firepower were needed.

The responsibility and final planning for this coordinated five-target strike fell to the veteran task force commander, Captain Bob Harward. Having commanded the Joint Combined Special Operations Task Force South in Kandahar during the Afghan campaign, and after a brief return to his duties as Commander, Naval Special Warfare Group One in Coronado, he was back to prepare the SEALs deployed to the CENTCOM theater for operations in Iraq. The general war plan for Iraq called for the inshore and offshore oil export facilities to be captured intact. The loss of future revenues and the cost of replacement aside, the military planners were well aware of the immense environmental disaster the sabotage of these installations could bring to the area. Saddam Hussein had demonstrated that he cared as little for the environment as he did for the welfare of the Iraqi people. The mechanics and tactics of the operation were left to Harward and his special operations task force planners.

At this stage war seemed probable, perhaps even imminent, but any number of things could prevent a U.S.-led coalition from going into Iraq. Saddam knew that the forces gathering around him could not remain staged in a battle-ready posture indefinitely; once assembled, they would probably either attack or leave. And there was always the chance that Saddam would wait until the buildup reached its peak and then comply with the UN mandates. Given French, German, and Russian opposition to a military incursion into Iraq, it seemed reasonable that compliance, or even a skillful ruse to abide by inspection requirements, would have kept foreign troops off Iraqi soil. But the military planners and logisticians had no choice but to prepare for war. To invade or not to invade was a political decision. General Tommy Franks's job was to make his forces ready and wait for the political dimension of the crisis to sort itself out. For the joint combined special operations task force under Harward that had just moved to Kuwait from Bahrain, the near-shore and offshore oil facilities were job one. It carried a priority equal to that of killing or capturing Saddam himself.

Two things were clear as the planners began their preparations. The first was that this conflict would be very different from the one in Afghanistan. The hastily prepared plan for that campaign called for a SOF-centric approach with Army Special Forces, Northern Alliance fighters, and American airpower taking the lead. The war plan for the drive to Baghdad that was taken off the shelf and dusted off in the fall of 2002 was a long-standing, comprehensive, well-thought-out document. Of course, it would have to be updated for the Iraqi order of battle and to reflect the makeup of the coalition force. Nonetheless, this was an American plan with American command and control, and the major forces in play would be American. That said, the contributions of the other coalition partners were significant, both militarily and politically. Within the special operations order of battle, the work of the Brits and the Poles was to prove operationally very significant.

The second thing clear to the SOF planners at KNB was that when the drive to Baghdad began, the heavy lifting would be done by armored columns. The U.S. forces would use their agility and skill in maneuver warfare to engage and defeat the static defenses of the Iraqi army. And if Saddam's army chose to respond and maneuver to counter the American armored columns, they would then be at the mercy of American airpower. SOF would be a player in the drive to Baghdad, but in a secondary role. In the south, special operations were to provide strategic reconnaissance as necessary in advance of the main-force elements, and SOF teams would be sent out to perform inspections on suspected weapons of mass destruction (WMD) sites as the ground was taken. Long before the SEALs attacked the oil targets, Special Forces were out in the vast Iraqi western desert to ensure that no Scud missile launchers were there to threaten Israel. Israel was not part of the plan. But no war plan is perfect, and as the battle was joined, SOF was to play a much wider role. When the 4th Infantry Division was denied the ability to stage in Turkey and attack Baghdad from the north, Army Special Forces teams, in mobilizing Kurdish resistance forces, were able to offset this loss. While they were not able to defeat the Iraqi forces north of Baghdad as the 4th ID would have, they were able to engage the Iraqis in such a way that the forces in the region were unable to abandon the northern approaches to Baghdad and relieve the beleaguered forces arrayed along the Tigris and Euphrates Rivers in the south. And, as they had during the Afghan campaign, the Green Berets were more than up to the task.

"For the first time I can remember," Bob Harward would recall, "the Naval Special Warfare components of SOF, along with our GROM brothers, were presented with a fixed, static, strategic target. My mission was clear. If war came, we would launch against the oil facilities on the al-Faw peninsula and the oil terminals offshore. The higher-ups made it plain to me that this was a critical target. SEALs in Afghanistan had been highly effective due to our ability to react quickly to perishable intelligence or to a tactical opportunity that might be short-lived. We learned to move very quickly. Now, for the first time, we would have the luxury of an extended planning window and ample time to rehearse. Given the size and importance of the target, it would tie up most of the Naval Special Warfare assets in theater and then some. As it was, we had to go out to PACOM to find more

SEALs. Thank God we had the GROM. From the outset, we knew it would be the largest coordinated SEAL operation in the history of Naval Special Warfare. As it turned out, more SEALs went in harm's way that night than were deployed at any one time during the entire Vietnam War. We had a lot riding on this one."

As Chief Morales struggled free of the concertina, the noise of the helo was replaced by automatic-weapons fire, most of it now coming from the Royal Marines as they took up a skirmish line inside the perimeter. The site itself was some nine hundred meters across and located on a shallow peninsula with water on three sides. The facility had been hit by air strikes from a dedicated Air Force A-10 Warthog and a special operations AC-130 Spectre gunship. A nearby SAM site and an Iraqi mechanized unit bivouacked along the road that provided security to the PPL facility had also been part of the prestrike package. The A-10 and the AC-130 ceased firing when the Pavelow arrived in the target area. This allowed the defenders to come out from cover and begin shooting at the inbound helo.

"Once those marines got themselves sorted out," Chief Morales said, "they laid down a good base of fire that allowed us to move into the facility. For a while, I didn't think we were ever going to get out of that damned wire. Once we got close to the structures, we went to work. Our job was to clear the bunkers and buildings while the marines moved with us to provide security."

The SEALs' first order of business was to deal with the two bunkers that guarded the facility from an attack from the sea. They were near where the Pavelow had inserted them on the perimeter. One bunker was heavily damaged from the air strikes, but the second was intact. As four of the SEALs closed on the damaged bunker, they began to take fire from Iraqis hiding in fighting holes a short distance from the bunkers. Apparently, when the bunkers were taken under fire from the air, the defenders sought shelter in defensive positions outside. Two SEALs circled the bunker and quickly took the defenders under fire, killing two of them. Six other Iraqi soldiers quickly surrendered. While the Royal Marines moved along the perimeter to provide security ahead of the SEALs, four other SEALs moved in on the undamaged bunker.

"Right next to the bunker," Morales recalled, "was a two-story building that had wires dangling from the upper floor down to and along the ground. We were briefed to be on the lookout for IEDs, improvised explosive devices, that may be set for us or to sabotage the pipelines. Seeing these wires, we immediately took the building under fire. We fired a half dozen forty-millimeter grenades into the building and the marines hit it with rockets. Then we set up on the door and prepared for an entry. Right after the breaching charge went off, three terrified Iraqis ran out and surrendered."

"What about the second bunker?" I asked. "The one that was undamaged?"

Morales chuckled. "Oh, the second bunker. Well, you always take the most immediate threat first. It was Lieutenant Thomas's call, and it was a good one. When we saw the wires, he had the Royal Marines cover the bunker while we moved on the building. After we cleared the building and cuffed the prisoners, we held our position while the marines took the intact bunker." Morales smile broadened. "One of the Brits tossed in a grenade, and a few seconds later the Iraqis tossed it back out. And man, everyone flattened out on the sand. We assumed it was a dud, but on later inspection, we learned that the guy hadn't pulled the pin. I guess even the pros make mistakes, but overall, those Royal Marines were fantastic. Anyway, they began to fire into the bunker. A few seconds later, three Iraqi officers filed out of the place with their hands on their heads."

"Were they compliant?"

"Pretty much, and they all spoke English. One of the officers began to get a little brave when we put him with some of the enlisted soldiers. I guess he wanted to show that he was macho in front of the troops. One of the guys had to put him on the ground to quiet him down. He got what he deserved, nothing more. Like I said, they all spoke good English. One of them even thanked us for not killing them. I think they were all surprised that we didn't just shoot them.

"From the second bunker and the larger building, we moved around the facility in a clockwise fashion, setting breaching charges on the other three buildings and clearing them. We took some fire from just outside the perimeter to the east, but the marines quickly suppressed it. Those Royal Marines took good care of us start to finish. Finally, we went to the pig building at the center of the facility. That was one door on which we didn't use an explosive breach, because we didn't want to damage any of the pipeline plumbing. Inside, we found everything in order. The big forty-eight-inch pipelines came out of the ground and into some valving, then back into the ground and out to sea to the loading platforms. The EOD guy checked everything out and found that there were no explosives on the pipelines or in the building that housed the valves.

"We called in that the facility was secure and for the backup complement of Royal Marines that were to occupy the site and keep it secure. While we were waiting for them, an armored vehicle approached our position along the access road. The Air Force controller called the A-10 back in. It was orbiting a short distance away. He rolled in on the armored vehicle and made a smoldering lump of scrap metal out of it. It was really impressive. After that, things got really quiet. In all, it was a good first operation for us. There were five Iraqi KIAs, two by us and three from the air strikes that went in ahead of us. There may have been more in the rubble of that one bunker and probably a lot more in the vehicle that the A-10 took out. By the time we secured the facility, we had taken a total of sixteen prisoners."

"Looking back on it, what would you have done differently?" I ask him.

He had to think on that. "We all probably would have gone in lighter. In later missions, we didn't carry nearly so much gear. Speed is everything when you're trying to clear and secure a facility like that.

And our TOT [time on target] was way over because of the concertina, and the time it took to clear the two bunkers and the two-story building. Our TOT was planned for about eight minutes, and it was closer to twenty by the time we called in secure. But," he quickly added, "that eight-minute TOT was predicated on the facility being manned by oil workers and a token security force. The guys we killed and captured were Iraqi army."

"Yet you got the job done," I offered, "and you didn't get anyone hurt, right?"

"Not if you don't count the damage from the barbed wire," he said with a grin. "We had all kinds of cuts and holes in us from the stuff. But we did get the job done. All the guys performed well, and Mister Thomas did great. He's going to be a fine team officer."

At the KAAOT PPL, the other platoon squad inserted by Air Force Pavelow overcame light resistance to capture that pumping station. A truckload of Iraqi soldiers responded after the fact, but the SEALs and Marines met this with overwhelming fire and set the truck ablaze. Both PPLs were captured intact and placed under tight coalition security. Further upstream, the large metering and manifold station at az-Zubayr was taken by elements of three SEAL platoons with relatively light resistance. At az-Zubayr, the SEALs came by land, making their attacks in Humvees and DPVs.

As for the oil terminal seizures, things changed dramatically less than forty-eight hours before the planned target window. Planning and rehearsals for MABOT and KAAOT were built around intelligence that the oil terminals were staffed by civilian oil workers with a token security force, just like the PPLs. Under this scenario, the assault forces were to first secure the valving that controlled the flow of oil to the terminals to prevent the oil workers from venting crude into the Gulf. Their primary job was to secure the pipeline terminal apparatus and safeguard the terminal storage tanks to prevent environmental disaster. Once the pipelines, valving, and storage tanks were secured, the assaulters would then move to clear the terminal of any Iraqi personnel. Plumbing first, then people. That was the plan right up until they approached the attack launch window. Then a contingent of the Republican Guards moved onto the MABOT platform and the oil workers went ashore.

"This really shook us up," Jan Watkins said. "Our focus had been on securing and controlling the terminal loading platforms. Now we had to take into consideration an armed force that could resist us with heavy weapons and who seemed to have the wherewithal to blow up the terminal. As the intel updates came in, I began to think that maybe we should be thinking about taking out the guard force, then securing the pipelines. I had visions of us moving to the valves and some Republican Guard dude sitting back there with a detonator in his hand, waiting for us to get close to the explosive charges on the pipelines. I talked it over with some of my senior enlisted men, and they concurred. So I took it up to Captain Harward. He readily agreed. At the eleventh hour, we decided to take out the opposition first, then secure the infrastructure."

"Jan Watkins was right on the money," Harward said. "When it became apparent late in the game that they had the means and now the opportunity to put charges on the critical valving of the loading platforms, we faced a much graver problem. I, too, had visions of our SEALs being blown off the terminal at the last minute and into a sea of burning oil. That was my first thought. Then, if the terminal valving of those pipelines was destroyed anytime before we could neutralize the guard force, we could do nothing but watch the gigantic oil slick that would blot the northern end of the Gulf from the Shatt al-Arab waterway to the Kuwaiti border. Eventually, it would work its way east and south, and foul the desalinization plants on the coast of Saudi Arabia. So at the last possible minute, we shifted the focus of the initial assault to the guard force on MABOT and quickly revised our final assault tactics. We made the same changes for KAAOT, but there was not the military activity on KAAOT that there was on MABOT. The pucker factor for those guys on the terminal assaults really went up when the Republican Guard arrived. I guess," Harward said with a grin, shaking his head, "you could say the same thing for their task force commander. The guys on the mission had a tough job, but I was sweating bullets the whole time."

"Our insertion point was the inshore end of seaward-most platform," Watkins said, "the one with the multistory berthing and living quarters. A security element with the EOD guys was to move back along the catwalk toward the loading platforms, while the rest of us concentrated on the housing facility where we assumed most of the Republican Guard force would be at that time of night. Even with the roar of the boats as we made the final approach, we still didn't know if they were aware we were coming to board the terminal. We swarmed over that housing complex as fast as we could get from the RHIBs up to the platform level and to the main structure. With the Republican Guard now in place, our ROEs were very liberal and for good reason. If there was any sign of noncompliance by an Iraqi or one of them made a sudden move, like he was reaching for a detonator or even a cell phone, we had authorization to shoot to kill. Any sudden movement was all it took for them to earn themselves a bullet. Really, we didn't know what to expect; we were ready for anything.

"It went down better than we had any right to expect. For the most part, the Iraqis seemed to expect us, if not at that exact moment, then sometime soon. They were more startled than surprised. As soon as they saw us, most of them put their hands in the air. But they didn't really seem to know we were coming at night. I guess you could say we had tactical surprise. We found food cooking over propane burners on the stove. Two of them were definitely noncompliant and outright defiant. But they were just being macho. I'm really proud of my guys for not shooting them. They rightly understood these two clowns were just being assholes and didn't need to die for being stupid. We brought them all out onto the open area by the building and cuffed them. A few of them we took down hard, so I had our corpsman check them out— a few bruises, nothing more.

"When I say things could have gone a lot worse, I mean a *whole lot worse*. They were very well armed. We found AK-47s, RPGs, antiaircraft guns, even SA-7s—the Russian-made heat-seeking antiaircraft missiles. And a ton of explosives. While most of us dealt with the Republican Guard, the search teams found charges made up to sections of the pipeline and the valving. They were not primed or wired up, but the charges were in place. It took a while to find all of it. From the time we went aboard until we had the terminal secure was about an hour and a quarter."

"Why weren't they capped in and ready to blow?" I asked.

"We wondered about that," Lieutenant Sean Yarrow, of Yarrow Entry fame, told me. He was back in the Gulf on his second SEAL deployment and was Jan Watkins's platoon AOIC. "It was as if they just didn't want to die for Saddam. That, or destroying their nation's oil export capability was just not in them. It was as if they were just going through the motions—doing just enough to make it look like they were going to fight or blow the terminal, but their hearts weren't in it."

I asked Lieutenant Rick Cotton how the terminal looked *above* the water. "Night and day. Things are always different on the surface, but the access routes from the surface up to the platforms were just as we described them from the SDV recon. The data and imagery we brought back allowed us to quickly find the access ladders up to the platforms. And after all the time I've logged in underwater, it sure was nice to be able to participate in a direct-action mission. Of course, it's easy to say that now, since we were able to get aboard those platforms virtually unopposed."

"What was your job in the assault?" I asked.

"My group was to manage the prisoners and marshal them as the other SEALs brought them out of the platform housing. We treated those Iraqis really well while the search teams moved about the facility. They were bound and gagged, but we drug out a stack of mattresses for them so they wouldn't have to lie on the steel decking. We were so relieved that they didn't put up a fight, we were downright nice to them. Jan Watkins and the task force planners deserve a lot of credit for getting that many people aboard the terminal that quickly. The Iraqis seemed to know we would come sooner or later, but were clearly surprised at how quickly we were on them."

By the time Watkins's SEALs had cleared the berthing and living platform, they managed to round up twenty-three Iraqi Republican Guardsmen. To all their relief, all of the priming charges and detonators were still in their packing crates. After declaring the facility secure, Watkins called in the U.S. Marine security force that would hold the terminal while the coalition forces occupied Basra and pushed northward for Baghdad. Joining the Marines were additional EOD personnel and oil service technicians who would fully inspect the facility and ensure that it remained in operable condition for future oil export duty. As the RHIBs and Mk Vs ferried the marines and the other support personnel to the terminal from the *Joint Venture* waiting offshore, Jan Watkins and his assault element were taken back to the *Joint Venture* for the return trip to KNB.

At KAAOT, the GROM enjoyed much the same success as the SEALs on MABOT, although there was not the same presence of the Republican Guard, nor were there the caches of weapons and explosives. With the taking and securing of the offshore terminals, along with coastal and inland infrastructure, the vital oil export capability had been made safe for the Iraqi people. Because of the fires deliberately set at some of the wells in the Rumaila oil fields and other infrastructure sabotage, it would be the better part of a year before the export capacity approached prewar levels. Problems still persist with the KAAOT facility, but MABOT currently handles about 80 percent of the more than 2 million barrels of oil exported each day from Iraq. Put another way, MABOT accounts for close to $60 million of revenue *daily*.

The SEALs, the GROM, and their security and support elements suffered no loss of life, and only a few combat wounds, that night of 20–21 March 2003. All five objectives were secured with minimal damage to the installations and no environmental consequence. High tribute, indeed, to the planning, training, and professionalism of the joint special operations task force. It was not until late April 2004 that the first fatalities occurred at MABOT, now the Basra Oil Terminal. Three suicide boats attacked the facility, but were stopped short of closing on the terminal and the single tanker that was alongside to take on oil. Three sailors and coastguardsmen were killed and four wounded in the attack. With the failure of this small-craft assault, saboteurs attacked a section of the pipeline two months later, destroying a section and closing oil export operations for ten days. This interruption cost the Iraqi people in the neighborhood of $700 million in oil revenues. The Iraqi pipelines and oil infrastructure now come under frequent attack. That they are still a viable economic target for insurgents in Iraq is an ongoing tribute to the brave men who took them from Saddam Hussein and gave them to the Iraqi people.

Following the initial fighting around Basra and the Umm Qasr, the world watched in wonder as armored columns from the 3rd Infantry Division and the 1st Marine Expeditionary Force drove into the heart of Iraq on their way to Baghdad. Many of the SEAL platoons were assigned to support these conventional armored thrusts. I asked a task unit commander what his SEALs were doing in support of the marines.

"There was some SR work for us at that time, but for the most part we just stood back in awe of those young marines. They were magnificent. They were professional, focused, and courageous. We do a lot of things that few other units can do, but when it comes to this kind of mechanized warfare, it was all we could do to keep up with those guys."

"It was a real eye-opener for me," one of the platoon SEALs said. "We do our best to avoid contact—to surprise our enemy and take him down fast. You know the deal—the element of surprise and violence of action. But those marines waded through that Iraqi fire and gave it back to them in spades. We used to joke a lot about the jarheads, but not so much anymore. We're proud to call them brothers. They were awesome."

The Special Boat Teams and the GROM turned their attention to clearing the waterways to bring in humanitarian aid. There were numerous hulks, mostly from the Iran-Iraq War, that littered the Khawr az-Zubayr waterway, the access to Iraq's only deepwater port at Umm Qasr. These were not only impediments to navigation, but a few provided shelter and hiding places for Baathist guerrillas.

"We had a few SEALs with us, but it was mostly the GROM who cleared these floating hulks," Chief Jim Collins recalled. "For the most part, it was boring work with a few anxious moments here and there. But we ran the legs off our boats—and our guys. There was one twelve-day period where we averaged close to twenty hours of operation per day. Fortunately, we had recently completed an extreme maintenance cycle on most of the craft, so we knew they would go the distance. It was just day after day of hard, dirty work with very little sleep. The boats and my SWCC guys did an incredible job."

"I can't say enough about those Special Boat Teams," said Captain Mike Tillotson. As the Commander, Explosive Ordnance Disposal Group One in Coronado, Tillotson then commanded all EOD assets in the Pacific. When the Iraqi campaign began, he was deployed and put in charge of clearing the sea approaches for the relief ships that brought supplies into Umm Qasr.

"Nothing was going to happen until we could make it safe for those ships to make the transit. The people in Basra were desperate for food, water, and medicines. The ships, loaded with all of the much-needed humanitarian aid, were just sitting out there in the Gulf, waiting for us to get our job done. The Special Boat Teams, the SEALs, the GROM, and my EOD techs worked around the clock to make it happen."

Shortly after the armored columns set off from Kuwait to Baghdad, another SEAL/GROM task element began planning a daring raid to protect another important piece of Iraqi infrastructure. It was the Mukarayin Dam, located some sixty miles northeast of Baghdad on a tributary of the Tigris River. This dam was important for three reasons. The first was that it held back an immense reservoir of water that would flood portions of Baghdad and the entire lower basin of the Tigris if it were breached. This much water would make it more difficult for the advance of the 1st Marine Expeditionary Force, approaching Baghdad from the south. Second, the two active turbines generated forty kilowatts of power for the suburbs of Baghdad and the surrounding area. Electric power is an important commodity for a population recovering from war. And finally, there was intelligence to suggest that weapons of mass destruction might be hidden within the concrete honeycomb of the dam structure.

The SEAL task unit held in reserve at Kuwait Naval Base was feeling left out of the action while just about every other SEAL in Central Command was involved in the operations at Umm Qsar. That they had only been at KNB for three weeks did little to soften the blow that the big one, the oil platform seizures, had gone down and they had been made to sit it out. They were then handed a target package for the Mukarayin Dam and hydroelectric plant and a three-day planning window to make it happen. They were given satellite and Predator drone imagery, but they had none of the detailed schematics and engineering drawings available to Jan Watkins and the SEALs for their missions at Umm Qasr.

"There was a Special Forces ODA team operating nearby," one of the platoon SEALs told me, "but about all they could tell us was that there were soldiers in the area, a military base nearby, and a whole lot of Iranians in the area—Iranians who were to become part of the insurgency once Saddam's regime was no more." The dam was only twenty miles from the Iraqi-Iranian border. "Normally, we would have tried to mount an SR mission into the area to get some eyes on the target, but there simply wasn't time. We learned as much as we could as quickly as we could, came up with a plan, and began rehearsing. You should have seen us at the rehearsal site at KNB. All of us yelling in English and the GROM yelling in Polish. But it all worked out."

The assault had to be aborted for two nights running due to weather. There were huge sandstorms across all of Iraq. On the third night, just before 2300, six MH-53 Pavelows lifted off in Kuwait. The lead helo had the ground force commander, his command-and-control element, and six snipers. The second helo carried twenty SEALs and two EOD techs. The third Pavelow carried all thirty-five GROM—a tight fit, to be sure.

Two other Pavelows, each with a DPV and a complement of SEALs, followed. The sixth MH-53 joined the formation as a backup and to serve as a CSAR (combat search and rescue) bird, if needed. The little squadron rendezvoused with their KC-130 tanker over Iraq and were over the target at 0415. They had been in the air just over five hours.

The lead Pavelow managed to land briefly on the flat roof of the three-story main power generation building. The ground element commander quickly set out his snipers in an overwatch position and called in his two ground assault elements.

"The two helos with SEALs and the GROM came in right after we got set," the ground force commander told me. "Because of obstructions on the ground, the helos couldn't land, so they had to fast-rope in. With that many guys, it seemed to take forever. Everyone is at risk when those helos are in a hover like that. I can't tell you how much better I felt after everyone was on the ground and those helos had cleared off. One of the Poles broke his leg on the insertion, but things went pretty well after that."

The two Pavelows with the DPVs made their planned insertions— one at each end of the dam. With six SEALs in one and four in the other, the DPVs took up defensive positions guarding the access road that ran across the dam from each side. The DPVs carried heavy machine guns and rockets, so they had the ability to engage trucks and armored vehicles. At the dam site, the assault elements moved to their assignments. The GROM broke into four sections and quickly cleared the four smaller support buildings. The SEALs headed for the big power generation facility.

"It was a large building with office space, control rooms, and two huge turbines," one of the assault element SEALs told me. "We had to cut our way through a chain-link fence with a Quicksaw to get to the door, but the door was unlocked. Inside, it was a well-run modern power plant. A few of the workers were hiding behind their desks and others were cowering out in the plant. They didn't know what to expect—and frankly, neither did we. We had to go in full tilt as if there would be active resistance. Having an armed bunch of SEALs descend on your world can be a terrifying experience. We searched them and cleared the building quickly. They were compliant, and as many of them spoke English, they did exactly as they were told. As soon as the building was secure, we brought in the command-and-control element and began a thorough search of the building. We had an interpreter with us, so he began questioning the Iraqis who didn't speak English."

"The assault elements immediately recognized that these were non-combatants," the ground force commander said. "They neutralized them and kept them safe while they cleared the plant. We treated them with firm courtesy. They were not only compliant, they helped us with a detailed search of the dam complex. We didn't find anything, but the EOD guys did get a couple of hits on their radiation test equipment. Hard to figure why there would be traces of radiation at a hydroelectric plant, but nothing ever came of it."

The SEALs in the assault element were pulled out the following day while the C2 (command and control) element, the GROM, and the DPVs remained in the area until they were relieved by units of the 1st MEF. With the dam and power generation facilities secure, the DPVs were able to roam around the surrounding area. The Iraqi military installation was deserted, and there were signs of looting. It seemed as if the garrison there had just picked up and left.

"We took no direct fire," one of the assault element SEALs told me, "but the locals were at it. At night we would hear gunfire and see tracers off in the distance. We could only guess that with us there and the Iraqi army gone, the Iraqis and the Iranians, or maybe some local clans in the area, had some things to settle. Every night they skirmished, but they left us alone. And that was fine by us. Our job was to take the dam and hold the dam. We didn't fight our way to Baghdad or anything like that, but we accomplished our mission. And when we finally did get to Baghdad and set up operations there, we soon had more than enough active opposition."

Chief John Morales is serving with the Training Detachment at Naval Special Warfare Group One, preparing SEAL platoons for operational deployment to the Pacific and Central Commands. "It was quite a challenge stepping into a platoon during the final days of predeployment training. I had to quickly learn to trust the men in the platoon, and they had to learn to trust me. Then we got the call to go to Iraq; we knew that we were going into combat. After all those deployments and all that training, I got to take a platoon into combat. I had the chance to make a difference."

Lieutenant (junior grade) Craig Thomas is serving in Europe as a NATO liaison officer. He expects to return to a SEAL team late in 2005 for duty as a SEAL platoon OIC.

Lieutenant Jan Watkins, the SEAL Navy nurse, is currently assigned as operations officer at one of the Special Boat Teams. After five operational deployments and three years of medical duties at Balboa Naval Hospital, he is preparing SWCC crews for operational deployment. "I'm not done operating," he assured me, "but I owe it to my family to spend some time at home. I'm hoping my next assignment will be to a SEAL team as the executive officer. Then I'll be back in the operational rotation."

Chief Jim Collins is the senior training chief at a Special Boat Team. His duties include the operational training of SWCC crews and the preparation of SBT assets for future combat deployment.

"I have been very lucky in my SEAL career," says Lieutenant Rick Cotton. "As OIC of an SDV platoon assigned to a SEAL squadron, I was in the right place at the right time to participate in the operation to secure the MABOT offshore oil platform. Then I was able to get orders to a SEAL team and to another platoon OIC job. Not many officers get back-to-back OIC jobs. I got these jobs because of the terrific support of my senior enlisted SEALs. My chiefs and leading petty officers took good care of me." He is currently deployed as OIC of a SEAL platoon.

Lieutenant Sean Yarrow, with two active SEAL deployments behind him, is now training with a platoon for operational deployment. He will soon be back downrange as OIC of a SEAL platoon.

CHAPTER 6

BAGHDAD AND BEYOND

Lieutenant John Rasmussen, Chief Cal Rutledge, and two other SEALs—Petty Officers Frank Ross and John Lopez—rolled cautiously up a side street in a Baghdad neighborhood in a Humvee. The chief was driving. The Iraqis along the streets stared blankly at them, and for the most part, the SEALs stared back. Occasionally, they exchanged smiles. Rasmussen and the others were trying to get a sneaky-peek at a target house in preparation for an operation they were planning for the following night. Their target, a Baath Party loyalist, visited his home only periodically, and their best chance to grab him was during one of his infrequent visits. They were being extremely careful, because they didn't want to tip their hand. Coalition forces had been in control of Baghdad for several weeks and the streets were relatively quiet. Rutledge pulled over near an intersection about half a block from the suspect's house. He and his lieutenant got out and spread out a city map on the hood of the Humvee and began tracing routes on the map with their fingers. Shopkeepers and other onlookers watched with guarded, neutral expressions. For outward appearances, they were just men who seemed

Desert patrol vehicles. SEALs and their DPVs train in the desert in Kuwait while they await the commencement of ground combat operations in Iraq. *Courtesy of the U.S. Navy (Eric Logsdon)*

temporarily lost and didn't want to ask for directions. What could be more typical?

"Boss," Rutledge said, glancing around as if he were looking for landmarks, "it's the third house down on the opposite corner—the one with the low concrete wall and iron gate."

Rasmussen bent low over the map then looked up and around the intersection. "Roger that, Cal."

He walked back to the passenger door of the Humvee and took up a radio handset. Without keying the radio, he said, "Frank, it's the third one down, the one with the concrete wall and what seems to be a small courtyard behind the wall."

"I'm on it, sir."

From the backseat of the Humvee, which was stacked with empty MRE boxes, Frank Ross framed the target house in the telephoto lens of his digital camera and clicked away. Rasmussen and Rutledge folded their map, exchanged a confused look, and climbed back into the vehicle. Rutledge pulled up into the intersection, hesitated, and turned from the target house as he sped away in the opposite direction.

Getting a firsthand look at the target is always helpful. At this juncture in the war, American vehicles routinely moved about the city. In this neighborhood, as elsewhere, the Iraqis on the streets were at best friendly, and at worst neutral. The reconnaissance drive-by in a Humvee with a stop to consult the map could be done without undue attention. Sometimes the SEALS would overfly the target in a helicopter or chance a drive-by of the target in a taxi or local truck. Seldom would they try to do a walk-by; an American in uniform on foot was simply too conspicuous. But for Rasmussen, who would lead the assault, seeing the physical layout in the daylight gave him a measure of confidence. This was Lieutenant John Rasmussen's third SEAL deployment, but this would be his first operation on this deployment. It would also likely be his first combat operation as a SEAL OIC. He and his platoon had arrived in Baghdad shortly after the Army and the Marines had secured the city.

When they wheeled back into the SEAL compound near Baghdad International Airport, Senior Chief Don Serles was waiting for them. It was 1800 hours—6:00 p.m. Serles, the task unit leading chief, was six-two and a solid 230. His head was shaved and he had a thick, brown mustache. He looked a bit like G. Gordon Liddy. He stood at the gate of the compound like a grade-school mistress waiting for her charges to come back in from recess.

"You get eyes-on, sir?"

"Affirmative, Senior Chief."

"That's good, because we go tonight."

"Tonight! You mean he's there—at the house?"

"He's there, or he will be tonight," Serles said. "That's what the informant tells us. Your patrol order goes at 2100, sir."

Rasmussen shot a concerned look at his platoon chief. "Relax, Boss," Rutledge said with an air of confidence. "We can make it happen."

Rasmussen quickly parked the Humvee and they piled out. Chief Rutledge went to round up the rest of the platoon SEALs and get them working on their assignments to prepare for the mission. Rasmussen followed Senior Chief Serles into the TOC to get a look at the latest intelligence on the target.

The task unit had been at this compound for a little over a week. Like the ones in Kandahar, Bahrain, and Kuwait, it already had the look of a SEAL compound. Those in and around the TOC were in shorts, T-shirts, and shower shoes. Some wore ball caps, while others had sunglasses parked on top of their heads. The atmosphere inside the SEAL compound was very informal, but whenever they left the interior of the compound, they were in operational gear or a proper military uniform and starched cap. SEALs and other special operators had long ago learned that when they were embedded with conventional service components, they needed to adhere to conventional force uniform requirements. It made for good relations. Since they would operate almost exclusively at night, they had already begun to keep vampire hours. Things were fairly quiet during the mornings, when most of the operators were sleeping. By early afternoon, most of the SEALs were up and about—preparing equipment, working out, washing clothes, or working on the vehicles. At night, they studied targeting folders, practiced mission-critical TTPs, or were out on missions.

The SEAL compound in Baghdad was the work of Senior Chief Don Serles and two other senior enlisted men assigned to the deployed squadron. One was Master Sergeant Will Mallory, an Army Ranger on loan to the teams, and the other was Chief Bill Flowers. Mallory was a wealth of knowledge about urban battle and close-quarter combat. While at the NSW Group One training detachment, he had trained Rasmussen and Rutledge in urban combat during their platoon's Unit Level Training. Flowers was a SEAL chief who was on his last war; his first was Vietnam. The compound had formerly been the maids' quarters for one of Saddam's palaces and contained several buildings. They converted one of the buildings into a multiroom barracks, while another that had a large open bay served as the task unit tactical operations center and briefing facility. It was situated in the middle of a larger military compound, so there was good security beyond the compound perimeter. There was a wall around the facility, so the SEALs could go beach-casual and not offend the conventional military components arrayed outside their compound.

When Serles, Miller, and Flowers were assigned the location for their operational compound, they set out to make sure their SEAL operators had everything that they needed in the way of tables, chairs, bunks, support equipment, washing machines, weight-training equipment, shower facilities, and all the creature comforts SEALS relish when they're not operating. What they could not requisition, they built; and what they couldn't build, they traded for. In short order, the veteran chiefs and the master sergeant had made this little compound in Baghdad a facility from which to stage SEAL operations and where the SEALs could work and relax between missions. It had the feel of a serious military post with just a hint of an athletic club.

"I had my heart set on a palace," one of the other platoon chiefs told me, "but we came in behind the main-force elements and all the good palaces were taken. But this was a good setup for us. We had good security, and no one bothered us there. We could relax between missions, and the TOC facility was more than adequate. We were not all that far from the Army chow hall, and the Army fed pretty well in Baghdad. Still, I had hoped for a palace."

Mission preparation is a collective effort for a SEAL platoon. Each man has an area of responsibility—communications, intelligence, weapons, demolitions, or vehicles, to name a few. They operate as a team, and they prepare and plan the operation as a team. If one of them finishes his area of responsibility, he immediately looks to see if he can help a teammate with his assignment.

The warning order, usually a briefing to assign equipment and duties for a pending mission, was not formally given but passed along among the assault and support elements. Everyone then went to work. At 2100, shortly after dark, they were gathered at the briefing facility in the compound TOC. It was time for the Patrol Leader Order, or PLO— the final premission briefing. Lieutenant John Rasmussen would not be the task element commander for the mission; Lieutenant Commander Alex Demming would have that job. But since Rasmussen was the assault element leader, he would give the briefing.

"Chief, we up?"

"We're up, sir," Rutledge answered, indicating that the assault element was all present.

"Alex, command and control?"

"We're up, John."

"Mobility?" They were the Humvee drivers and gunners—all SEALs.

"Mobility's up."

"Security element?"

"The security element is all present," said a thickly accented voice.

Most SEAL missions employed a security or blocking force that allowed the assault element to focus exclusively on their mission, knowing their backs were covered. For the mission that evening, the blocking force would be the GROM.

"The GROM are our brother warriors," a task unit commander told me. "We now work with them on a regular basis. They've learned a lot from us, and we've learned from them. They're real pros, and I can't say enough about these guys. When we assault, they watch our backs; and when they assault, we're proud and honored to cover them."

The GROM, arguably the finest European SOF fighters, was formed in 1990. They are built on the British Special Air Service (SAS) model. Their selection process and rigorous training deep in Poland's Carpathian Mountains is a great deal like SEAL training. To find one good man, they begin with five good men. The members of the GROM are very fit and love working alongside Navy SEALs.

"GROM also means 'thunder' in Polish, and it's a deserving title," the task unit commander said. "These guys are awesome."

Few of the GROM speak English, so there is little integration with the various elements on an operation, since rapid communications within the element in a tactical situation is critical. The GROM will assault, block, or drive as assigned for a given mission, but seldom do SEALs and GROM work within the same element. The SEAL-GROM oil platform assaults and the vessel-clearing operations at Umm Qasr cemented the close working relationship between the Poles and the Americans. That night, while John Rasmussen gave his brief in English, a SEAL officer who speaks Polish quietly translated for the GROM.

"Okay, guys, tonight we go after Abu Masharib. He's a bad guy and a committed Baathist; we want him, and we want him alive. He is a key lieutenant of Uday Hussein, and we know that Uday recently gave him the equivalent of one million dollars in Iraqi dinar. He's supposed to take these funds to Basra to finance the planned resistance there. Our job is to stop him before he leaves Baghdad and is able to get those funds south.

"We will operate in four elements. There will be ten SEALs from my platoon in the assault element as listed on the board." Rasmussen turned to the ten names neatly blocked on the white board behind him. "Lieutenant Commander Demming and Senior Chief Serles, along with the source and the agent handler, are the C2 element. Chief Stone and his drivers and gunners are the mobility element, and the GROM will be the blocking element."

Rasmussen went quickly through the movement to the target, communications, friendly force disposition, danger points, and other known elements of the target area. As with many SEAL operations in Baghdad, their target and the target location came from an informant. For this particular operation, which was the preferred way of doing business, the informant and his CIA case officer would be with the command element.

In Iraq and Afghanistan, the CIA, the FBI, and other federal agencies were referred to simply as OGAs—other governmental agencies. Increasingly, in the Afghan operations and in Iraq, the OGAs supplied the operational intelligence for SEAL operations. And increasingly, the OGAs were CIA case officers. Whatever might be the political or jurisdictional turf issues between the Department of Defense and the CIA in Washington, it did not get to the operational level, or at least not that I heard about. The CIA case officers I spoke with had nothing but good things to say about the SEAL operators, and the same was true with the SEALs regarding the CIA officers. On the ground, they worked well together.

"They had the contacts, the money, and the language skills," one SEAL candidly told me of the operations in Baghdad, "and they were able to get the good Iraqis to drop a dime on the bad Iraqis. They came to us because we were the reaction force that was fastest out the door. And they respected us if we turned down a mission for tactical reasons. Sometimes the importance of the target didn't justify the risk, and sometimes there was just too much opportunity for collateral damage—the target was in an area where there were too many civilians. One of our constant fears was getting in a shooting situation with a lot of civilians around. The bad guys never gave this much thought, but we sure did."

"It was always nice," Rasmussen told me, "when the guy who provided the information you're operating on is taking some of the same risks you are. Often, we had the OGA and the informant right there with us on the operation. You know you got the right house when he points and says, 'That's the house—his bedroom is on the third floor, at the top of the stairs on the left.' And the informant knows that if it goes badly for us, he's going to have a few questions to answer."

When Rasmussen got to the critical mission areas and danger points, he slowed the speed of his briefing. For this mission, the transition from the Humvees to the door of the target house would be a vulnerable time. If for some reason their visit had been expected, crossing the ground from the door of the vehicle to the door of the house would be dangerous. Another danger point was the entry. Again, if somehow their arrival at the target house was expected, the first SEALs through the door would be severely at risk. Rasmussen quickly went through actions on target, time on target, and rally points along the route in and along the route out. Most of what they will do in operations like this are governed by TTPs—standard close-quarter combat and close-quarter defense procedures. Even though it is early in the deployment of this task unit and this SEAL platoon, they already constitute a reasonably well-oiled machine. The SEALs know how to move, shoot, and communicate in any number of tactical situations. They have trained together for close to eighteen months, and each of them has a great deal of confidence in his brother SEAL.

"That concludes the PLO," Rasmussen said. "Any questions?" There were none from the assembled elements. "Alex?"

"Good plan and a good briefing, John," Alex Demming said, stepping to the front of the assembled group. "Once I get a confirmation from the source that we, in fact, are setting up on the right house, I'll confirm that on the net. But don't waste any time getting from the vehicles to the door. Let's keep the command net clear and free of chatter, but keep me informed."

"Understood," said Rasmussen. "Commander?"

Commander Matt Kelso currently served in the role of their task force commander. He was a combat veteran, having made a deployment to Afghanistan. The Joint Special Operations Task Force, or JSOTF, would not be up and running in Baghdad for another week. Until then, he held go/no-go authorization for this task unit's operations, which at this point was all the SEAL operations in Baghdad. Even when the JSOTF became fully operational, most of the operational planning and execution decisions would be made at the task unit level.

"Give me your backup commo plan again, John." Rasmussen did, and Kelso nodded. "All right, I buy it. We're on for the operation, subject to a good rehearsal. Good luck, gentlemen. Let's make it happen."

The SEALs filed out into the compound for inspections and rehearsal. Neither were fancy nor elaborate. The element leaders inspected their men to make sure they had the right equipment and that their gear was in place. All wore Kevlar helmets and body armor. Some of the vehicle gunners had only "chicken plates," frontal chest armor that were lighter and less protective but afforded them more freedom in the use of their guns. They boarded the Humvees and took their defensive positions. Senior Chief Serles inspected each vehicle to make sure it had 360-degree security, and that the men and guns had proper fields of fire. The SEALs had modified the Humvees so that the rear passenger seats faced outward for good firing positions. Serles made changes and adjustments to each vehicle until he was satisfied they were in the best defensive posture for the run to the target.

"Okay, you've just pulled up to the target house," the senior chief said to the assault SEALs. "Pretend the TOC is the target. Let's see you set up on the entry door. First time is a walk-through."

The SEALs poured from the first two Humvees and approached the door like a football team coming to the line of scrimmage. The GROM in the blocking element moved off to the side in their security role. Several SEALs formed a stack-file to the left of the door, opposite the door hinges and several yards back. Each had his hand on the shoulder of the man in front of him. The breachers came forward and simulated placing their breaching charge on the door. The other SEALs in the assault element took up fields of fire out from the door to protect those working on the entry. Serles stood back, arms folded, critically watching their setup.

"Okay, I like what I see." He made a few recommendations on position and said, "Now let's do it a few times on the run. And don't forget, you have a wall to hop over before you can get to the door. We can't simulate that here, but think about it."

Following the run-throughs, they practiced their door entry. SEALs have a number of ways to breach a door—an explosive breach is just one of them. Taking the door with a small explosive charge is fast and has the advantage of making it very uncomfortable for someone waiting just inside, but it lets everyone inside, and outside, know that a raid is in progress. Other methods of entry range from a kick to a two-man iron battering ram to the bumper of a Humvee. Sometimes the assault element will try a window entry or get to a window to cover those entering through the door. Each situation is different; each calls for a different tactic or a shift to an alternate tactic as the operation unfolds. After several entry rehearsals, Senior Chief Serles pronounced the task element ready to move. Commander Matt Kelso also watched closely and was satisfied. The SEALs remounted their four Humvees. A man in civilian clothes and body armor, accompanied by an Iraqi, materialized, and the two men climbed into the back of one of the vehicles. Both were dark complexioned and both had broad, thick mustaches. Often, personnel from the OGAs can pass as one of the locals. It was 0100 by the time the four Humvees rolled out of the compound. They ran their proscribed route to the target, driving very fast and fully blacked out. The drivers wore night-vision goggles, and the safety of the little convoy rested primarily with their skill. Everyone in the convoy was on full alert, looking ahead and to each side for any sign of danger. Approaching the target house, they slowed and quietly rolled to a stop. The informant again identified the house, and his verification was passed to Rasmussen and the assault element. Everyone had a radio, but each element was on a different frequency. The element leaders could also speak with each other on a separate frequency, and with Lieutenant Commander Demming with the command-and-control element. While elements moved into place, Demming and his C2 element took a position across the street from the target house.

As the SEALs in the assault element poured from the two lead Humvees, members of the GROM moved from their Humvee to the side and rear of the house to provide security. The gunners in the ring turrets of the vehicles swept their assigned sectors of responsibility. The gate was locked, so the SEALs had to climb the concrete wall to get to their positions for entry.

"No matter what kind of a look-see you get ahead of time," one of the platoon SEALs told me, "it's always different when you do it for real. The wall was a little taller than we thought it would be, so it took a little longer to climb over it. And moving across that courtyard area, it seemed like we made a lot more noise than we should have. When you're in an exposed position like that, you seem to hear everything. And looking up at the windows of the target house and the house next door, well, you just feel vulnerable—naked almost. If there were any guns in those windows, they could have made it very hard on us. Of course, you're all keyed up and excited; all your senses are working overtime. That's the time you have to focus on your area of responsibility and know that the other guys are doing their jobs. It comes down to a matter of trust. You have to do your job and trust that your teammate is doing his."

"Luck was with us that night," Chief Rutledge said. "The first they heard of us was when the door blew. It took us a matter of seconds to clear the first floor and leapfrog up the stairs. We spent a lot of time and effort on our close-quarter battle drills, so the guys can be both fast and deliberate."

"My job is to let the guys do their job," Lieutenant Rasmussen said of his role as the assault element leader. "I try to stay focused on the big picture inside, as well as listen up for the ground force commander if he has something to pass along that may be happening outside. I don't say anything unless I see something that my guys clearing the rooms don't. I also have to be ready to make good decisions if the tactical plan breaks down or needs to be changed."

The assault element usually enters a target house in an ordered and prescribed manner, as it was briefed and rehearsed. What happens after that will be dictated by the tactical situation. Sometimes the intelligence can be precise enough that they know where the person they're looking for might be in the house—where he sleeps or whether he is sleeping alone. Most high-value target individuals, like the one they were after tonight, have to remain on the move to avoid capture. They know that they are wanted, and they know that any adherence to a pattern puts them at risk. After the blast took down the front door, all was ordered confusion. Voices rang out:

"Clear left!"

"Clear right!"

"Moving!"

"Move!"

They quickly cleared the first floor and re-formed to move up to the second. It was on the second floor that they began to encounter the residents. In this case, their information was spot-on. Their man was reported to be married and have four sons. The first two bedrooms the assault element cleared each yielded two sons. The boys ranged in age from nine to fifteen. All were compliant.

"It's hard when you're dealing with kids," one of the platoon SEALs told me. "Hey, that was me fifteen years ago. But the safest thing for them, and for us, is to come at them full tilt until they show compliance and do exactly as they are told. These kids were compliant; we quickly got them searched and in one place where we could keep an eye on them. The problem comes when a kid doesn't do what he's told. You're thinking, 'Does he not understand what we're telling and motioning for him to do, or is he too scared to move?' With some of the surly scumbags we encounter, you know they are testing us. They get dealt with firmly and efficiently. With kids, it's always a judgment call as to how much force to apply. Bottom line, we have to keep them safe, and we have to keep ourselves safe. And in a tactical situation, we have to do all this very quickly. That's where all our training comes in. And it's amazing just how many times we encounter an operational situation that is exactly like one of our training scenarios."

While the second-floor rooms were being cleared, the other SEALs poured onto the third floor. By that time, the target was up and running. He bolted from the door of a bedroom toward a room across the hall, but he didn't get far.

"There was a big debate during the debriefing," John Rasmussen said with a chuckle, "as to who took him down. Chief Rutledge said he tackled him, and Sam Crenshaw, my AOIC, said he took him down. I think they both hit him. They had him cuffed and on his way downstairs in a matter of seconds."

"What about his wife?" I asked.

"We found her in the bathroom, hiding behind a door. She was scared to death. We put her with her sons while we searched the house. She spoke good English and asked what we were going to do with her husband. I told her we were going to put him in jail. She seemed genuinely relieved. 'That is good,' she told me, 'because he is not a good man.' It's been our experience that a lot of the Iraqi men don't treat their women all that well. She was glad to see him led away, or she was one hell of an actress."

"How about the money?" I pressed.

"We found some of it, but not all of it. Once we had the place secure, we began a thorough search. We found a few weapons. It seems every house has at least one or two AK-47s. This one had more than that."

"Sounds like you couldn't have had a better break-in op."

"It was a great first mission. Seeing the guys perform so well, doing exactly what we had trained to do all those months. It was a real credit to the senior chief and the other task unit personnel. Those guys worked so hard, both with the intelligence product and helping us get our target package ready. It was a team effort by the planners and the operators. Alex, in his ground commander's role, coordinated the operation and allowed me to focus on the assault. And a lot of credit for our success goes to Commander Kelso. I'm just now beginning to appreciate him. Right before we rolled on that operation, he took me aside and said, 'Get the job done; bring 'em all back.' Then he turned and walked back into the TOC. What he was saying was that he trusted me enough to take men in harm's way. You don't want to disappoint someone who places that kind of trust in you.

"That operation kind of set the tone for our task unit's work in Baghdad. The CIA guy was really impressed that we could move on a target, set up security, and conduct an assault that quickly. They began to give us a lot of business. Our TOT that evening was seventeen minutes. Later in the tour, we got so we could do it faster, safer, and make a better search of the target area. But it's always a learning experience. Always, even at the end of our tour when we felt fairly confident about what we were doing, there is always something we could have done better—always. A good portion of every debriefing after an operation are the lessons learned. The guys don't hesitate to be critical of themselves or each other—or of me. Anything that can make us better or safer is fair game. One thing we learned from our success in Baghdad was that you could never take anything for granted. After every mission, we had talked about how we could have done it better, or how we could do the next one a little differently to avoid a pattern in our tactics. Every time you go out you learn something, and that changes how you do it the next time."

I spoke with any number of SEALs returning from deployment. And I consistently heard the same thing from the platoon leadership: "We had great guys in our platoon." When they weren't praising their SEALs or other platoon leaders, they were complimenting the efforts of the task units and task forces in looking out for them and helping them to succeed. And they had nothing but good things to say about their dealings with the CIA and other OGAs. They were no less vocal in praising the components that supported the SEAL assault elements. That doesn't mean that a deploying SEAL squadron or support element did not have problems with personnel, equipment, leadership, or performance. But the rigorous predeployment process tends to iron out most of the wrinkles before the SEALs and other squadron elements go in harm's way. That's why the deploying squadron commanders do everything they can to get the diverse elements of their squadron to attain a maximum level of interoperability.

"The platoon SEALs," one task unit commander told me, "pretty much perform to standard or they wouldn't be here. That's not to say that we don't occasionally have a problem, but it's generally a personality problem, and that gets fixed in a hurry by the senior enlisted leadership. The surprises are how the guys break out on the upside. Some of them just have a natural instinct for this business; it's like they have a nose for it. And I'm not talking about shooting. All of them shoot well—some better than others. It's recognizing a potential threat, a situation that could get out of hand if not addressed quickly and professionally. Some guys do that instinctively. They seem to know how to deal with the locals—when to be a hard-ass and when to soften up. The Iraqi people understand and respect force. You really have to have a good feel for when it's safe to back off, or when it's right to be aggressive. The making of a SEAL, a combat SEAL, is an evolutionary process—perhaps even a maturity process. A new guy, a SEAL here on his first deployment, may have been undistinguished in BUD/S or SQT or even during the predeployment workup. But when he gets here and goes downrange, he suddenly finds himself in his element. Most platoons I see will have at least one guy, sometimes a very unlikely platoon SEAL, become a go-to guy by the end of their tour. And I'll tell you this, it's a validation of our whole basic, advanced, and predeployment process when one of these new guys steps up and becomes an impact player within his platoon. And better yet, it keeps the veteran SEALs on their toes and encourages them to take their game to a higher level."

It was also my sense, mostly from my discussions with platoon SEALs and the junior leadership within the platoons, that the operations in Iraq after the fall of Baghdad enjoyed excellent leadership at the task unit and task force level. The maturity and reach of this senior leadership was also an evolutionary trend. The task units were often staffed by officers and senior enlisted leaders who had been platoon

OICs and platoon chief petty officers in Afghanistan. Most were combat veterans. This experience and perspective can't be overvalued as new SEALs and new SEAL platoons rotate into theater.

"The TUs and TFs did a lot of things," one platoon LPO told me, "but one that's often overlooked is the sanity check. We get so buried in the details of mission preparation, and which tactics to use, that sometimes we didn't see the obvious. What is the risk and reward of doing this mission? Is this a good SEAL mission; does it match up with our capabilities and training? A few times, someone up the chain of command would pull the plug on an operation, and we down in the platoons would really be pissed about it. But when we thought about it, we realized that maybe it wasn't something we should be doing in the first place. We were so busy getting ready, we just didn't see it. And there's always the question of the intelligence and the reliability of the intelligence. We can do everything right on the ground, but if the intel is bad, then we're going to have problems and not complete the mission. More than that, we might get someone hurt."

Intelligence in the war on terrorism has always been crucial, and never more so than in Iraq after the end of main-force combat. The success of SEAL operations is a near-linear function of the quality of intelligence. The mechanics of getting the intelligence from various sources into the hands of the SEAL operators in a usable form was, in itself, an evolutionary process. Each deploying squadron and task organization, and every SEAL element, no matter how remote, was always on the hunt for good intelligence. There was no "centralized intelligence distribution network" as such, nor was there any single clearing entity that an operational component could tap into to access the intelligence product. Most of the operable intelligence that contributed to SEAL operational success in Baghdad was the result of the initiative of the task unit and task force personnel. They didn't develop this intelligence product; they went out and found it. The secret weapon in this intelligence-generation effort were senior enlisted petty officers, like Senior Chief Don Serles, who, in the course of their decades of service, had developed a lot of contacts—both in and out of uniform. They know how to make friends. When a SEAL task unit or special operations task group moves into an area, these wily veterans are out making contacts, finding out who has the best intelligence on the AO, establishing relationships with other service components and OGAs. A great deal of good intelligence in Iraq was developed by the Army Special Forces. This is often done over a cup of coffee or a beer. Veteran SEALs were very good at this. When I hear about this in Iraq, I immediately flash back on the work of my senior petty officers in Vietnam. When we set up at our base in the lower Mekong Delta, they were out pressing Army intelligence officers and nearby village chiefs for information on local Vietcong movements. It's as if it's in the blood of a good SEAL petty officer to do this.

"I'd walk into a joint headquarters command," a SEAL chief petty officer told me, "and I'd see a familiar face in baggy trousers sitting over in the corner. We'd make eye contact, he'd smile at me, and I'd smile at him. Usually he was CIA, a Special Activities guy. We worked with them in Afghanistan and again in Iraq. They get a bad rap sometimes by us in the military, but I took every opportunity to make friends with them. Most of them I got to know were patriots and professionals. We were delighted to work with them."

In addition to the snooping about of the SEAL petty officers, there are formal military intelligence channels. The broad specialty of operational intelligence in the Navy, both officers and in the enlisted ranks, is a community unto itself. Navy SEALs may depend on intelligence and work closely with those tasked with developing and providing operational intelligence, but there are no SEAL intelligence officers, nor are there designated, rated intelligence specialists (the IS rating in the Navy) who are SEALs. Embedded within a deploying squadron and the composition of a TU or TF is an intel section. The personnel in that section are tasked with the collection and management of actionable intelligence. Their job is to take requests for intelligence support that come from the SEAL operators and go to the proper sources to find that information. They also attend the debriefings of the operators when they come back in from a mission. Here they collect documents, information, and observations from the SEALs for future operations, and later they pass this material along to higher headquarters. SEAL element leaders and SEALs tasked with platoon intelligence responsibilities may conduct field interrogations for quick-response, tactical exploitation, but little more than that. TU and TF intelligence sections, depending on the situation, may also conduct interrogations when the detainees are brought in from an operation. But neither the task units nor the task forces are interrogation centers, and neither are equipped to handle detainees or EPWs—enemy prisoners of war—for any length of time. EPWs brought in from the field are passed along to the detention centers.

Who mans these intel sections? The best answer is whoever the task force or task unit commander can find to do the job. Depending on the size of the staff, they are rated intelligence specialists or intelligence officers, but a commander will not hesitate to assign a SEAL operator to his intel section if he's a fit. The management and delivery of actionable intelligence at the operational level are one of the most important tasks of a task unit or task force. The same is true for the squadron intelligence detachments. And sometimes the best man for the job is a woman. A deploying SEAL squadron is a male-centric organization, but among the headquarters' element there are female clerical, logistic, and intelligence personnel who serve in these important support roles.

"We had a female third class petty officer in Baghdad who was nothing short of phenomenal," one of the squadron commanders told me. "To look at her you would have thought she was some gum-chewing Valley girl, and well, she was. But she was bright and a tireless worker. She had only been in the Navy a few years, and this was her first deployment of any kind. We had a chief petty officer in charge of my intel section for a while. He had to rotate out, and they were going to give me another chief. I said, 'No way; I'm putting my third class in charge.' She took over and ran the section, and our intel product was first rate. I was lucky to have a number of breakout performers within my support components. They stepped up and did the job." He broke out in a smile. "But this lady was something special. I'd see her buzzing about the intel section, ponytail poking out from the back of her ball cap, making assignments, giving orders, taking charge. My SEALs had all the respect in the world for her."

The operational environment in Baghdad from the cessation of major combat operations became one of identifying bad guys and grabbing them when they weren't expecting it. There was the occasional raid on a makeshift bomb factory or a weapons cache, but most operations focused on taking a bad guy off the street. Early on, the hunt was for Baathist leaders. As time went on, this became the Iraqis and non-Iraqis who opposed the emerging government of Iraq—the insurgents. This usually meant working at night. The operations began to fall into a pattern, and patterns are dangerous for SEALs. Yet there are only so many ways to get to the target individual in an urban environment and only so much that can be done to keep a street-smart, indigenous enemy from hurting you. The very nature of these operations meant moving in vehicles at night, usually the specially configured Humvees. Without getting into detail that might be inappropriate, the SEAL Humvees moved as fast as possible, and they made sure to avoid dead-end or restricted areas that could curtail their speed or mobility. Unless it was unavoidable, they never left the target by the same route as they went in.

"We're just like fighter pilots," one of the SEAL drivers told me. "Speed is life. We move as fast as we can and as safe as we can at night, using our NVGs. Sometimes we had to be out in the daytime for one reason or another. We use different tactics in the daytime, partly because of the traffic. When they can see us coming, we play the game a little differently. Sometimes we have to move through a bad neighborhood, and we try to always make it a point to know if it's a bad one. If there's a slowdown due to traffic, the guys are out of the Hummer and on both sides of the street, looking for trouble before trouble finds us.

It was certainly like that in Fallujah. We had to drive through Fallujah several times, and we never felt all that comfortable there. When the guys come out of the Hummer ready for business, people usually shrink back and get compliant. A lot of Iraqis have guns, and I guess some of them think it's okay to take a shot at an American. By taking an aggressive posture when we get slowed by traffic, it hopefully discourages some idiot from doing something stupid. They want no part of you if your guard is up. You can see it in their eyes. In some of the more militant neighborhoods, you could tell they didn't like us. But when we dismounted the vehicles and walked along the roadway, ready for business, you could see that they respected us."

When they can, SEALs prefer to work at night. For the most part, there was very little shooting on these nocturnal urban raids. "That's the way it should be," one of the task element ground commanders told me. "It's all about the element of surprise and violence of action. When the intelligence is right and we do our thing properly, the first time they know we're there is when the front door lands in the middle of the living room. Then we have to get through the house as quickly as possible. And," he added soberly, "carefully sort out the residents until we find the guy we're looking for. For the most part, it's a CQD drill; we have to maintain control of the situation. The guys always have to be ready to dial it up if someone goes off on them, and that means going to their guns. You've probably heard this a lot, but the other guy always gets only what he deserves. They dictate the level of violence; our job is not to exceed it. Even when things are going well, the SEAL operators have to be totally alert. They can take nothing for granted. They have to be ready to respond with lethal force while looking out for the welfare of noncombatants. It takes a lot of training and teamwork to get to that level. After a while, we did it routinely."

"You never quite know what to expect," a platoon officer told me, "because they're not like us, and in many ways they're not like each other. In some neighborhoods, they were genuinely friendly to us, especially the kids. But in another neighborhood, you'd get nothing but hostile glares. There were some really bad parts of Baghdad, and it was our job to go there. I don't know if it's a cultural thing or comes from years under Saddam Hussein, but the Iraqis think differently. Sometimes we'd get shot at and we'd look at each other and say, 'Was he shooting at *us*?' A lot of times, we'd take a few rounds from a house and just let it go. I think they shoot at us as a macho thing, almost like giving us the finger. It's as if they make sure not to shoot too near us because they know we'll come for them. One time a guy took a shot at us from a window of a target house just as we were about to breach the door. When we got inside and up to the room where he was, he was standing there with his hands on his head and a smoking AK-47 lying on the floor at his feet. He then swore up and down that he wasn't the one who shot at us. Go figure. They perceive things differently, and they don't react like we do. They know that if they put their hands up, no matter what they've done, we won't kill them. It's as if they count on us to play by the rules. Well, they're right. There are rules, and we, at the least, have to play by them."

Any number of SEAL operators told me that they never really knew what to expect from the Iraqis on any given day or any given mission. And, quite often, the people they were after were non-Iraqis who came to Iraq to participate in the insurgency. And there were a number of operations that were less than textbook in the quality of the intelligence or the execution of the mission.

"It was right before dawn when we took the door down," a platoon chief told me, "and the lead SEALs in the assault element burst through the door. We always try to spread out once we get inside so we don't present a concentrated target, and it was a good thing this time. An Iraqi stepped out from around the corner and opened up on us with his AK, full automatic. He only got off four or five rounds when we shot him. His rounds missed all of us, but they spattered the wall right behind us. But we didn't miss. Our guys can shoot, and you could tell that we were very focused on his weapon. We found that several rounds had gone through his hands and the weapon itself, and more than a few were in his chest. Every round was center of mass. That entry shook us up pretty good. After that, we started thinking of how we could make entries safer. A few weeks later we were setting up on a target house and one of the guys moved to a side window to see inside. Right next to the window was a bad dude with an AK-47 aiming at the door. He took the barrel of his weapon right through the glass and into the side of the guy's head. The guy we were looking for wasn't there, but we dragged off the guy with the AK. He was lucky, and we were lucky. For a single guy to shoot at a squad of SEALs is usually a death sentence."

"And once in a while we got it wrong," one of the task unit commanders said. "One night we took down this door, and"—he broke into a sad smile—"it was a big wooden door, really a nice one. Many people sleep on their roof when it gets hot, so this guy came down the stairs just as we finished clearing the ground floor. Often the Iraqis are excitable and start yelling and waving their arms when we come in, and we have to sort it out. This fellow calmly asked who we were looking for. When we told him, he simply said that we had the wrong house. 'The man you are looking for,' he informed us, 'lives two doors down and across the street.' By the time we did get to the right house, our target had fled. But that left us with an Iraqi citizen with a ruined door. We came back the next day and paid him the equivalent of some four hundred dollars for the door and the repairs to the casing, and for the scare that we gave his family. It was something he didn't expect, and he was very grateful."

In talking with one of the squadron commanders, I asked him about the tactical shift from Afghanistan to Iraq. His was the first squadron tasked with operating in Iraq on a full-time basis, so this was the first time SEALs had conducted operations primarily in an urban environment for an extended period.

"We make these transitions easier than you might think," he told me. "Right after 9/11, our platoons were quickly ashore, doing business in Afghanistan and in mountainous terrain without the benefit of a predeployment workup for extensive inland operations or operations at altitude. Because we operate in the sea, in the air, and on land, we have a diverse skill set; there is a built-in flexibility in how we do business. We're good at improvising and adapting existing tactics to new situations. And shame on us if we had found ourselves in Baghdad or Mosul and were not ready for operations that involved advanced mobility and CQD techniques. While Secretary of State Powell was taking our case to the UN for armed intervention, my senior petty officers and training cadre were working up mobility scenarios. We focused on urban mobility—getting around in Humvees and getting out of them quickly to take the fight into a building. We also focused on room-clearing techniques and close-quarter shooting. We asked the group training cadres for more CQD training and MOUT training. And the guys spent a lot of time on the vehicles, learning what they could and could not do. Driving a Humvee in a hostile situation isn't for everyone, but some guys really like it. I guess they were the ones who were into hot rods in high school. On a mobility operation, our drivers will make dozens of mission-critical decisions—life-and-death decisions. A lot is riding on them, no pun intended.

"And, of course, there were the things that you can only learn through experience. We kind of expected to be operating in an urban environment, but we didn't know what the climate would be—how the people would receive us. I had to consider that it could possibly be like the liberation of Paris or a bad day in Mogadishu—or anything in between. As it turned out, it was just that—anything in between. I was very concerned about our projection of force. That's why the CQD training is so valuable. We had to be prepared to hurt, maim, or kill one minute and to give aid and comfort the next. In Baghdad, we did it all. In one room we would be taking a bad guy to the floor because he didn't do as he was told, and in another you'd be trying to quiet his wife and mother down—to let them know we weren't there to hurt them. Our issue was with him, not the women in his family.

"Tactically, we did everything we could to accomplish our mission, keep our guys safe, and bring the appropriate amount of force to bear. We learned as much as we could about the target and the target area before we launched on a mission. Whenever possible, we had an AC-130 gunship standing by and an MH-53 in case we needed to evacuate a casualty. The Navy HCS crews were always ready with their Blackhawks to fly us around to recon the target or the general area. And they were always on standby when we were on an operation. During the course of the deployment, we also learned a few tricks to keep us safe and to keep civilians safe. Like the use of lights. Most of our M4s are set up with both high-intensity white lights and the red-dot targeting lasers. Usually, we were out looking for a single individual or individuals, so everyone else was considered a noncombatant unless they showed us otherwise. Sometimes, especially coming off target, they would gather on rooftops looking down on us, which always made us very uneasy. So the guys would illuminate them with white light or put the red dot on them. They all knew what the red dot was and would usually move back out of the way.

"One thing that began in Afghanistan and continued in Iraq and during our operations in Baghdad was the size of our units. SEALs have traditionally trained to work in small units—usually squads with no more than eight men. If it was an SR operation, the number going forward to put eyes on the target could be as few as two. Now we operate with multiple elements—an assault element, a blocking or security element, a mobility element, a command-and-control element, and perhaps some sort of a mission-speciality unit. This calls for close coordination between the elements, and that's the job of the C2 element. Command and control is essential. Most of our platoon OICs, and even the AOICs, train to be in command on the ground—to be in charge and to make all the tactical decisions. And so they should. But now there is usually a ground force commander in a C2 element on the operation. Often, it was the task unit commander, and he made many of the operational decisions on the ground. That didn't mean that the element leaders didn't have the latitude to make tactical calls during a mission, especially the assault element leader. But it wasn't often that a platoon OIC was in charge of an operation of any size. Usually, there was someone more senior there to coordinate things and exercise over-all operational control. There is good reason for this. It's hard to be aware of what is going on outside the building and in the surrounding area if you're inside managing a room-clearing operation. But we've been at this business a while. Most of our task unit commanders have now had combat experience as a platoon commander, so they bring that experience to their ground force commander's role. Experience counts. Many of them are on their fourth or fifth deployment. Some of the platoon OICs and AOICs who cut their teeth on combat opera-tions in Iraq are going to become great ground force commanders and task unit commanders. We're going to need them; this is going to be a long war."

Not all the operations in Iraq were urban, and not all urban operations were in Baghdad. Several months after the occupation of Baghdad and the conduct of SEAL operations from the task unit there, two other task units were established. One of them operated near Mosul.

"Mosul was an interesting place, and a lot different from Baghdad and a lot farther north," one of the task unit operations officers commented. "We set up at the air base there in Mosul, along with a number of the SOF aviation support assets. We lived in trailers until Navy Seabees could get us set up with modular-construction huts. For quite a while, it was a SEAL trailer park. The whole time we were there, our camp was a construction site. KBR [Kellogg, Brown & Root] kept us well fed for most of that time—there were no com-plaints about the chow. Our camp was well within the secure perime-ter of the airfield. The bad news was we had to contribute to the security, which meant I had to put our SEALs on perimeter security duty. It was just the cost of doing business in Mosul.

"We were colocated with the Army Special Forces detachment, so we felt right at home. It was an ODB team or headquarters element. We never operated with them, but they were able to provide us with some good intelligence that we reacted on successfully. They had a much different role, which was primarily working with and training the Kurds, but it was nice to have our SOF brothers nearby.

"Operationally, what we did in Mosul looked a lot like what we did in Baghdad. The reputation of what the SEALs were doing at the task unit in Baghdad made it easy for us to go right to work. Pretty much from the start, we had good intelligence, and we enjoyed good operational success. And like in Baghdad, we fell right in with the OGAs." He paused to frame his words, not wanting to stray into areas that were operationally sensitive. "You see, by this time, we were becoming the go-to direct-action force when a quick and measured response was needed. Often, our target was a low-level bad guy, someone who could lead us to bigger fish. So the drill was to scoop him up, quickly and professionally. We'd try to take him with as little force as possible and avoid bringing any harm to his family. When some former Baathist or dissident is ripped out of his bed in the middle of the night, and none of his family are hurt—and he's treated humanely and with respect—the word gets out. The guy who we want information from also knows this, so he's more willing to cooperate with us. In many cases, that surgical-snatch capability was pretty much unique to SEALs. And, once again, all those CQC [close-quarter combat] and CQD drills paid off.

"Mosul seemed to have a high concentration of former regime members. Maybe it was because it was the closest major city to the Syrian border. There were many pockets of resistance and cells plotting against Americans and the Coalition Provisional Authority, and later on the new Baghdad government. Thanks to the quality of our intelligence, we were able to hit a few weapons caches and IED factories. In Mosul, it seemed there was always some group of bad guys stockpiling weapons or making bombs. Usually, they were troublemakers in the neighborhood, and one of the neighbors would rat them out. Even in Mosul, there are a lot of Iraqis and more than a few Kurds who wanted nothing to do with members of the former regime."

"We ran our operations out of Al Hillah," yet another task unit commander told me, "and we had none of the infrastructure to work with they had in Baghdad or Mosul. We had to build our facility there from the ground up. We found a piece of level ground that afforded us reasonable security and began living out of tents inside concertina wire. We went from ground pads to air mattresses to cots. As soon as we could, we built bunkers and went underground, as much to hide from the heat as for security. Most of the time, we had civilian contractors providing us with messing facilities. When those weren't available, we broke out the MREs.

"Our operations in Al Hillah were different from those in Baghdad, but there were some similarities. We operated out of a more remote location, but most of our work involved urban operations. Like operations in Baghdad, we functioned best when we had good intelligence, and that intelligence usually kept us busy at night. And like in Baghdad, we put our CQB and CQD skills to good use."

I pressed him on just how different things were in Al Hillah. "We looked for every opportunity to conduct good operations and to stay out of the vehicles. By that, we did what we could to keep our operations from falling into a pattern. But a lot of what we had to do meant that we had to use Humvees. It probably wasn't a lot different for you SEALs back in Vietnam. Most of your traveling was done by water, right?" I had to agree with him on that one. If my platoon was out at night in Vietnam, we were on the rivers and canals in boats—sometimes in SEAL support craft and sometimes in sampans. And like the SEALs in Iraq, we did everything in our power to vary our operations and avoid patterns. "We did have one operation that gave us the option between Humvees or boats," he said. "We chose the boats. It was an island in the Euphrates that was served by a single bridge. We drifted down on the island in two CRRCs and were able to slip ashore without being detected. We left two men with the boats and headed out. We patrolled to the target house, kicked the door, cleared the house, and found our man. As is often the case, by the time we were coming off target, the locals were awake and wondering what was going on. Some of them were bad guys. While they grabbed their guns and headed for the bridge, we patrolled to our CRRCs."

I talked with a great many SEALs about their work in Iraq. As this book goes to press, they have been conducting operations there for more than two years. Each deploying SEAL squadron built on the operational success of its predecessors. And each squadron continued to develop and modify its tactics to respond to the quality and availability of the intelligence. Tactics also had to adapt to the changing conditions as the Iraqis moved along the tortuous path toward sovereignty, and the insurgent challenge became stiffer. As the SEALs went about their business, they had to be innovative in how they conducted their operations—their actions on target, as well as their methods of getting to the target. Maintaining the element of surprise meant that they had to avoid patterns and avoid becoming predictable. Because they were usually bringing violence of action to a situation or confined space in which there were noncombatants and innocents close at hand, they had to be professional and exercise a great deal of judgment. And there is the changing nature of the enemy. As the operations went forward, there seemed to be an increasing number of non-Iraqis—Chechens, Malaysians, Saudis, Iranians, and any number of Islamists who had come to Iraq—to deal with. They were in Iraq to kill Americans, but they were also there because al-Qaeda knows that a sovereign Iraq with a viable economy will be a huge setback for the fundamentalists.

The SEAL squadron that deployed to CENTCOM from April 2004 through October 2004 took a detachment of U.S. Marines with them to the fight. It was an eighty-six-man contingent that carried the title of U.S. SOCOM Marine Detachment One. The SEALs called it the Marine Corps Det, or simply the McDet. The detachment OIC was a Marine Corps lieutenant colonel and was broken down into four elements. First, there was a recon element of thirty marines that consisted of four six-man recon teams and a recon headquarters element. Then there was an intelligence element with capabilities in signals and human intelligence, and a sophisticated communications suite. Next, there was a headquarters component with artillery and naval gunfire liaison officers, forward air controllers, and radiomen. Finally, the medical support element was staffed with five senior corpsmen—Navy corpsmen, as the Navy has traditionally supplied the Corps with medics.

"It was a very impressive group," the SEAL squadron commander told me. "I think the most junior man was a staff sergeant. Most of them had at least five years with a Marine recon unit. They really knew what they were doing. The detachment trained at Camp Pendleton for six months and joined us for six months of Squadron Integration Training. But the liaison work had been going on well before that."

When the U.S. Special Operations Command was established in 1986, the Marines Corps declined to become a supporting service component of the new force. Instead, it focused on building a special operations component within its force structure. Marine Expeditionary Units, or MEUs, began to deploy with a specially trained reconnaissance component that supported their battalion landing teams with "special operations." These became known as MEU(SOC)s, or Marine Expeditionary Units (Special Operations Capable). With kind respect to a superb fighting force, there was very little within the capability of a MEU(SOC) that met the test of special operations as practiced by Army Special Forces or Navy SEALs. The Marines have not had good success with elite units—units composed of Marine infantrymen who have been selected from the ranks and, with additional training, been given a special, narrow, or more difficult mission. I believe this is because the Marine Corps, being a small, integrated, expeditionary force, is special in its own right. For whatever reason, they simply have not done well with elite units for an extended period of time. Marines do what Marines do—they can storm a beach or storm a city, as we saw in their magnificent assault in Fallujah. They are highly professional in a very basic, straightforward, professional context. And they are one of the crown jewels in our military force structure.

In late 2001, the commandant of the Marine Corps and the commander of the U.S. Special Operations Command signed a memorandum of agreement (MOA) that they would explore the integration of Marine elements within the existing SOF structure. This MOA led to the formation of the SOCOM Marine detachment and its deployment with a SEAL squadron. The creation of SOCOM Marine Detachment One was a rare move for the Marines and was to be a one-time-only, proof-of-concept outing. Candidly, it would create a serious talent drain on the Corps to support SEAL squadrons on an ongoing basis. Those senior enlisted marines are needed to train and lead marines for MEU deployments. Since their return, both SEALs and marines have said little publicly about their joint deployment.

"We got on well at the command level, and the SEALs and the marines operated well together in the field," the SEAL squadron commander told me. "Great bunch of warriors; it was a privilege to be their commander. I'd go to war with them anytime."

Whether there will be future Marine Corps detachments deploying with SEAL squadrons—and if so, in what size—is currently under review. But on an operational level, this was nothing too different from the marines assigned to Task Force K-Bar. The experience level of SOCOM Marine Detachment One and its inclusion into the predeployment workup certainly make for a more integrated force from the get-go. But that was to be expected; the guys on the ground always seem to find a way to get the job done. It is my guess that there will be some ongoing formal Marine Corp involvement with special operations, and that this involvement will affect SEAL operations.

"And I'll tell you something else," the same SEAL squadron commander added. "We conducted some incredible operations in Iraq, but then we had an overwhelming supply of talent and experience and the best supporting arms available in theater. We operated at night with good intelligence; we were always on the offensive. Sure, it was dangerous, but we had no excuse not to perform well. But let me tell you who my hero is. My hero is that E-4 Army specialist sitting out there on some checkpoint for eight hours a day, checking papers and IDs. He's exposed and vulnerable, yet does a dangerous and necessary job. That takes courage—and that soldier is my hero."

Going forward, it is hard to imagine just what form the war on terrorism will take. It seems that we will not be leaving Iraq or Afghanistan soon. I would assume that military operations, even SOF activity, will take on a new look as the current insurgency waxes and wanes, perhaps with Iraqis and Afghans accompanying SEALS on operations on a regular basis. Certainly, it will change as the Iraqis field their own national force.

"Dick, we'll be doing what you guys did in Vietnam," a squadron commander told me.

"Excuse me," I said quite candidly, "but I'm not seeing a lot of parallels here." What I didn't say is that I'm not sure I wanted to. We lost that one.

He grinned. "Well, it was all before my time, mind you, but didn't you have ex-VC who worked for you and led you on operations because they knew the land, and they knew the good guys from the bad guys?"

"Well, yes," I replied.

"And didn't you guys develop intelligence and try to find informants who could identify targets for you? Weren't you trying to find some farmer or villager who could lead you to the hooch of a senior Vietcong cadre member? And then when you had the intelligence and the guide who would take you to his hooch, didn't you try to capture him if you could, kill him if you had to?"

"That was what we tried to do," I replied.

"When you did make a successful snatch, didn't you immediately try to see if you could get information from the guy you just grabbed that would lead to another good operation?"

"Yeah, that was usually the intent," I said. "It didn't always work out that way; but again, that's certainly what we tried to do."

"We do the same thing in Iraq," he replied, "only instead of jungle and grass hooches, our AO was concrete streets and buildings. You went out at night in boats, we used vehicles. You had the Seawolf gunships from HAL-3 [Helicopter Attack (Light) Squadron Three] and we had the Navy helos from HCS-4 and HCS-5."

He was making his point. HCS-4 and HCS-5 were, in fact, the direct descendants of HAL-3, the Huey gunships that supported SEALs throughout the Vietnam conflict. Our boats carried .50-caliber and

M60 machine guns, just like the SEAL Humvees and the current Special Boat Team craft. And perhaps the special operations AC-130 Spectre gunships that watch over today's SEALs are not unlike the Black Ponies of VAL-4 (Light Attack Squadron Four) who flew top cover for us when we patrolled inland from our boats. We didn't call them task units back then, but there were three or four firebases in Vietnam where SEALs lived, ate in someone else's chow hall, and set up a TOC-like operation to gather intelligence and plan missions. We liked operating at night much more than in the daytime, and our life blood was good, actionable intelligence.

"We still have a lot to learn," the squadron commander continued. "Most of our intelligence in Iraq came from outside sources. From what I've heard, in Vietnam the platoons developed their own intelligence networks and reacted on that intelligence. We need to do some of that so we don't have to be so reliant on others. We need to continue to work at being more proactive in the gathering of intelligence."

In Vietnam, we did in fact generate most of our own operational intelligence. My best operations were the result of my SEAL petty officers getting close to some village chief who provided us with a guide to take us to a weapons cache or point out the hooch where some VC cadre was sleeping that night. In that way, SEAL operations in Iraq were quite similar to those in Vietnam.

"We were in Vietnam for seven or eight years," I replied. "We had the time to develop those contacts and intelligence networks. Reporting assets were passed along from platoon to platoon. But our overall mission in Vietnam was to help make the South Vietnamese free so they could hold elections and govern themselves. In that regard, we failed. I can only hope that the SEAL task units and SEAL platoons operating in the current conflict will have a better outcome for the people of Iraq."

"My brother and I were worried that it would be all over in Iraq before we got there in April," Lieutenant John Rasmussen told me. I had been with him and his brother Phil, also a SEAL platoon commander, as their platoons conducted their Unit Level Training during their pre-deployment workup. The training of their two platoons is well documented in *The Finishing School*. "As things worked out, there was plenty of work for us when we got there." I remember getting an e-mail from their dad in October 2003. He was a platoon officer when I was in the teams. It simply read, "My boys are home and they are safe!"

Lieutenant John Rasmussen is currently deployed as a task unit commander. His brother, Lieutenant Phil Rasmussen, is preparing for his sixth SEAL deployment.

"This was my last platoon, and it was a good one to finish up with," Chief Petty Officer Cal Rutledge said. "The guys did a great job. Most of them will be staying in the Navy and with the platoon. With their experience, they're going to be simply awesome on their next squadron deployment."

Cal Rutledge has retired from the Navy. He is currently working for a contract security firm and is deployed overseas.

Petty Officers John Lopez and Frank Ross are still with the platoon. They are currently on deployment with a SEAL Squadron in the CENTCOM area. John Lopez is now a chief petty officer and has replaced Cal Rutledge as the platoon chief.

Senior Chief Don Serles is currently serving on a Naval Special Warfare Group staff. His duties include developing tactics and training to make future SEAL squadron deployments more effective. His advice is much sought after by those SEALs returning to Iraq on deployment.

CHAPTER 7

MAN DOWN

When a man goes down or goes missing during a mission, things change. The recovery of a brother warrior or a fellow citizen has a unique priority in our military culture, and certainly in our special operations culture. It is almost a sacred covenant that we do not leave one of our own behind or abandon his remains on the battlefield. When a man is missing or down, a different set of priorities and emotions begin to drive what happens next.

In this chapter, I will address those Navy SEAL missions that may be sensitive or classified due to the issues that relate to the closely held TTPs that govern or modify personnel recovery missions conducted by SEAL elements. The notion of never abandoning one of our own falls more heavily on our special operators because they often fight behind enemy lines and against numerically superior forces. Quite often, deployed SOF forces are beyond the reach of a strong conventional rescue force or may lack the ability to defer to higher command authority for a resolution. Men on the ground and junior commanders have to make timely and critical life-and-death decisions. These judgment calls are often made in the heat of battle and under a great deal of pressure. When a man goes down, or is unaccounted for, the complexion of the

A SEAL takes a prone security position in order to cover his teammates while they close on the target. *Courtesy of the U.S. Navy (Tim Turner)*

mission or an operation is altered. A leader, usually a junior leader, has to decide: "Do we continue the mission or abort? Do we go back for him now or later?" And then comes the toughest decision of all: "How many men do I put at how much risk to recover the remains of a fallen brother?"

Unfortunately, this is an issue that now has to be dealt with in the context of the current war on terrorism, which has added some new and disturbing wrinkles to an already difficult task. We are dealing with an enemy that is without state sponsorship and feels that it has a religious mandate to torture and murder prisoners and to abuse their corpses. We are not talking about Abu Ghraib–style humiliation or mistreatment. I'm speaking of dismemberment and mutilation. We first saw this with the dragging of bodies through the streets of Mogadishu, Somalia. Now we see videotaped beheadings of contractors, civilians, and Iraqi security forces taken hostage. It takes no stretch of the imagination to picture the inhumane treatment that awaits an American special forces warrior who has the misfortune to be taken alive by this enemy. A captured or fallen warrior knows his brothers will, if at all possible, come for him. Unfortunately, so does the enemy. They know we value the lives of our comrades and will make every effort to return for a fallen brother, dead or alive. This presents a whole other set of problems and priorities. Indeed, our most revered special operations warriors are those who have gone back for someone, or refused to leave a downed man in the face of overwhelming odds and certain death. The honor we afford those warriors is a basic tenet of our special operations culture.

Three Navy SEALs were awarded the Medal of Honor in Vietnam. Two of those awards involved the rescue of others in harm's way. In November 1972, Lieutenant Tom Norris and Petty Officer Nguyen Van Kiet made their way across the Demilitarized Zone into North Vietnam to find and bring out a downed Air Force pilot. After successfully locating and rescuing the pilot, they returned a few days later to also bring out his copilot. These stunning rescues were made in the final days of the war when the North Vietnamese Army was massing its forces above the DMZ for a final push south.

"We stayed in the water and traveled by sampan most of the way in and out," Tom Norris said of his storied mission. These courageous rescues were later made into the movie *BAT*21*, starring Danny Glover and Gene Hackman. "Sometimes we'd have to turn the boat upside down to hide under it in the tall grass along the bank. The North Vietnamese were marching south along the edge of the river, four abreast. There were even tanks moving along the roads. By the time we located each of the pilots, they were in pretty bad shape. Once they realized that I was an American and spoke English, they were able to rally and do what we told them. Kiet and I put them in the sampan and covered them with palm branches. There were NVA everywhere. We hid by day and passed ourselves off as fishermen at night. We were lucky as heck to get away with it once, let alone twice. If we hadn't gone after them, those two pilots would have become POWs—or worse." Tom's rescue of the two Air Force pilots stands as one of the great personnel recoveries in the history of special operations.

Tom Norris is an unprepossessing SEAL hero. Then, as now, he stands five-nine and weighs about 145 pounds. He was one of the fifteen survivors of BUD/S Class 45, the last winter class conducted at the Naval Amphibious Base in Norfolk, Virginia. Sixty-five men began that class. At the end of his Hell Week, Tom Norris weighed barely a hundred pounds. But he never quit; he never gave up. Likewise, he never gave up until he had both of those pilots safely out of North Vietnam. I was also in that last East Coast winter BUD/S training class. Tom and I were in the same boat crew during that very nasty and cold January Hell Week.

The rescue by Tom Norris was dramatic; the rescue *of* Tom Norris was equally so. Shortly after Tom had the downed Air Force pilots safely in friendly hands, he was leading a squad of South Vietnamese SEALs on a patrol just south of the DMZ. With him was another Navy SEAL, Petty Officer Mike Thornton. Mike, at six-two and 220 pounds, dwarfed his lieutenant. Tom's squad managed to ambush an enemy patrol, killing all of them. Only then did they learn that they'd ambushed the point element of an NVA battalion. The two Americans and their Vietnamese allies found themselves overwhelmingly outnumbered and outgunned. Their only option was to make a desperate fighting retreat to the shores of the South China Sea. When in trouble, and when they can, SEALs head for the water.

"We were out of ammo and options," Mike said of that desperate fight. "Tom told us to make a run for the surf while he covered us. I led the Vietnamese into the water and looked back for Tommy, but he was nowhere in sight. I shouted to the man closest to me, 'Where is the *Dai-uy* [Vietnamese for lieutenant]?' The guy said, '*Dai-uy* is dead.' I really didn't want to go back onto that beach, but what choice did I have? I couldn't leave Tommy—no way. So I left the water and retraced my way back over the beach. I found Tom lying at the dune line, and for a moment, I thought he was dead. The bad guys were closing in and surrounding us from three sides. Now I thought we were both dead."

As Tom covered his squad's retreat, an AK-47 round entered his right eye from the front and took out much of the right side of his skull. "I was still conscious when Mike got to me," Tom told me. "I remember that Mike grabbed me and said, 'Can you run?' I said, 'I can run, but I can't see.' He pulled me to my feet and said, 'Hang on and run like hell.' Then all I remember was running through sand and Mike pulling me along. When we hit the surf, he started dragging me through the breakers."

Mike had been wounded by an enemy grenade during the running firefight to the sea, and again on his second dash for the water. Yet he managed to keep Tom afloat and alive for six hours until they were picked up by a Navy warship. Mike refused treatment for his own wounds until he was sure Tom was being cared for. Tom Norris was given no chance for recovery. He was taken to Japan, where his parents were flown in to be with their dying son. But Tom recovered and went on to complete an illustrious career as an FBI field and undercover agent. For his gallant action in saving the life of his officer, Mike Thornton was awarded the Medal of Honor. It is the only time in history that a Medal of Honor recipient has been awarded the medal for saving the life of another recipient. It is my high honor to call both of these SEALs my brothers.

The last two Medals of Honor awarded to special operations warriors were for events that took place in Somalia, on the mean streets of Mogadishu. I personally feel that this was one of the most selfless actions in the history of SOF. Master Sergeant Gary Gordon and Sergeant First Class Randy Shughart had come to the aid of a downed Blackhawk helicopter. The crewmen, severely wounded and trapped in the wreckage of the helo, were at the mercy of the onrushing Somalian militia. When the situation became hopeless, Gordon and Shughart refused to leave their dead and wounded brothers. With nothing but their professional skill and courage, they stayed and fought to the death. When all their ammunition was finally gone, they used their rifles as clubs against their attackers. A great many Somalian militiamen died before the two Green Berets were finally overwhelmed. These gallant warriors embody the ethos of never leaving a wounded comrade. At Fort Bragg and Camp Mackall in North Carolina, where new men are tested and trained for Special Forces, the heroic legend of Master Sergeant Gordon and Sergeant First Class Shughart is passed on to future generations of Green Berets.

In the current war on terrorism, there have been a number of occasions for personnel recovery. Men have had to go in harm's way or back into harm's way for a fallen brother. In the naval service, the highest award for bravery is the Navy Cross, second only to the Medal of Honor. Two of these have been awarded to Navy SEALs, and on both occasions, they were the result of personnel recovery. Both involve extraordinary acts of bravery on the part of these two SEAL warriors. Since there are security issues that surround both of these actions, I will tell their stories with a great deal of care. Security issues aside, both are very private men, and both still have their guns in this fight.

The first of these actions took place in November 2001, barely two

months after the attacks of 11 September. In the early days of the liberation of Afghanistan, the Taliban and their al-Qaeda allies were resisting the movement of the Northern Alliance fighters every step of the
way. In the vast reaches of northern Afghanistan, there were pockets
of fierce resistance. Americans on the ground at that time were of
two persuasions: Army Special Forces and CIA personnel. Sprinkled
among them were some British special operators and Navy SEALs. All
of them worked closely with the Afghan resistance under the banner of
the Northern Alliance, whose members were fighting to reclaim their
country—or, to be more honest about it, their tribal territory. Early
on, CIA officers in the area had the best working knowledge of the
Northern Alliance and some of the best Arabic language skill. On the
ground, the CIA men and the special operators, with a few exceptions,
worked well together.

While a group of captured Taliban and al-Qaeda fighters were being
questioned at the prison at Mazar-e Sharif, fighting broke out and the
former captives gained the upper hand. Using smuggled weapons, they
broke into the prison armory. In short order, the former captives were
armed and in control of two-thirds of the prison compound. The large
prison courtyard became a battleground. In the fighting that followed,
two CIA operatives were separated from their element, and their status
was uncertain. In spite of repeated attempts to get to the two CIA men,
the rescue team that was sent for them was driven off with heavy volumes of fire from the former captives. As the battle raged, a lone Navy
SEAL, then working with a British commando unit at the prison,
crawled forward under heavy fire to assist the two fallen men. In part,
the citation reads that he ". . . was engaged continuously by direct
small arms fire, indirect mortar fire, and rocket propelled grenade fire.
He was forced to walk through an active anti-personnel minefield . . ."
They had located one of the CIA men and he was alive, but the second
man was still missing. After darkness settled onto the battlefield, the
SEAL again moved forward ". . . by himself under constant enemy fire
in an attempt to locate the injured citizen. Running low on ammuni-

tion, he utilized the weapons from deceased Afghans to continue his rescue attempt." In noncitation language, after dark he fought his way to the downed American, who had been killed in the fighting. When our SEAL ran out of ammunition, he took weapons from the enemy dead, many of whom he had personally consigned to their martyr's paradise, and kept going. He didn't know the dead American, but he willingly put his life at risk to reach him and recover his remains, those of the first CIA officer to be killed in Afghanistan. His name was Johnny Spann.

In the lobby of the CIA at Langley there is a permanent memorial plaque that commemorates those at the CIA who gave their lives in the service of their nation. There is always a vase of fresh-cut flowers resting under it. Many of the entries have a date and no name because the operation in which these brave men or women were lost is still classified. When I was last there, Johnny Spann's name was one of the more recent additions.

Months later in Afghanistan, in March 2002, the man on the ground was one of our own—a special operator. He was Petty Officer Neil Roberts. During Operation Anaconda in the Sahi-Kot Valley, Neil and his teammates comprised a reconnaissance element that was attempting to insert on a ten-thousand-foot mountaintop in support of a joint special operations mission. The helicopter took enemy RPG and small-arms fire on insertion. The helo, though badly damaged, managed to clear the insertion site and crash-land a few miles away. But as it veered away from the insertion, Neil Roberts fell from the helo and found himself on the ground, alone and surrounded by an entrenched enemy. His teammates at the helo crash site, as well as other SOF elements in the area, knew immediately that Neil Roberts was still fighting but was in mortal danger. He was heavily outnumbered, and time was against him.

The senior chief petty officer in charge of the element immediately set security at the helicopter crash site and directed the rescue of his team and the helo aircrew. But knowing that Neil was on the ground, alone and fighting for his life, the senior chief immediately asked to lead a team back to the original insertion site, in spite of the numerically superior force that held the ground. His citation reads: "After a treacherous helicopter insertion onto the mountain top, [the senior chief] led his team in a close-quarter firefight. He skillfully maneuvered his team and bravely engaged multiple enemy positions, personally clearing one bunker and killing several enemy within. His unit became caught in a withering crossfire from other bunkers and closing enemy forces. Despite mounting casualties, [the senior chief] maintained his composure and continued to engage the enemy until his position became untenable."

This story does not have a happy ending. This valiant rescue attempt by Neil Roberts's teammates was met and defeated by an overwhelming force and overwhelming firepower. It ended in a fourteen-hour running firefight in rugged mountain terrain and waist-deep snow. The senior chief did a magnificent job of caring for his wounded men and fighting off a determined enemy, but he had no choice but to withdraw. In the end, Neil Roberts fought the enemy alone and died in that fight. In his honor, the ridge that led to their mountain objective was informally named Roberts Ridge. In the larger fight to save Neil, and then to successfully recover his remains, *seven* special operators died on that mountain in Afghanistan. The loss of these men sent a shock wave through the special operations community, and a sobering look at the cost of going back for one of our own. Yet it remains an embedded tradition in SOF culture that the many, at substantial risk, will come back for the one.

There are three notable postscripts to the tragedy that took place during Operation Anaconda. The first was penned by Neil Roberts himself. He had left a letter with his wife with instructions that it should be opened if he failed to return. It read in part:

> *My time in the teams was special. . . . I loved being a SEAL. I died doing what made me happy. Very few people have the luxury of that.*

The balance of the letter was devoted to thanking his family for their love and support. Strong and courageous words from a magnificent warrior.

The second is the action that followed quickly on the heels of Operation Anaconda. It has been proven, by body count, that many al-Qaeda fighting in Afghanistan are not Afghans but Arabs, Chechens, Iranians, and Islamists from many other nationalities. The hard-core al-Qaeda that fought so fiercely in the Sahi-Kot Valley were thought to be Chechens. This was confirmed when some thirty of them were spotted leaving the valley on foot. SEALs and other special operators from Neil's unit managed to be inserted by helo in the path of the fleeing Chechens. Though this SEAL element was outnumbered two to one, they were now the ones waiting in ambush. After a fierce firefight and with only minor SEAL casualties, they killed them to a man. No quarter was asked, and none was given. I like to think of this action as Roberts's Revenge. Yet no amount of enemy dead can, or should, compensate Neil's family for their loss, nor the families of the seven brave special operators who died while trying to rescue their SOF brother. There was some degree of satisfaction in this ambush, however, for Neil's teammates who have to continue the fight in which he perished.

And, what of those warriors who survive a vicious firefight or a prolonged engagement such as Operation Anaconda? They know full well that there will be other firefights in which *they* might be the one to make that last long, refrigerated flight in a special C-17 for stateside burial. Yet many of them will go to great lengths to keep their guns in the fight, and this brings us to our third postscript. One of the men that the SEAL senior chief carried through the snow as they were driven off from the rescue of Neil Roberts had his lower leg severely mangled. He was rushed back to the States, but nothing could be done to save his leg. It was amputated just below the knee. A year later, this *same* SEAL warrior was back in Iraq and had his gun back in the fight—on a prosthetic leg. He was behind enemy lines conducting special operations as the 3rd Infantry Division and the 1st Marine Expeditionary Force pushed toward Baghdad.

"Not a problem," he told me. "The docs did a great job. I can do anything on the new leg I could do on my old one. I'm still good to go; I'm still in the deployment rotation."

In describing these combat actions and citations for bravery, one might get the impression of the fast-moving, well-choreographed combat action scenes from *Saving Private Ryan* or *The Dirty Dozen.* It's not like that in real combat. There is confusion, uncertainty, second-guessing, and mistakes—usually a lot of mistakes. Mostly, it's men who found themselves in a terrible situation and bravely did the best they could to go to the aid of a man down.

I know these guys well and they never cease to amaze me—never. I only hope our nation appreciates the quality of warriors that risk so much and willingly return to the fight, deployment after deployment. Sometimes I feel like Paul Newman's character in *Butch Cassidy and the Sundance Kid,* who asks, "Who are those guys?" Where do we find these kind of warriors and patriots? I seldom hear them complain—except, maybe, when they are asked to deploy to the South America or Africa theaters, which they feel is away from the center of action. They truly are a magnificent band of brothers.

To my knowledge, there is no protocol or standing mission order for what happens when a brother special operator is separated or goes missing. Often, the operational planning of a recovery is ad hoc due to time and circumstance. But there is a collective understanding that when this happens, we will do all in our power to recover that man—or that woman. As we have seen, this can lead to further casualties. It can draw rescue teams into the thick of the fight, perhaps by design on the part of a clever and ruthless enemy. And the pain and suffering can expand exponentially. For every warrior lost, there are family and extended family who must deal with that loss. Quite often, a personnel recovery or rescue mission is brought on by a combat action that has gone against us. It really doesn't matter why the man was lost or became separated. What does matter is that he has to be accounted for. It is important to the families of the dead, and it is important to the warriors who have to continue the fight. They know that if the fortunes of war go against them, their brothers will come—to save their lives if they can, or for their remains if they cannot, but they will come. General Hal Moore told the troopers of his Air Cavalry battalion who followed him into the Ia Drang Valley in 1965 that he would bring them home. And he did, every single one of them. Three hundred and five of those fine soldiers came home in caskets, but they all came home. Hal Moore did not let it stand there. Over the years, Hal and his wife, Julie, made time to meet with every family and asked to pray with them for their loss. (This past year, Hal lost his wife and companion of more than sixty years, and now we pray for him.)

There is a special mind-set in those who feel duty- and honor-bound to go on a personnel recovery mission. Occasionally, they may be members of a personnel recovery team, but usually they are not. Often, word simply comes in that a team has been hit and that it cannot extract on its own. The news may come as a shock, but it is not entirely unanticipated, nor entirely unplanned for. A SEAL element leader will stick his head in the platoon hut and say, "Saddle up, guys; there's a team in trouble. We launch in five minutes." There is not a more important or emotionally charged call to action than a personnel rescue mission. Still, amid the emotion and anticipation, the SEALs have to methodically gear up for battle. A personnel rescue mission, like any other special operation, depends on attention to detail and professional execution. In January 1971, at our firebase on the Cu Long River in lower Mekong Delta, I told my team to saddle up. There was a team in the field, and they had been hit.

A team of American and Vietnamese SEALs had gone on a mission the night before and had been ambushed on the way out. Their SEAL support craft had taken two RPGs that killed or wounded every man on the boat. The Vietnamese SEALs managed to fight their way ashore and set up a security perimeter. It wasn't until late morning that the boat, which miraculously was still afloat and running, got back to the base, where the crew let us know that their team had been hit. But most of the team were still at the ambush site, waiting for a rescue team. The previous night, I had been drinking beer with two good friends: Lieutenant Jim Thames, the senior Vietnamese SEAL adviser; and Lieutenant Bob Natter, the OIC of the SEAL boat unit detachment that supported the American and Vietnamese SEALs. Both Bob and Jim were on the operation. As I tore down the river in another SEAL support craft to the ambush site, I didn't know the fate of either of them.

The ambush site had been abandoned by the Vietcong, so the rescue was unopposed. There were twelve men on the operation; five were dead, and the others were badly wounded. Six were still in a defensive perimeter on the river. The senior Vietnamese petty officer and three of his men were dead. Jim Thames had died instantly when the first rocket hit the boat. Bob Natter, his eardrums blown out and his arms riddled with shrapnel, had been set on fire when the boat was hit. He and others who were still alive had gone over the side to extinguish themselves. A brave boat crewman (this was before we called them SWCCs) got to an extinguisher and put out the fire on the boat. He saved his boat. I've forgotten a great deal about that awful day, but two things are as clear as if they had happened yesterday. The first was the anxiety and anticipation of that ride to the ambush site, not knowing what we would find when we got there. Would there be a fight? Would the team of SEALs that went in ahead of me by helo be engaged? Were the VC setting up to hit us on the way in? *Who was still alive and who was not?* The second was sitting in the back of the Navy Huey as I took Jim Thames up to our parent base. He was in a body bag, but his head was in my lap. I'd known Jim only for about six months. I had known Bob for over six years; we were classmates and close friends from the Naval Academy. And I thought, What could I have done to have kept this from happening? If I'd been on that boat, could I have made a difference, or would it be me in the body bag? Jim Thames was on his way home. So was Bob Natter, but he recovered from his wounds and went on to become a four-star admiral and to command the Atlantic Fleet and the Fleet Forces Command. *C'est la guerre.*

Most personnel recovery operations are ad hoc in nature—men down, men unaccounted for, saddle up and go. These operations are not done without some form of planning, but clearly they are mounted with much dispatch. There may be risks taken that would not be acceptable for other kinds of operations. Most special operations teams have the skills to recover captured personnel—POWs. Some special mission units have had enhanced POW recovery training associated with their predeployment workup. When possible—that is, when time and proximity allow—these units will be called in to deal with POW rescues. These are difficult and dangerous missions. The lives of both rescuer and rescuee are at risk. Our nation has had some notable successes and failures in this area.

Among the most notable of these successes was the rescue of 513 American POWs from the Japanese prison camp at Cabanatuan in the Philippines during the closing days of World War II. It was one of the Rangers' finest hours. After a long foot patrol through Japanese lines, they set up on the camp at night, executed a clever diversion, and made a coordinated attack. The main assault was led by the unflappable Robert Prince, a quiet Stanford graduate. It was over in twenty minutes. The Rangers escorted and carried the freed Americans back through enemy lines to safety. It was a magnificent raid—a classic that has been studied by generations of special operators. This daring rescue is the subject of the bestseller *Ghost Soldiers,* by Hampton Sides.

On November 21, 1970, a contingent of Army Special Forces launched a personnel recovery operation into North Vietnam. It was an airborne assault on the American POW compound at Son Tay. Tactically, the operation was as textbook in its execution as the Cabanatuan raid. But a typhoon blowing in from the Pacific had caused the North Vietnamese to move the American POWs a few days earlier. The raiders stormed into an empty compound. While it had been a superb piece of planning and execution, no Americans were brought out. I can only imagine the disappointment of those Army raiders as they secured the compound and found no fellow Americans.

Operation Eagle Claw, mounted on 25 April 1980, was a bold rescue attempt to free the fifty-three U.S. Embassy personnel held in Tehran. The Americans were taken hostage by the Iranians after the fall of the shah and the return of Ayatollah Khomeini. The mission was launched from the aircraft carrier *Nimitz* by a Joint Special Operations Task Force. Problems stalked the mission from the beginning, including glaring communications and intelligence shortcomings. The mission plan called for the forces to stage at an intermediate base called Desert One, located some two hundred miles from Tehran. A ground collision of two aircraft with the loss of both at Desert One led the mission commander to abort the mission. This final indignity in the last year of President Jimmy Carter's administration ultimately led to the formation of the U.S. Special Operations Command for the conduct of military special operations. The hostages were released shortly after Ronald Reagan took office. Many feel that this taking of American hostages was one of the initial actions in the current conflict with Islamic fundamentalists. So that brings us to the current fight, specifically the ongoing operations in Afghanistan and Iraq.

As the American armored columns raced up the Tigris and the Euphrates toward Baghdad, the logistics train that supported that effort was enormous. One of those vital support convoys was badly strung out and running about twelve hours behind its lead armor units. It lost radio contact with the other support vehicles, and made a wrong turn near Nasiriyah. On 23 March, three days into the war, several vehicles from the Army's 507th Maintenance Company were now in deep trouble. As a result of an ambush, the American vehicles were severely mauled by RPG and automatic-weapons fire. All of them were destroyed or wrecked, and the Americans aboard killed, wounded, or captured. One soldier who was severely wounded was Private First Class Jessica Lynch. Her capture and subsequent treatment at Saddam Hussein Hospital, and then her dramatic rescue by special operations forces on 1 April, quickly became a national focus. There were few details about the rescue other than some infrared video footage of Pfc. Lynch being taken down a stairwell and onto a special operations helicopter, and that there were Navy SEALs in the rescue team.

At the time, I was in New York—one of those talking heads on

Fox and MSNBC offering technical comment during the nonstop, twenty-four-hour coverage of the war. The saga of Jessica Lynch and her rescue became a media circus and a case study in news management—or mismanagement. There was a great deal of hype and hyperbole surrounding Pfc. Lynch's actions when she was captured and those of her rescuers in securing her release. On camera, I was often asked about the men who came for her—the armed men we saw on TV in green-lit stairwells of that hospital. When it became known that they were Navy SEALs, the network anchors pressed me for details. Who were these men? What unit did they come from? Those details were and are classified, of course. Amid all the speculation, the only comment I offered that I knew to be true was this: The men who rescued Jessica Lynch were practicing for that mission, and missions like it, when she was in grade school. These were serious men in a very serious business.

The action that led to her capture, her treatment at two Iraqi hospitals—one military and the other civilian—her rescue, her repatriation, and her recovery have been analyzed to death. The media's handling of the event is a story unto itself. Let's step past all that and look at this from the special operator's perspective—from the perspective of the team leader who was tasked with this personnel recovery. The mechanics and procedures that govern such an operation—the all-important TTPs—are very closely held. I have no knowledge or direct access to men on that particular recovery, but I know what goes through a team leader's mind as he prepares for such a mission. I did this a time or two, years ago and in a very different setting.

The crux of any recovery mission comes down to three basic elements: accomplish the mission, don't get any of your men hurt, and avoid collateral damage—which means don't get any noncombatants hurt. It's that simple and that difficult. In this case, the mission was the safe recovery of Pfc. Lynch. On a recovery mission, the SOF imperatives of surprise and violence of action still apply, only the violence has to be measured and appropriate. And recovery operations are always dicey, in that time usually works against the rescuers. The more time the rescuers take to gather intelligence and prepare, the more time the enemy has to move his prisoner, kill his prisoner, or prepare for the arrival of the rescuer.

The team that stormed into Saddam Hussein Hospital in Nasiriyah had a good knowledge of the building and the exact room where Lynch was being kept. That she was being afforded as good care as was available in an Iraqi hospital and that there was no opposition probably did little to alter the tactics of the rescue team. The team leader had to prepare his men for active opposition and use tactics that would lead to mission success and that best ensured the safety of all. I found it amusing that the medical staff, when questioned later by reporters about the team's entry into the hospital, found it odd that the rescuers refused help, like the keys to locked doors or the offer to lead them to Lynch's room. They thought it strange that the special operators kicked doors, tossed flash-bang grenades into rooms prior to entry, and leapfrogged down corridors in full-tilt tactical fashion. After all, the staff knew all the soldiers had left; they even told the Americans they had left.

That SEAL team leader was focused on his task. His mission was to secure Jessica Lynch, and so he wasted no time in getting to her room and getting the medical personnel on his team to prepare her for movement. After she was secured and ready for transport, they were only half-finished. He had to get her safely out of the building and aboard the waiting helo. Again, he and his team wasted no time in doing this. Time on target also works against the rescuer. The aggressive SWAT-like tactics used by the team, even in a hospital staffed only with caregivers, was standard procedure. The team leader had to play the game like there was a Fedayeen Saddam down every corridor and behind every door. As the operation wore on, I can imagine that this leader began to realize that there was no active resistance in the hospital. It didn't matter. His standard procedures are to move with authority under full tactical discipline, start to finish. In this way, he did all in his

power to ensure the safety of his men and the safety of the noncombatants in the hospital. In the subsequent scrutiny of the Lynch rescue,
which has been exhaustive, a great deal has been made of the Rambo-
like procedures and shock tactics of the rescue force. Why, the investigative reporters ask, was there such a fuss to take down what proved
to be an unarmed hospital? Was not the hospital staff compliant?
Didn't they give assurances to the raiders that they would meet no opposition? Why, indeed?

In special operations, there is an old saying: Hope for the best, but
plan for the worst. That is exactly what that team leader did in the rescue of Jessica Lynch. I can, from experience, tell you that he did a lot
of playing the "what if" game. What if they, the bad guys, know that
we are coming and this is a setup? What if they have RPGs and are
waiting for the helos when they slow and flair to land? What if they
have rigged doors, access ways, or even the captive's room with explosives? Is there a suicide bomber waiting to rush down a corridor at
them? What if there is a command-detonated bomb or IED waiting at
the exit? That team leader thought about this all through the planning
process and the rehearsals, if there was time for them, and it never left
his mind while he executed his mission. What if? What if? What if?

In the press reports, the rescue had gone off without a hitch. Pfc.
Lynch was safely in American hands and the citizens of Palestine, West
Virginia, rejoiced. The remains of nine other soldiers were recovered in
or near the hospital, so there was confirmation and closure for those
families and friends. While the nation cheered for Jessica, my thoughts
went immediately to those men in the recovery team and their leader.
As soon as that extraction helo cleared hospital grounds and gained
enough altitude to be safe from ground fire, imagine the pride and
sense of relief they felt. *We did it! We got in, we accomplished the mission, and got out. And nobody got hurt!* It's a feeling that is hard to
put into words. It's a sense of pride at saving one of your own, and it's
a validation of your professional military skills. It's the World Series
and the Super Bowl. Certainly, there is a measure of relief. But more to

the point, you have just cheated death in the company of warrior brothers, and that sense of accomplishment is almost narcotic. It is also short-lived. After the high fives and some attaboys coming off the extraction helo, there are debriefings and after-action reports that need immediate attention. In the hot washup following a mission, no matter how successful, there is a sober look at what went well and what could have been done better. Even with the textbook operations, there is always room for improvement. But somewhere along the way, the task group commander or task unit commander pulled that team leader aside and said, "Good job, Lieutenant. That was a nice piece of work." That may be all. The members of the team that brought out Jessica Lynch will get no public recognition for their effort. They knew that going in; it is the lot and life of the quiet professional warrior.

In the days that followed, America rejoiced, and the media converged on the Lynch family like livestock at a feedlot trough. It was made public that U.S. Marines and Rangers were used in a diversionary role and as a blocking force. Official sources put Navy SEALs in as the rescue team, but did not elaborate on who or how many. And there was immediate speculation about active resistance and heroic action. I have learned not to speculate about those things. What happens on the ground in a high-visibility operation and how it gets played in the media are two very different things. I was pretty sure of two things, which I have since validated through the old warriors' grapevine. The first was that the team that recovered Jessica Lynch was indeed a mature, experienced, and very, very professional force. The second was that while America swooned and the media did its Hollywood thing with this event, the guys who made it happen checked their equipment, reset their radios, and focused on their next operational tasking. They may or may not have been aware of the spectacle that was unfolding here at home, but I know they were far too busy to pay it much attention. Again, it's part of the role of a quiet professional warrior.

It's not going to get any easier for those who may be asked to make personnel recoveries in the future. With the rise of the Islamists and their contempt for life and modern Western values, we can expect neither mercy nor civil treatment for Americans who become prisoners of war. The policy of nations is now influenced by hostages and beheadings. For those who oppose us in this fight, hostage taking and executions are not a by-product of war, they are a tactic of warfare. This enemy may take hostages with the sole purpose of trying to lure a rescue team to their death. They may plan well ahead of time to kill the hostage and themselves in an effort to do this. In short, the enemy knows full well the value of taking hostages and the value we place on their safe recovery. Will this bring a change in our national and warrior cultures that urges us to risk many to go to the aid of one? Perhaps. In some ways I hope so, entirely for selfish reasons. I personally know a great many young men who may be asked to perform one of these dangerous and difficult rescue missions. However this deadly game unfolds, the guns in the fight, those SOF professionals who may have to board the insertion helos, will adapt and tactically evolve to meet this threat—to maintain the element of surprise and violence of action. May God watch over them as they go downrange to save others.

EPILOGUE

This book has been a selected review of Navy SEAL operations in what we now refer to as the war on terrorism. It is by no means a complete accounting of their operational history in this fight, or even one that could address many of the classified combat operations that SEALs have performed. I believe that it is representative of what these dedicated and talented warriors have done and are continuing to do as this work goes to press. The past several years have redefined the SEALs and their role as the maritime component of our modern special operations forces.

The Navy SEALs have their roots in the Underwater Demolition Teams that served in World War II and Korea, but they were born as a force in 1962, during the Cold War, to fight Communism and Communist insurgents. For the first ten years, almost a quarter of their existence, they were committed in Vietnam, much as the SEALs of today are committed in Afghanistan and Iraq. The development and maturity of the Navy SEALs has largely evolved in two venues: the Vietnam era and the era of the fundamentalist Islamists. Not to say that there were not some important contributions of SEAL operators during the intervening years. Navy SEALs saw combat in regional undertakings such as Panama and Grenada, and were very much a part of the Gulf

---

A SEAL element moves into an enemy-controlled area. SEALs will continue to maintain their maritime skills, but the war on terrorism may keep them active on land. *Courtesy of the U.S. Navy (Eric Logsdon)*

217

War in 1991. They remain involved in the peacekeeping and stabiliza-tion of the Balkans. And there have been any number of foreign inter-nal defense missions on which they have deployed in hostile—if not combat—environments. Navy SEALs have been killed while serving as advisers to elected governments resisting insurgencies. But for direct sustained combat, there are still only Vietnam and the current war on terror, with the Vietcong and the North Vietnamese Army now re-placed by al-Qaeda and the Islamists.

Yet there is a crucial difference between these two foes: The Viet-cong and the NVA never threatened Los Angeles or New York. Neither one of those Communist, Cold War–era adversaries had the ability or the willingness to strike us here at home. That, if nothing else, is what makes this fight so much more important. But there is also a difference in the generation of SEALs that oppose this new threat. As a Vietnam-era SEAL who has spent a great deal of time with the current crop of Navy SEALs, I can say, without reservation, that they are better than we ever were. It's a good thing. Today's Navy SEALs have a far more challenging and important task than we ever did.

One thing Vietnam-era SEALs share with the current guns in the fight is the narrow focus on a particular enemy. Back then, SEALs could do a lot of things—direct action, strategic reconnaissance, un-conventional warfare, and foreign internal defense—and they still do them today. Back then, SEALs commuted to the job site in the same ways that they do today—from or under the sea, through the air, or across the land. But when you are in a protracted struggle with a single enemy, you tend to focus your efforts and training on the enemy you have to fight. During the Vietnam era, we still parachuted and main-tained our combat scuba capability, but our focus was jungle warfare. The deployments that counted were combat deployments to Vietnam, and our enemy was the Vietcong infrastructure. Our predeployment training focused on finding enemy leaders and killing them, primarily in the Mekong Delta. On deployment, we commuted to work in boats, SEAL support craft driven by our Special Boat Team brothers, often paddling the last few miles to the target in sampans. Sometimes we walked down jungle trails with an indigenous guide or a paid informant showing us the way. Occasionally, we operated from helicopters, and quite often we patrolled across rice dikes or waded through mangrove swamps. Most of the work was at night. Among the most effective Navy SEALs of that era were the advisers. SEALs served as advisers to the South Vietnamese SEALs and the Provincial Reconnaissance Units. In the final tally, the PRUs and their SEAL advisers were the deadliest forces of their era. Almost everything we did back then was direct action, after sunset, and usually in areas controlled by the enemy. It was miserable work. I can still remember returning to our firebase from those nights in the mangroves, muddy from head to foot and covered with leeches. But we learned to be as good, if not better, than the enemy on his own ground, and that made all the difference.

Today, the focus of SEAL operations is Afghanistan and Iraq. SEALs are in the mountains, towns, and cities of those nations, because that's where the bad guys are. They are deployed elsewhere as well, as our current foe is a global one. After 11 September, when the enemy fled to the mountains, SEALs became mountain fighters; and when the enemy hid in the cities, SEALs became urban warriors. And when new technologies or perishable intelligence presented opportunities with short lead times, SEALs became adept at compressing their reaction time to take advantage of this real-time intelligence capability. That's what SEALs are best at: changing tactics and adapting methods to meet new threats and changing environments. One thing has remained constant from Vietnam up through the intervening years to the current conflict: Good intelligence makes for good operations. It was as true then for my platoon in the mangrove swamps of the Mekong as it is for today's SEALs, whether they are in the mountains of Afghanistan or the streets of Baghdad. And it's hard to find good intelligence without help from the locals. Most of my success in Vietnam was due to good intelligence and the help of the ex-VC scouts who led us through enemy territory.

The Vietcong and al-Qaeda also share a certain methodology that allows for a tyranny of the minority. Ten men with guns can intimidate a village or a neighborhood of two hundred, so long as those ten are prepared to kill indiscriminately. They can compel the two hundred to give them shelter and safe haven, to oppose a reformist government, and to give over their sons and daughters for their cause. The Communists did it for an ideology; the Islamists, for their religion. Both are about power and control. In either case, the goal is to establish a tyranny of the minority based on resistance to any form of democracy, whether political or economic. Given the choice, without oppression or coercion, people will choose freedom every time. We have only to witness the power of the ballot box in Iraq. The people there may hold on to their ideologies and their religion, but they still want a vote and a say in their own affairs. Today, the Islamists cannot tolerate a secular Iraq on the model of a secular Turkey. If that kind of freedom takes hold, they are finished. But if they prevail, they are on their way to spreading their brand of theocratic rule over the Middle East. And that is why so much is on the table in Iraq, for the Iraqis and for us.

So, going forward, what is the future for Navy SEALs in this struggle? Indeed, what role will SOF play as this war unfolds? Not an easy question as SOF, along with its component commands, is experiencing some dramatic changes. It is a very dynamic landscape, both operationally and politically. In 1962, President John F. Kennedy ordered the Army, the Navy, and the Air Force to develop capabilities in unconventional warfare. This led to the birth of the Navy SEALs, but it was not until 1986, when Congress directed the formation of the U.S. Special Operations Command, that SOF had a legitimate chair at the DoD table. The new organization would be headed by a four-star commander in chief, or CINC, and would have parity, at least on the organizational chart, with warfighting commands like Pacific Command, European Command, or Central Command. The creation of SOCOM was an unpopular decision among the service components who have traditionally resisted elite units, and especially those elite units who seriously compete for talent and treasury. There was even resistance within the SOF components that were made to leave their parent service for duty under the fledgling SOCOM. I can remember senior SEAL commanders saying that we would regret the day that the SEALs left the protective skirts of the Navy; they said we would be awash in Army green as the smallest service component of the new joint command.

There are certainly a lot more green Army uniforms than blue Navy uniforms at the Special Operations Command headquarters at MacDill Air Force Base in Tampa. In reality, the working uniform at the headquarters is battle dress utilities, or BDUs, generally referred to as cammies—albeit starched cammies and spit-shined boots at the headquarters. But in the decade and a half that followed the birth of SOCOM, the force has thrived and matured. With the fall of the Berlin Wall and the rise of terrorism in the 1990s, the traditional armed forces saw the new Special Operations Command as a useful tool against the emerging threat of terrorism. The new upstart command still drew less than 1 percent of the DoD budget and had at best, a limited warfighting role. In reality, SOCOM—and by extension, the Naval Special Warfare Command—were training commands. SOCOM was a stateside support command and responsible only for the training of special operations forces. WARCOM's role as the SOF maritime component was not to fight wars, but to train Navy SEALs and to provide combat-ready SEALS and Special Boat Teams to the theater commanders. So the theater commanders had Rangers and Special Forces to support their major ground components and SEALs to put aboard ships for fleet duty or to assist with amphibious operations. There are special mission SOF units that have always operated independently, but conduct of war still rested with the theater CINCs.

Theater commanders often don't understand their SOF warriors or how to use them, so they are prone to go with what they know—their conventional forces. A case in point was the Gulf War. General Norman Schwarzkopf, the CENTCOM commander, kept his SOF forces on a tight leash while he readied his conventional forces for an armored dash across southern Iraq. To some degree he was right; entrenched armored opposition needs to be met with armor—armor and a good dose of American airpower. That said, I don't believe Schwarzkopf really wanted a lot to do with his SOF assets. The general used his Army Special Forces in a main-force reconnaissance role and to keep an eye on the Kurds in northern Iraq, but little else. He employed his assigned SEALs for downed-pilot recovery and to feign an amphibious landing on the Kuwaiti beaches. In spite of the picture of a SEAL desert patrol vehicle rolling into Kuwait City on the cover of *Newsweek,* they had little to do with resolving the issue. SOF operations can sometimes be high-risk undertakings, and General Schwarzkopf saw their behind-the-lines capability as a source of potential POWs or casualties. Our commanders often ask, and the American people have come to expect, that our armed forces engage and kill the enemy without American casualties and without an Al Jazeera camera crew providing live coverage of manacled American POWs. This level of expectation leads the public to think that we will always be able to exchange *our* technology for *their* blood. Nice work if you can get it—or, stated differently, if you can get your enemy to go along with the idea. As for special operations in the Gulf War, I think Schwarzkopf neither understood nor trusted his SOF operators.

General Tommy Franks, on the other hand, had an excellent feel for what his SOF assets could and could not do. And more important, perhaps, his secretary of defense and his commander in chief listened to him. Franks knew that Afghanistan could easily turn into a tar baby and soak up his conventional armor and infantry, as it had Soviet armor and infantry for close to a decade. So he sent his Army Special Forces to lead the Northern Alliance to victory, a role for which they were superbly suited. This proved to be a classic unconventional warfare operation. A few hundred SOF personnel, primarily Army Special Forces working closely with the CIA, organized the Northern Alliance into an effective irregular force. Then, making use of precision munitions, they directed the rout of the Taliban. There was a lot of pressure on Tommy Franks to bring in more conventional forces, but he demurred. It was an SOF game start to finish with the Green Berets taking center stage. When it came time to take down Iraq, Franks let the 1st Marine Expeditionary Force and the 3rd Infantry Division make the dash to Baghdad with a British division to guard their rear. On the eve of battle, when his 4th Infantry Division was denied a staging area in Turkey, he sent Army Special Forces and the CIA to work with the Kurds to open a second front in northern Iraq. Before commencing main-force action, he sent SOF units into the Iraqi western desert to destroy Scud sites and blow up bridges—bridges that the mobile Iraqi units would need if they were to block the 1st MEF and the 3rd ID on their way to Baghdad. SEALs and British Royal Marines, as we saw in chapter 5, were able to seize and secure the Iraqi oil infrastructure intact. Yet with American and British divisions massed on the Kuwaiti border and SOF forces loose inside Iraq, Franks still managed to direct his conventional forces in such a way as to achieve a measure of tactical surprise.

A word about the theater commander who engineered the Afghan and Iraqi campaigns. Tommy Franks is a measured, rawboned, nononsense man from Midland, Texas. An artilleryman, he hasn't the flash and dash of an infantry or armored commander. The task of taking Afghanistan and then Iraq were thrust on him without much warning or time to prepare. And in Donald Rumsfeld, he had a strongminded, overbearing, and often difficult boss. Many in uniform admire Rumsfeld, but few really like working for him. The war plans Franks developed for both campaigns were not an easy sell for this understated Texan. But each, in its conception and application, was brilliant. America likes colorful military leaders. When compared to an imperial MacArthur, a theatrical Patton, or the taciturn and mercurial Schwarzkopf, the publicity-shy Franks might seem like a letdown. But seldom has a commander so ably and effectively served his nation. He did it perfectly in Afghanistan, and he did it perfectly again in Iraq—right man, right place, right time. I believe he is a strategic and tactical genius without modern peer, and I think that history will rank him as one of our greatest military leaders. The fact that he avoided publicity and shunned the press during both conflicts only made him more endearing. We were privileged to have a warrior leader of his stature and competence to lead our forces during the opening campaigns of this war.

While Saddam Hussein hadn't the talent or the force to stop Franks, he had learned something since his army and his Republican Guard units had been carved up a decade earlier. The resistance Saddam placed in front of Tommy Franks's armored columns was both token and suicidal. While talking tough and waiting for France and Germany to intervene on his behalf, and camouflaging his ability to produce WMDs, Saddam was preparing for an insurgent campaign. I believe that he knew he did not have a prayer of keeping the Americans out of Baghdad, but he did harbor the notion that he could make an occupation force pay—that the American people would have little patience for a protracted struggle. And not being a fool, he probably rightly predicted that al-Qaeda (who reviled Saddam only slightly less than George Bush) and a whole host of stateless insurgents would be drawn to an American-occupied Iraq. He did not, however, foresee that a relentless SOF special missions element would drag him out of a hole and throw him in jail.

The days of defeating armies and occupying capital cities may be over, but not the need to project force in regions where our enemies take up residence. What the 1st MEF and the 3rd ID accomplished in Iraq will not soon be forgotten by those in power in Damascus and Tehran. Nor will our difficulties in trying to bring stability and peace after any cessation of major combat operations. We now face an enemy that will not put an army in the field, nor will it conform to international boundaries. I don't see an end to the regional threats and the need for theater commanders who must deal with those threats. But there may be an end to our theater CINCs' role as the end users of our SOF components. Two years ago, Donald Rumsfeld ordered the commander of the Special Operations Command to prepare to conduct special operations as a *supported* commander. In order to better prosecute the war on al-Qaeda and their sponsors, state or otherwise, the secretary ordered SOCOM to develop the ability to take the lead in fighting this enemy. This means that an SOF commander may well be given a regional responsibility for conducting operations against terrorists, and the assigned conventional Army, Navy, Air Force, and Marine units in that region will *support* that SOF commander. This announcement was met with much incredulity by the regional CINCs and by General Charles Holland—then Commander, U.S. Special Operations Command. SOCOM was unprepared to field the command-and-control elements, and the battle staffs, to fight a regional war. While Holland backpedaled, he put the machinery in motion, made possible by additional DoD funding, to begin the training and development of the command and staff components needed for SOCOM to function as a supported command. This is easier said than done. Fighting wars takes a great deal of vision, experience, and talent. The Tommy Frankses of the world don't come along all that often. And it takes time to design battle plans and to perfect those plans in military training exercises. Any SOF commander who goes forward to manage the fight on a regional scale as a supported commander will have to have a broad understanding of the conventional forces that support his SOF elements and how best to use them. What will be his relationship with the regional CINC? And who will that SOF commander be?

Each theater CINC has a senior SOF officer on his staff—his SOC, or special operations commander. During the Afghan campaign that officer was Rear Admiral Bert Calland. He held the title of SOCCENT—Special Operations Commander, Central Command. He worked directly for Tommy Franks, and it worked well. The Army Special Forces and CIA elements that managed the Northern Alliance's ouster of the Taliban worked under Calland's direction, but under Franks's command. So did the SEALs, the U.S. Marines, the GROM, and the Danish and German special operators assigned to Captain Bob Harward with Task Force K-Bar at Kandahar. Since the Afghan campaign,

Calland has moved on to serve as Commander, Naval Special Warfare Command, and is now the associate director of Central Intelligence for Military Support at the CIA. I think Rumsfeld's direction that SOCOM prepare to fight as a supported command reflected the secretary's desire that his special operations forces not be restricted by conventional command thinking. This would allow them to be more agile and flexible, and therefore more effective in pursuing al-Qaeda. The idea is not a bad one, if it can hold up in practice. I would hope that the staff and senior command talent are being developed within the SOF community to meet these dramatically enhanced responsibilities.

Rumsfeld's vision for an extended role for SOF was not only reinforced by the findings of the 9/11 Commission, but that body called for an expansion and an acceleration of the vision. The commission recommended that the "lead responsibility for directing and executing paramilitary operations, whether clandestine or covert, should shift to the Department of Defense." So the U.S. Special Operations Command, in addition to undertaking theater and even global command responsibilities in this war, may be asked to take a larger role in developing allied paramilitary fighters, a key element in developing moderate Islamic resistance to the fundamental Islamists. If we do not find a way to empower and motivate the moderates to oppose the fundamentalists, then we will certainly lose this war and all of Islam to the dark, regressive world of the Islamists. Yet we cannot allow 300 million souls and the wealth of the Middle East to be controlled by someone like Musab al-Zarqawi. In dealing with that volatile region, we must never forget Lawrence of Arabia's dictum: "It is their land and their war, and your time here is limited." We have to help and encourage the moderate Islamic majority to stand against the extremists.

The future of covert activity is a whole other kettle of fish with significant operational and political dimensions. SOF and the CIA worked well together on the ground in Afghanistan and Iraq. Nevertheless, the 9/11 Commission concluded, "The United States cannot afford to build two separate capabilities for carrying out secret mili-

tary operations . . . and secretly training foreign military and paramilitary forces." The commission clearly favored an expansion of the DoD
in these areas.

Before we go further, let's define some things. A clandestine operation is one that is carried out in secrecy, which is often necessary to
achieve the all-important element of surprise. A covert action, as
defined by U.S. law, is designed "to influence political, economic or
military conditions abroad where it is intended that the role of the
United States Government not be apparent or acknowledged." Covert
activity under the aegis of the CIA must, with few exceptions, be authorized by a written presidential finding in advance and followed by
the notification of the House and Senate intelligence committees, again
in advance. The U.S. military does not operate under these restrictions,
nor with this oversight. The law that governs covert activity does not
address what has broadly come to be known as "traditional military
activities" that in time of war may be undertaken in anticipation of
hostilities or preceding them. Tommy Franks sent SOF elements into
Iraq well ahead of main-force operations. Their operations in some
cases may have met the test of a covert action, but under the law, it did
not require a presidential finding or congressional notification. These
activities came under the blanket heading of "preparing the battle-
space." SOF is now being asked to lead the fight with an enemy who is
a nonstate player and who does not respect international boundaries.
How will the line be drawn between traditional military activity and
covert activity by the military? And just how long are the tentacles of
the Pentagon's secret Strategic Support Branch, instituted by Secretary
Rumsfeld to lessen his reliance on the CIA?

This leads to the question of who will provide oversight for any future SOF paramilitary or covert activity. It is easy for a politician to
call for more funding for SOF or for a committee to recommend that
SOF be given a broader charter in the fight. But what laws will govern
when clandestine operations become covert activity—when the nature
of the enemy demands that effective action may indeed cross the line

from traditional military activity to covert action? This consideration alone will have a bearing on an important aspect in the war on terrorism. I see a food fight looming between Congress, the State Department, and the DoD on this one.

Then there is the sticky question of the special operators themselves. Are they ready to expand their paramilitary activity and move into the covert arena? In his role as a supported commander, General Bryan Brown—a veteran Special Forces warrior and a fine commander—has said that he will "plan and selectively execute combat missions against terrorists and terrorist organizations around the world." I can only assume that these actions may take place in sovereign nations, with or without their knowledge, and that we may want to avoid U.S. government attribution for these actions. Case in point: When we do find bin Laden, do we want him killed by a U.S./SOF hunter-killer team or by the locals? What if bin Laden's exact location is in Syria, where we are not welcome, or in Pakistan, where our presence would be embarrassing for the Musharraf government? Getting bin Laden under these conditions could be a classic covert action. That action may require that our special operators act while not in uniform and with no official portfolio. When they do this, they do so with no international protections such as the Geneva Convention. If we continue down this road, then SOF has to come to terms with operating, as the Agency guys say, "out in the cold." Our SEALs, Rangers, and Special Forces joined the military to serve as special operations soldiers. Are they prepared to take the next step and become covert operators without official portfolio? Most men in uniform did not sign up to be spies.

It is one thing for Secretary Rumsfeld or his successor to direct that SOF take the lead in the war on terrorism. Making that a functional reality is quite another. Competent special operations forces are not something that can be grown overnight. Special operations personnel have a series of maxims for this: They are called the SOF Truths, and they've been around the SOF community for years. Perhaps the policy makers in Washington need to be aware of these as well:

Humans are more important than hardware.

Quality is more important than quantity.

SOF cannot be mass-produced.

Competent SOF cannot be created after the emergency arises.

Unfortunately, the last of these truths may not be so valid, because this war—this emergency—is likely to be with us for some time. The bottom line is that it takes time to make these guys. The average age of the men in a deploying SEAL platoon is about twenty-eight; that of those in a Special Forces ODA team, thirty-two. The special mission units are typically more mature and more seasoned. This is a business where experience counts. These components are not like a conventional Army or Marine platoon with a capable but inexperienced first lieutenant and a cadre of competent, battle-tested NCOs leading a group of nineteen-year-olds. Like night follows day, seasoned SOF operators leave the service, through retirement and for other opportunities. If SOF is to take on expanded duties, then we will have to grow the force, and that will take time. It will also take money; these warriors do not come cheap. You can train a surprising number of soldiers, sailors, or marines for what it costs to find, train, and develop one competent SOF operator.

The special operations force currently stands at about fifty thousand personnel. Only about a third of those, or some sixteen thousand, are "shooters," men capable of ground special operations. Stretching it for a limited time, we can keep a third of those deployed and in the field. That comes to some fifty-three hundred on deployment, with perhaps four thousand of those at the tip of the spear in Afghanistan and Iraq. Breaking it down further, there is something on the order of two thousand Navy SEALs on active duty, which includes training cadres and those at the senior command and staff level. Keeping five hundred trained SEAL operators deployed and on the job is pressing our capability at this time. Regarding funding, special operations now commands close to $7 billion of the $400+ billion defense budget. For the force that is being positioned to take the lead in the war on terrorism, that seems a little low. But the secretary of defense, be it Rumsfeld or another, has no magic appropriations wand, nor has he the discretion to reallocate funds from other DoD programs on any scale. Special operations may be an obsession with this secretary, but there are two forces that will fight him every step of the way.

The first is the conventional military. The admirals and the generals are slow to change; but to be fair about it, they have their service responsibilities and their own soldiers, sailors, airmen, and marines to look after. They always have and will continue to do what they can to protect their fleets, divisions, and squadrons, including finding the means to fund them. That said, the SEALs probably have the best relationship with their parent service. Unlike the Army, there is no shared capability or potential mission overlap between the blue-water Navy and the Navy SEALs. Perhaps the strongest competitor for the special operations dollar within the Naval Service is from the Marine Corps. The Corps currently deploys its forces in Marine Expeditionary Units with a special operations capability, which it calls MEU(SOC)s. While this "SOC" component does not meet a strict test of a true special operations capability, it cannot be overlooked, especially considering the strong standing of the Marine Corps on Capitol Hill. Congress has a history of giving the Corps what it asks for. The marines have earned it; they have a history of noble and gallant service. Nonetheless, the issue of funding needs to be reviewed in light of the current threat. It's a matter of focusing the dollars where they will be most effective in the current war against terror. We have to make good choices.

The second opposition force to allocating more resources for special operations is Congress. It's a rice bowl issue for the military contractors who build destroyers, jet fighters, and tanks, but it's a jobs issue for those politicians in those states that produce this hardware. For example, our Navy has more amphibious assault ships than it needs or can effectively man, but Senator Trent Lott will see that the yards in

Pascagoula, Mississippi, will continue to build them. They're great ships, but we really don't need more of them. While special forces cannot be mass-produced, their training can be made better with more money—and the sooner we find the appropriations to pump up the training pipelines, the easier it will be for the SOF training cadres to grow the force. I have spent a great deal of time in Coronado, where the SEALs train, and at Fort Bragg, where Special Forces train. Given the funding, they can and will train more special operators. It is my sense, born by close observation, that these training cadres are sensitive to the need for more SOF operatives, but that they also recognize the danger of cutting quality. In World War II, we trained Navy frogmen in a matter of weeks and sent them forward. Basically, training time was a function of the schedule for the next amphibious landing. The lives of our marines depended on the reconnaissance of enemy-held beaches. We are again at war, but in my opinion, the nature of this war and the character of this enemy dictate that we dare not sacrifice quality in the SOF operators we send forward. Do we need more SOF? Yes, but only if they can be recruited, trained, and fielded with close attention to maintaining a very high standard.

There is another issue in creating a more robust SOF capability, and it is at the other end of the effort to find good men and train them. It deals with keeping trained SOF operators in uniform longer. The backbone of our SOF capability is the senior enlisted personnel—the SEAL senior and master chief petty officers, and the Special Forces master sergeants and sergeant majors. These talented and experienced men earn something on the order of $60,000 a year. At any time after twenty years of service, they can retire with half of their active-duty pay plus a tidy benefits package. This means that we are asking a special operator, whose talents are at their peak and essential to prosecute this war, to work (taking into account the $30,000 he could claim if he retired) for $30,000 a year. In the 1990s, these men retired and found work in law enforcement and as security guards. Many entered the corporate world because of their leadership skills, but most business organizations were not looking for fortysomething managerial talent with a strong military résumé. The attacks on 11 September changed all of that as well.

Security is a cost of doing business in the post-9/11 world, and not just in the reconstruction of Afghanistan and Iraq. Security costs are going up in Saudi Arabia and Russia, in Europe and in Asia. If there is another event on the magnitude of 11 September in America, the cost of goods and services due to increased security measures will run into the tens of billions. Security is a big business and a growth business, and few individuals are as attractive to those companies in the business of providing overseas contract security services as experienced SOF operators—SEALs, Rangers, and Special Forces. What's not to like? These men are skilled, mature warriors who understand rules of engagement and can follow directions. They are used to living overseas and under harsh conditions. And more to the point, they are accustomed to danger; and if required, they can fight. Just how well they can fight was illustrated in March 2004 when hundreds of militia fighters attacked a regional Coalition Provisional Authority facility in Najaf. The building was guarded by one marine, four Salvadoran soldiers, and eight Blackwater private security personnel. As security contractors, they were there to guard the building, not conduct offensive military operations. The bulk of those Blackwater personnel were former SOF operators. When the attack came, they coolly took the measure of the attackers and, outnumbered twenty to one, decimated them. When the U.S. military units finally arrived, the area around the facility was littered with corpses, and the Blackwater personnel were preparing to drive off yet another assault. Men like this are rare—and in this time of immediate need, they have become expensive.

Firms like Blackwater, Triple Canopy, and Custer Battles are stepping up to meet this demand. There is no way these private companies can train men to a high standard, even if they had the time, so they are in what I call the skills-validation business. They are looking for men who have maturity, experience, and a reputation for excellence.

Regarding the latter, the SOF community is a small fraternity. While the Blackwaters of the world do not actively recruit from the active forces, which would be counterproductive to their ongoing military training operations, they can always make a phone call to an active or retired SOF operator to get a line on a new hire. In the SEALs, as in the Special Forces, reputation is everything. When the call is made and the employer hears, "Great operator and a solid performer. He was in Afghanistan in early 2002 and back in Iraq for the push to Baghdad. Great guy; his stuff is tight," the former SOF operator is hired on the spot. In SOF, everyone knows everyone else—or knows someone who does. An SOF operator's reputation follows him while in the service and from the service into the private security world. The prize catches for the security contractors are the senior enlisted cadres with solid reputations—the very people SOCOM does not want to lose if it is to effectively grow the force. For these experienced SOF operators, the security contractors are willing to pay up to $1,000 a day, or more. I have spoken with former Navy SEALs who left the teams they love for the private sector because they could bank a quarter of a million dollars for a single year's work. It's not easy work, and it's dangerous, but no harder or more dangerous than what we taxpayers are asking them to do for an additional $30,000.

"I have no problem with serving my country," one ex-SEAL told me. "Hell, I did it for twenty-two years, and I have two ex-wives to show for it. But this is my chance to make some decent money. Why shouldn't I be able to send my son to Duke and my daughter to Stanford like the doctor living down the block? I've paid my dues in this profession; I have a master's degree and a Ph.D. in kicking ass and taking names."

The military has recently begun paying bonuses for selected SOF personnel to stay in uniform—up to $150,000 to stay on active service for another six years. Selected SOCOM enlisted billets are slated to receive $375 per month in Special Duty Assignment Pay. Only time will tell if this inducement is enough to stem this critical loss of talent.

There is another source of competition for experienced special operators that is a little closer to the taxpayer's wallet. The Special Activities Division at the CIA is also looking for a few good men, and while the role of SAD is not within the scope of this book, I believe they have an important role to play in this fight. Whatever comes of any intelligence community reorganization, we will still need this capability—men who are *not* in uniform and who can take the fight overseas to our enemies. I have spoken with more than one SEAL officer who, after his tour as a platoon OIC, elected to leave the Navy for the business world. The Agency does not contact them while they're in uniform, but they certainly do after they become civilians. The same applies for the senior enlisted operators. This work differs from that of the corporate security sector, but they are competing for the same talent. I doubt that the Agency pay scale can match that of the security contractors, but it is more than competitive with the salary paid to a corporate junior executive. And the CIA officers do go downrange. Publicly, two case officers have been killed in the line of duty since 11 September, both in Afghanistan. The Special Activities folks are good people. After my duty in the SEAL teams, I served at the CIA in the forerunner of the current Special Activities Division. I am proud to call *them* brothers, as well.

Looking ahead, I believe that special operations forces and that subset of SOF, the Navy SEALs, will have an important role to play as the current war unfolds—perhaps a pivotal one. The challenge for our nation and our military is to use our resources wisely and effectively. Failure to do so will make us hostage to those who use terror as a weapon. The Islamists who embrace terror have demonstrated that they are masters of change and evolution—that they can and will adapt. The question is, can we make the changes to effectively engage them? One of the chief reasons we have not had a domestic terrorist event since the attacks of 11 September is that we have kept the pressure on al-Qaeda—and those states that have supported al-Qaeda—financially, religiously, and politically. We need to continue to make the battle against terrorists an away game—played on their turf. The Islamists may not be able to focus on bringing terror to our shores if we continue in our efforts to bring fundamental change to the Middle East. Iraq was a bold gamble. If it ultimately succeeds, and a form of representative government with economic democracy ensues, then the Islamists will have been deeply wounded—perhaps mortally. Freedom and economic democracy are the enemies of the Islamists. They envision a world governed by strict eighth-century religious practice. Free people will not choose to live in that world.

There are, however, some creditable arguments that claim our venture in Iraq is a distraction from pursuing al-Qaeda and their like. One such reasoned and frightening perspective is the subject of Graham Allison's recent book, *Nuclear Terrorism: The Ultimate Preventable Catastrophe*. Graham, a professor at Harvard's Kennedy School of Government, makes a good case for the prospect of nuclear terror. He feels we should focus on Iran and North Korea, not Iraq. He feels that the ultimate contagion is nuclear weapons in the hands of terrorists. On that point I would agree with him, but what do we do about it— how do we proceed? In the case of North Korea, I think we can work with that country's Asian neighbors to reign in Pyongyang's irresponsible nuclear ambitions. North Korea has rational neighbors, nations that want to trade with us. It's a problem that can be addressed, with our help, by regional consensus. As for the Iranians, they are dangerous and they are dirty. The regime in Tehran is a state sponsor of terror. Most notably, they directed the death of 241 Marines in Beirut in 1983. A National Security Agency (NSA) intercept put the smoking gun in Iranian hands, yet we did nothing about it. More recently, al-Qaeda leaders like Musab al-Zarqawi used Iran (and Iraq) as a safe haven after the fall of the Taliban in Afghanistan. Sadly, Iran does not have a rational neighbor—not yet. But Iran has an ongoing problem with its young people, who are educated and susceptible to an enlightened secular government. Educated young Muslims do not want to live under the restrictions of sharia, strict Islamic law. A thriving democracy on Iran's western border may cause the Iranians to change the corrupt theocracy currently in power, as well as their nuclear ambitions. We have everything to gain by doing all in our power to make Iraq an economic success. It is the one thing that Iran *and* al-Qaeda fear. In the meantime, our enemy is the Islamists—al-Qaeda and their related factions in Afghanistan and Iraq, who continue to use terror and indiscriminate violence as their weapons of choice. The fight, at least for now, is in Afghanistan and Iraq, and that is why SOF is so committed to this region.

Regarding our military, there are three things that will need close attention if we are going to shape the force to deal with this vicious and elusive foe. The first is to redefine and develop the command relationships between our theater commanders and our SOF commanders. Given the large numbers of soldiers and hardware in theaters like Central Command, there will be a need for a conventional commander for the foreseeable future, but that commander will have to allow SOF to operate as a supported command within his area of responsibility. That means that when an SOF commander is charged with special operations in an area like the Afghan-Pakistani border region, he must be given what he asks for in the way of conventional support *and* that support will have to be provided with no strings attached. Subordinate conventional commanders cannot go running back to the theater CINC when or if they don't agree with the way the SOF commander is handling things. On the ground, conventional forces and SOF work well together, but it gets a little turfy up the chain of command. This has to change. For example, a theater CINC will have to yield some of his authority while maintaining much of the responsibility. It's like this: Traditional military organizations like direct lines of command and accountability. Allowing SOF to do what SOF does best will place a four-star CINC in a position where he may not control what SOF does in his theater, but if something goes terribly wrong, he may have to answer for it. Not an easy or natural thing for a regional commander, but necessary if we want to take full advantage of SOF's operational capabilities. And changes like this will not take place without pressure from the highest levels of the Defense Department.

In keeping with the concept of allowing SOF to take the lead in this fight, it is necessary to accept that SOF will have to be able to operate in their own way. That means there could be a mix of direct action, unconventional warfare, and now perhaps covert activity, all going on at the same time. For this to be effective, there will have to be a more decentralized chain of command than exists in conventional military organizations, with junior SOF leaders making decisions in the field. Navy SEAL lieutenant commanders in charge of task units will plan and carry out direct-action missions, often notifying higher headquarters with the standard Navy catchall term UNODIR, which means "unless otherwise directed." Further defined, it implicitly says that unless I hear differently, we are hitting this target. Army Special Forces team leaders—in many cases, Army captains and warrant officers—will develop intelligence and react on it immediately, notifying higher headquarters while they carry out the mission. This, if for no other reason, is why the quality of our SOF operators cannot be allowed to deteriorate. This uniform quality allows SOF to operate without a cumbersome command structure and senior command micromanagement. It's not cowboys and Indians, as some senior conventional commanders would have it; it's agility and flexibility that can only be achieved with a high order of competence and professionalism in the junior ranks.

The second thing that must be done is to put our intelligence house in order. This may be much harder than settling food fights between SOF and conventional forces in the military. A robust intelligence capability is of the utmost importance. It is essential for special operations, as well as for covert and paramilitary activity. We are blind in this fight against terrorism without a continuous flow of operable intelligence. In the words of John Lehman, former secretary of the Navy and a member of the 9/11 Commission, "We have allowed our intelligence community to evolve into a bureaucratic archipelago of baronies in the Defense Department, the CIA, and ninety-five other different intelligence units in our government." This mosaic of intelligence agencies, civilian and military, is inefficient, ineffective, and expensive. Yet within each there are dedicated professionals who work hard to provide a valuable and needed product. How this mess gets reordered and streamlined is as difficult as it is important. Allocating responsibility and defining working relationships between civilian and military intelligence organizations will be difficult and important. It is a very crucial issue. It's my opinion that the "intelligence czar" must be talented, an individual of immense character and patriotism, and have control of the intelligence budget. We will see how John Negroponte, a diplomat, fares as the first director of national intelligence. I wish him well. It is essential that he quickly find a solution to interagency turf wars that have hamstrung our intelligence production. We simply must find a way to get the right information into the hands of those who can convert it into operational opportunity. It goes without saying that the policy makers need a quality intelligence product for strategic purposes, but we desperately need a timely, tactical intelligence capability to support the men down range. We used to need informants who could tell us what the ol 1 men in the Kremlin were doing. Now we need young Muslims to tell us where the bad guys are hiding in their village.

Third, we have to grow and invigorate our SOF capability if it is to lead us in this fight. This means giving as much attention to our SOF command-and-control capability as to our shooters. With the SOF Truths in mind, we can grow this force, but only so fast. Additional funding can help with this growth. With more money, we can train new men a *little* faster while maintaining the quality. But the men entering SOF training today will not be impact players in the force for another six to eight years. Those now beginning training will not be ready for deployment for two to three years. They will not have the experience to be team leaders until well into the next decade. While SOF may be our best and brightest, it is not so much a question of pure talent when comparing an SOF warrior to a conventional warrior; it is simply that the SOF skill set takes longer to master and longer to season under operational conditions. In spite of the recent bonus program, we are still losing our experienced SOF operators at an alarming rate. This is no flesh wound; it is arterial bleeding. Any formula for growth through recruitment and training will make the force younger, less experienced, and less special in a business where experience *really* counts. How do we encourage more of our senior enlisted SOF operators to stay in uniform another five or ten years? In addition to bonuses, one formula would be to pay a proven SOF operator his active salary *and* his retired pay. Given the cost and lead time of selecting and training a new man, this is cheap. In the context of a $400+ billion defense budget, it is cheap. *Given the expense in terms of the treasury and the human suffering of another 11 September–type event, it is a bargain beyond measure.* If SOF are to lead this fight, quality has to be the priority. However it is done, we simply have to find a way to keep SOF talent from leaving the force while we buy time to front-load the system with new men.

Finally, what about our Navy SEALs going forward? They've done some incredible things in the war on terrorism, but what about the future? As we have seen, they were very quickly able to morph from a maritime-centric SOF organization into the premier direct-action SOF force. SEALs were able to take their lengthy, Cold War mission-planning process and shrink it to meet new operational requirements. They quickly learned to compress the time from target acquisition to rounds on target from a matter of days to a matter of hours, even minutes. These warriors were able to do this because every SEAL from team new guy to team leader has been drilled in the mechanics of operational planning since he was in BUD/S training. Oddly enough, when it became necessary to think out of the box and modify old ways of doing business, it was the "old SEALs" who often as not came up with the new ideas and tactics. All this had to be done while carrying out combat missions down range with lives on the line. It's a matter of training, experience, and adaptive thinking, as well as the desire to solve tactical problems in unconventional ways.

We have SEAL squadrons deploying with men who are "shooters" in the purest sense of the word, but who can also think and improvise. The squadron SEAL platoons are well-oiled direct-action teams that are also very good at conducting special reconnaissance missions. In the current vernacular, they are door kickers with the ability to sneak and peek when needed. Given the pace of operations in Afghanistan and Iraq, they have struggled with their mandate to "keep one foot in the water," but they've maintained that capability. If it's a maritime target, like the oil infrastructure at Umm Qsar, they will get the job done. If it involves a strategic reconnaissance on an inland mountaintop, they will do that as well. I guess one could say that about the entire spectrum of what Navy SEALs may be asked to do: They will do what is necessary to accomplish the mission. They are the masters of adaptability. They will find a way to make it happen.

What's next? Much of that will be dictated by the enemy. And this is a very determined, unpredictable enemy. Since 11 September, we have killed or captured 70 percent of the al-Qaeda leadership, yet it still remains a deadly threat, regenerating itself and attracting new followers to its ranks. It is a secretive and elusive foe that can hide in austere mountain terrain or in large cities—they are as comfortable in Karachi as in New York City. This enemy employs state-of-the-art communications technology and modern money-laundering tactics, yet will use archaic religious dogma to incite young women to strap explosives to their bodies and detonate themselves in a crowded market. It is a lethal brew of technology, religion, and fanaticism, and its weapon of choice is terrorism. I doubt that the mistakes they made in Afghanistan and Iraq will be repeated. The SEAL direct-action elements enjoyed a measure of success because of our technical collectors, such as drone aircraft and cell-phone intercepts, but also because of locals who would rat out the enemy for money. Al-Qaeda has already begun to work around our technology, and we can be certain that they will be quite ruthless in dealing with those, including moderate Muslims, who provide us with information.

Operable tactical intelligence is and will continue to be the key element in finding and killing this enemy. The best source of this intelligence is that which comes from the local population, especially in areas where tribal loyalties and animosities govern. This information needs to be very carefully managed and vetted. SEALs—indeed, all of SOF—will need to be involved in the gathering and processing of this intelligence. Without intelligence, we will be unable to target the leadership and infrastructure of this enemy. I don't believe that whatever comes from the reorganization of our intelligence community will be totally suited to SOF tactical intelligence requirements. This means that Navy SEALs will have to learn from their SOF brothers in Army Special Forces how to be more culturally proactive. Building relationships with local populations means understanding their problems and helping them to solve those problems. It is often more difficult than kicking down a door, let alone kicking the wrong door and exacerbating the problem. But getting close to the locals is the best way to generate good intelligence. Sometimes an SOF medic who is caring for a woman and her baby in a village may be given information that is more honestly rendered and tactically relevant than that obtained by some guy in civilian clothes named "Bob" who speaks the language and has a satchel full of money.

We can only grow SOF within certain constraints, and we can continue to field superbly capable tactical elements. But only through unconventional warfare and paramilitary activity can we leverage our deployed SOF forces and enlist the locals to help us. It's their land, but with respect to T. E. Lawrence, it *is* our war. We may not be able to do it without their help. The SOF "hunter-killer" teams that Secretary Rumsfeld is so fond of are great for killing bad guys. But while their success is a function of the quality of the intelligence, their primary worth is more psychological than strategic. Al-Qaeda has to know that anywhere, at any time of night, men with guns and blackened faces can be upon them. But if the swamp is breeding rats faster than we can kill those rats, then time is on their side. We have to drain the swamp, and that means local help. A representative government and economic democracy in Iraq will help to take a lot of water out of the swamp. While sacrificing none of their direct-action and strategic-reconnaissance capability, or their maritime skills, SEALs will have to become more proactive in developing intelligence. This means that they will have to add enhanced language capability and cross-cultural skills to their combat load. It means that they will have to become more than the superb pure shooters that they are now.

I have no doubt that our Navy SEALs are up to the task, because their greatest talent is not their ability to shoot or to kick down doors or to conduct reconnaissance. Their greatest talent is their ability to change to meet an emerging threat. It is this creative, ongoing, adaptive warfighting ability that will keep them in the forefront of the war on terrorism.

GLOSSARY OF ACRONYMS
AND ABBREVIATIONS

AO

Area of operations. Can be regional, like Central Command, or more limited, like a mountainous region in Afghanistan.

AOIC

Assistant officer in charge. The officer who is second in command of a SEAL platoon.

APL

Assistant patrol leader. The leader of a SEAL element is usually called the patrol leader, or PL. His designated second in command is the APL.

ARG

Amphibious Ready Group. An naval task group or force that is built around a Marine Expeditionary Force embarked on naval ships.

ASDS

Advanced SEAL Delivery System. Similar to the free-flooding SDVs, these craft are small dry submarines with extended on-station and operational capability.

BDU

Battle dress utilities. The camouflaged-patterned uniform worn by SOF operators and other military units. Also referred to as cammies.

BUD/S

Basic Underwater Demolition/SEAL (training). The BUD/S program at Coronado, California, is the basic training for all Navy SEALs.

CCT

Combat Control Teams. Air Force SOF operators who are specialists in the calling in of close air support. One of the Air Force's special tactics teams.

CENTCOM

Central Command. An area that includes the Middle East and Southwest Asia. The command held by General Tommy Franks during the prosecution of the war in Afghanistan and Iraq.

C4

Command, control, communication, coordination.

CINC

Commander in chief. Four-star commanders charged with area or theater command responsibilities. Often used in the context of theater commands such as Central Command or Pacific Command.

CPO

Chief petty officer. Usually the ranking enlisted man in a SEAL platoon, where he is recognized as the platoon chief.

CQB

Close-quarter battle. Close-in fighting, and a term that is often synonymous with close-quarter combat.

CQC

Close-quarter combat. This usually refers to combat inside a confined area like a room or the compartment of a ship.

CQD

Close Quarter Defense. A system of "behind-the-gun" skills used by

SEALs for the projection of lethal and nonlethal force, urban assaults, weapons flow, and prisoner management. Developed by Duane Dieter.

CRRC

Combat Rubber Raiding Craft. A Zodiac-type rubber boat that can carry four to eight SEALs, usually with a 55-hp outboard engine.

CSAR

Combat search and rescue. The location and rescue of downed pilots or other personnel who are in enemy territory or in a hostile situation.

C2

Command and control.

DA

Direct action. Refers to a combat mission directed at a given target, such as an enemy compound or a safe house occupied by a high-value al-Qaeda leader.

DPV

Desert patrol vehicle. Specially made and heavily armed vehicles, similar to dune buggies, used by SEALs for mobility in open terrain.

Endex

End exercise. A command used during SEAL training exercises to bring about an end to exercise. Usually used in mock close-quarter combat.

EOD

Explosive ordnance disposal. A technical specialty that deals with the handling and render-safe procedures of U.S., foreign, and improvised explosives and ordnance.

EPW

Enemy prisoner of war. In the current lexicon, EPWs are enemies captured by U.S. or other coalition forces. POWs are U.S. personnel who are captured by the enemy.

GOSP

Gas and oil separation plant. In this context, a piece of the Iraqi oil export infrastructure captured by U.S. Marines in the early days of the Iraqi campaign.

GROM

Grupa Reagowania Operacyjno Mobilnego (in English, Operational Maneuver Reconnaissance Group). Acronym for Polish special operations forces that work closely with SEALs.

HCS

Helicopter Combat Support Special Squadron. Designation for any of several Navy H-60 squadrons operating in Iraq that often supported SEAL and SOF operations.

HUMINT

Human intelligence. The gathering of information from human sources, typically by individuals, as when a villager tells an SOF operator where the enemy is hiding in his or her village.

Humvee or Hummer

HMMVW—high-mobility multipurpose wheeled vehicle. Humvees currently used by SEALs are highly modified vehicles for SOF/SEAL missions.

ID

Infantry division. Shorthand for an Army infantry division.

IED

Improvised explosive device. An improvised explosive, used often by insurgents in Iraq against coalition targets, sometimes detonated by cell phones and garage-door openers.

Indoc

Indoctrination Course. Precedes the three phases of the regular BUD/S training curriculum.

IS

Intelligence specialist. A dedicated enlisted rating in the Navy. Intelligence specialists assigned to SEAL teams help SEALs plan missions.

JCSOTF/G

Joint Combined Special Operations Task Force/Group. "Combined" refers to the inclusion of SOF elements from allied nations.

JDAM

Joint Direct Attack Munition. A smart bomb. This precision munition can be guided by laser illumination or a set of GPS coordinates.

JSOTF/G

Joint Special Operations Task Force/Group. A task force or group tasked with the conduct of SOF operations that include multiservice U.S. SOF units. Task forces are normally larger than task groups, which are usually larger than task units.

KAAOT

Khor al-Amaya Oil Terminal. Smallest of the Iraqi offshore oil terminals. Captured by the GROM in the opening days of the Iraqi campaign.

KBR

Kellogg, Brown & Root. A subsidiary of Haliburton and one of the major contractors that provide services to coalition forces in Iraq and help in reconstruction efforts.

KNB

Kuwait Naval Base. U.S. naval facility located on the Persian Gulf near Kuwait City.

KSK

Kommando Spezialkrafte. The German SOF component that served in Afghanistan.

LAR

Lung-activated rebreather. Usually used in context with the Draeger LAR V, a German-designed closed-circuit scuba used by SOF divers.

LIO

Leadership interdiction operation. The interdiction of ships at sea that are thought to have senior al-Qaeda or terrorists aboard.

LPO

Leading petty officer. In the context of a SEAL platoon, the ranking enlisted man who is not a chief petty officer, usually the second-ranking enlisted man.

LUP

Layup position. A rally point or secure, concealed position for a SOF element, one near the target objective and usually chosen by the element leader.

MABOT

Mina al-Bakr Oil Terminal. Now called the Basra Oil Terminal, located offshore in southern Iraq near the town of al-Faw. Captured by SEALs during the opening days of the Iraqi campaign

MCADS

Maritime craft, air deployable system. This refers to the capability to parachute SEALs, SWCC crewmen, and an eleven-meter RHIB from a C-130 into the open ocean for an SOF mission.

MCT

Mobile communications team. An NSW component charged with the secure and reliable communications within Naval Special Warfare units and as directed, other SOF units.

MEF

Marine Expeditionary Force. A division-size Marine Corp unit, usually configured for a specific purpose, like the 1st Marine Expeditionary Force in Iraq.

MEU

Marine Expeditionary Unit. A contingent of U.S. Marines embarked on an Amphibious Ready Group, or ARG. Supported by the ARG, they can be deployed ashore by helicopter or landing craft.

MEU(SOC)

Marine Expeditionary Unit (Special Operations Capable). A MEU that has a special operations capability.

MIO

Maritime interception operation. In this context, the interception of ships at sea for inspection and possibly seizure of waterborne cargoes.

Mk V

Mark V combatant craft. This eighty-two-foot aluminum-hulled boat is the largest and fastest combatant craft in the SBT inventory.

MOPP

Military Operational Prevention and Protection (suit/gear). The cumbersome suits worn by American forces at the beginning of the Iraq campaign to prevent exposure to chemical, biological, or nuclear agents.

MOUT

Military operations in urban terrain. This refers to combat operations in an urban setting, out in the street as opposed to close-quarter combat (CQC) inside a building.

MRE

Meals ready to eat. Combat rations currently in use by the U.S. military. A man needs two of these a day, but can get by on one.

NSA

National Security Agency. Located between Baltimore and Washington, D.C., this secretive agency maintains a global surveillance network and has highly sophisticated computer and communications capabilities.

NSW

Naval Special Warfare. Encompasses all Navy SOF assets, including SEAL teams, Special Boat Teams, and a host of command, staff, administrative, and logistical components.

NSWTU

Naval Special Warfare Task Unit. A NSW unit, usually with one or more SEAL platoons, that is tasked with conducting NSW operations in a given area.

NVGs

Night-vision goggles. Worn by SOF operators and other military personnel to see at night. Uses ambient light or infrared illumination.

ODA

Operational detachment, alpha. This refers to the standard Army Special Forces A-team. An ODA is a twelve-man team that includes two officers.

ODB

Operational detachment, bravo. The bravo detachment is a company-size headquarters element that supports and often controls several ODAs operating in the field.

OEF

Operation Enduring Freedom. The military designation for operations in Afghanistan.

OGA

Other governmental agency. Could be any governmental agency, but most usually refers to the CIA.

OIC

Officer in charge. In this text, it refers to the senior officer in a SEAL platoon. The OIC is often referred to as the platoon commander.

OIF

Operation Iraqi Freedom. The military designation for operations in Iraq.

OP

Observation post. A vantage point near the target objective where the target can be safely observed.

PACOM

Pacific Command. With headquarters in Pearl Harbor, this theater command encompasses the broad reaches of the Pacific Ocean. It gives way to Central Command at the entrances to the Indian Ocean.

PL

Patrol leader. The designated leader of a SEAL element when it is of platoon size or smaller. Usually the PL is the platoon OIC or AOIC.

PLO

Patrol Leader Order. A preoperational briefing usually given by the SEAL element or assault leader.

PPL

Petroleum pumping lock. The final valve / pumping station in the Iraqi oil export infrastructure, which permitted oil to flow from land to the offshore oil terminals.

PRODEV

Professional development (training). The initial six-month period in the predeployment workup of a SEAL team. Focuses on individual warfare skills.

RHIB

Rigid-hull inflatable boat. In this text, RHIBs are combat craft with rigid hulls and inflatable sponsonlike gunwales. The workhorse in the Special Boat Teams are the eleven-meter RHIBs.

ROEs

Rules of engagement. Guidelines and rules that govern units in combat. ROEs can vary, depending on the threat environment and the mission requirements.

RPG

Rocket-propelled grenade. A shoulder-fired, bazooka-like rocket launcher effective against buildings, vehicles, and armor. A favorite of insurgents.

SAD

Special Activities Division. A division at the Central Intelligence Agency that deals with paramilitary activity and some aspects of covert action.

SAS

Special Air Service. The lead British special operations component, and a force model for the SOF components of many other nations.

SATCOM

Satellite communications. Refers to tactical radios that rely on communications satellites to send and receive messages. Secure and usually very reliable.

SBT

Special Boat Team. NSW teams charged with the operation, maintenance, and deployment of NSW combatant craft.

SDV

SEAL delivery vehicle. A small wet (free-flooding) minisub that carries SOF operators. SDVs can be launched from the surface or a submerged parent submarine.

SEAL

Acronym for sea, air, and land. Given this name for methods of infiltration—from the sea, through the air, across the land. The SEALs were formed in 1962.

Sims

Simunitions. Paint pellets used in training exercises to simulate 9mm ammunition. Designed for military weapons that have the same short-range trajectory and cyclic rate of fire as the real thing.

SIT

Squadron Integration Training. The final six months in the predeployment workup of a SEAL team. The Seal team becomes a SEAL squadron with the augmentation of a number of non-SEAL combat and combat-support components.

SITREP

Situation report. A report sent from lower to higher—from a unit in the field to the TOC, or from the TOC up the line to a reporting senior.

Smee

Subject-matter expert. Usually the assignment for a new SEAL officer's first deployment. His expertise could be a range of disciplines, including close air support or intelligence.

SOC

Special operations commander. Usually used in a regional context, such as SOCCENT, which refers to the Special Operations Commander, Central Command.

SOCOM

Shortened acronym for United States Special Operations Command; also USSOCOM. Located at MacDill Air Force Base in Tampa, Florida.

SOF

Special operations forces. Refers to all special operations components, including Army Special Forces and Rangers, Air Force Special Tactics Teams, and Navy SEALs.

SOP

Standard operating procedure. An established method or set common practice for conducting an aspect of a SEAL operation. Often used in conjunction with TTPs.

SQT

SEAL Qualification Training. An advanced course of instruction that follows soon after BUD/S and qualifies a man as a Navy SEAL.

SR

Strategic reconnaissance. A mission to gather information and/or put "eyes on" a target. May precede an air strike or a DA mission.

SWCC

Special Warfare Combatant Craft. SWCC personnel are trained in weapons, navigation, engineering, and combat operations specifically tailored to the operation of NSW small craft during SOF missions.

TCCC

Tactical combat casualty care. Battlefield first aid. This is first-line care given by SOF corpsmen or SOF operators while under fire or during a mission and away from a field medical facility.

TF

Task force. A large command staff that may have task groups and task units working under it.

TG

Task group. In this text, usually a joint or combined special operations task group.

TOC

Tactical operations center. The room or space, ashore or afloat, dedicated to management and coordination of special operators in the field; a command post or center.

TOT

Time on target. A very critical period of time beginning with the initial assault or entry into the target area. Short TOTs make for high mission-success rates and the safety of the operators.

TRADET

Training Detachment. In the lexicon of this text, Training Detachments located in Coronado and Norfolk with the NSW group commands. These units are charged with conducting SEAL predeployment training.

TTPs

Tactics, techniques, and procedures. Standard operating methods and procedures common to a tactical unit. Usually not classified but closely held information.

TU

Task unit. In this text, an NSWTU.

UAV

Unmanned aerial vehicle. An unmanned drone aircraft. Often called a Predator, because the Predator was the UAV most commonly used in Afghanistan and Iraq.

ULT

Unit Level Training. The middle six-month period in the eighteen-month predeployment workup of a SEAL team. Focuses on training SEAL platoons and is often referred to as platoon training.

VBSS

Visit, board, search, and seizure. Refers to the boarding by SOF of a ship or offshore oil platform. May be opposed or unopposed.

WARCOM

Shortened acronym for Naval Special Warfare Command, located in Coronado, California.

WMD

Weapons of mass destruction. Typically WMDs are thought of as biological, chemical, or nuclear weapons.